MONKS, NUNS AND MONASTERIES

Sacheverell Sitwell

MONKS, NUNS AND MONASTERIES

WEIDENFELD AND NICOLSON
20 NEW BOND STREET LONDON WI

Text printed in Great Britain by
Morrison and Gibb Limited,
London and Edinburgh
Illustrations printed by
Jarrolds of Norwich

In loving memory
of my sister

Contents

Illustrations

Illustrations

Audience-hall at St Florian (*Guillemot – Connaissance des Arts*)
Grand portal at St Florian (*Toni Schneiders*)
Grand portal at Kremsmünster, Upper Austria (*Guillemot – Connaissance des Arts*)
Colonnaded fishponds at Kremsmünster (*Österreichische Lichtbildstelle – Bavaria*)
Monastery of Melk, Lower Austria (*Toni Schneiders*)
Crypt at Altenburg, Lower Austria (*Toni Schneiders*)
Refectory of the Monks by Alessandro Magnasco. Abbey of Seitenstetten, Lower Austria
    (*Bundesdenkmalamt, Vienna*)
Tree of Life (detail) by Bartholomäus Steinle. Monastery of Stams, Tyrol (*A. Demanega*)
Monastery of Stams, Tyrol (*A. Demanega*)
Church at Wilhering, Upper Austria (*Hans Wöhrl*)

ROCOCO IN BAVARIA (*between pages 82 and 83*)

High altar at Rohr, Lower Bavaria, by E. Q. Asam (*Hirmer Fotoarchiv, Munich*)
Group above high altar at Weltenburg, Lower Bavaria, by E. Q. Asam (*Hirmer Foto-
    archiv, Munich*)
Interior of abbey church at Ottobeuren, Suabia (*Toni Schneiders*)
Choir-stalls at Zwiefalten, Wurtemberg (*Toni Schneiders*)
Choir-stalls at Ottobeuren (*Toni Schneiders*)
Interior of church at Zwiefalten (*Toni Schneiders*)
Pulpit at Zwiefalten (*Renner – Bavaria*)
Central altar at Vierzehnheiligen, Upper Franconia (*Eva Meyerweissflog – Bavaria*)
Library at Wiblingen, Wurtemberg (*Leonard von Matt*)
Library at Metten, Lower Bavaria (*P. Damm – Bavaria*)
Statue of *Death* by J. T. Stammel in Library at Admont, Styria (*Toni Schneiders*)
Library at Waldsassen, Upper Palatinate (*E. Schmachtenberger – Bavaria*)
Library at Schussenried, Wurtemberg (*Toni Schneiders*)
Church of Steinhausen, Wurtemberg (*Fritz Eschen – Ullstein*)
Interior of church at Steinhausen (*Toni Schneiders*)
Detail of colonnade in church at Steinhausen (*Toni Schneiders – Bavaria*)
Pulpit at Irsee, Suabia (*Toni Schneiders*)
Pulpit at Traunkirchen, Upper Austria (*Toni Schneiders*)
Font-cover at Ufford, Suffolk (*Edwin Smith*)
Wrought-iron gates in church at Einsiedeln, Switzerland (*Bildarchiv Foto Marburg*)
Grand Stair at Kloster Ebrach, Upper Franconia (*Emil Bauer – Bavaria*)
Kaiserstiege at Göttweig, Lower Austria (*Toni Schneiders*)

MONASTERIES OF NORTHERN ITALY (*between pages 106 and 107*)

Certosa del Galluzzo near Florence (*Robert Descharnes*)
Cloister in Certosa del Galluzzo (*Ente Provinciale per il Turismo, Florence*)
The Church Militant and Triumphant (detail) by Andrea da Firenze. Spanish Chapel,
    Florence (*Anderson*)
Church of Certosa di Calci near Pisa (*Ente Provinciale per il Turismo, Pisa*)
St Dominic Blessing a Lay-brother of his Order by G. B. Tiepolo. Gesuati church, Venice
    (*Alinari*)

Illustrations

Marriage at Cana by Paolo Veronese. Louvre (*Alinari*)
Scene from the Life of St Benedict by Luca Signorelli. Monte Oliveto Maggiore (*Alinari*)
Monte Oliveto Maggiore near Siena (*Ionesco – Réalités*)
Camaldoli, from *Vita del beato Michele Flammini* by M. Brocchi, 1761
La Verna, from *Descrizione del Sacro Monte della Vernia* by L. Moroni, 1612
Cloister in Certosa di Pavia, Lombardy (*Alinari*)
Church at Fossanova, Latium (*Fototeca di Architettura e Topografia dell' Italia Antica, Rome*)
Triumph of the Name of Jesus by Baciccia. Gesù church, Rome (*Leonard von Matt*)

OLD KINGDOM OF THE TWO SICILIES (*between pages 122 and 123*)

Façade of Santa Croce, Lecce, Apulia (*J. Allan Cash*)
Courtyard of Seminario, Lecce (*J. Allan Cash*)
Street in Noto, Sicily (*J. Allan Cash*)
Cloister at Monreale, Sicily (*Leonard von Matt*)
Monte Cassino, from *Historia Abbatiae Cassinensis* by Erasmo Gattola, 1733
Cloister of San Gregorio Armeno, Naples (*Collection Édition Arthaud*)
Cloister of Poor Clares at Santa Chiara, Naples (*Collection Édition Arthaud*)
Double stair at Certosa di Padula, Campania (*Prof. Sir Anthony Blunt, Courtauld Institute of Art*)

ROYAL FOUNDATIONS IN SPAIN AND PORTUGAL (*between pages 138 and 139*)

Tomb of Charles V by Pompeo Leoni in the Escorial (*Ampliaciones y Reproducciones Mas*)
Double tomb of Alfonso VIII of Castile and his wife. Burgos, Las Huelgas (*Ampliaciones y Reproducciones Mas*)
Tomb of Isabella of Portugal by Gil de Silóee. Burgos, Cartuja de Miraflores (*Ampliaciones y Reproducciones Mas*)
Tomb of Dona Ines de Castro at Alcobaça, Estremadura, Portugal (*Secretariado Nacional da Informação*)
Nuns in the cloister at Sigena, Aragón (*Ampliaciones y Reproducciones Mas*)
Wooden coffin of Beatriz Cornel of Sigena (*Ampliaciones y Reproducciones Mas*)
Sacristy at Guadalupe, Estremadura, Spain (*Éditions du Temps*)
Moorish patio at Santa Clara, Tordesillas, León (*Ampliaciones y Reproducciones Mas*)
'The Entrance of the Mausoleum of Emanuel the Great King of Portugal' from *Plans of the Church of Batalha* by J. Murphy, 1795
Doorway leading to Sacristy at Alcobaça
Three Cistercian Monks of Alcobaça by Nuno Gonçalves. Museu de Arte Antiga, Lisbon (*Royal Academy of Arts*)
Convent church at Tomar, Ribatejo (*Secretariado Nacional da Informação*)

OTHER MONASTERIES IN SPAIN AND PORTUGAL (*between pages 146 and 147*)

Relief of Walk to Emmaus in cloister at Santo Domingo de Silos, Old Castile (*Jean Dieuzaide – Yan*)
Cloister of Santo Domingo de Silos (*Jean Dieuzaide – Yan*)

Illustrations

Illustrations

Acknowledgements

The author and publishers would like to thank the institutions and photographers mentioned above, for kind permission to use their photographs.

Photographs from books were taken by J. R. Freeman and Co from copies in the British Museum.

The layout of the illustrations is by Arthur T. Lockwood.

The author would like to acknowledge his constant indebtedness to Dom David Knowles, whose books on English Monasteries, and particularly *The Monastic Order in England*, Cambridge University Press, 1963, provided much valuable material for Chapter One; and to Miss Joan Evans, whose books on French Monastic Architecture were an important source of information for Chapter Five, and by whom the author's attention was drawn to the words of Edmund Burke, quoted on page 2.

Introduction

THIS beginning sentence of mine marks the opening or unfolding of an immense theme of which a necessarily inadequate account is given in the pages that follow. How could it be otherwise with so huge a subject which is no less than the attempted description and enumeration of the buildings and works of art with which the monks and nuns had contact in their daily lives! This, in England, Southern Germany, Italy, Spain and Portugal, and France, with a glance, if no more than that, in the final chapter at the monasteries of the Eastern Church. But this implies an essential or fundamental contradiction which it may be better to excuse or explain at once. For it is when the ascetics of both sexes are surrounded by the luxuries of art that they become our subject. Not that this means any lessening in the rigours of their régime and rule. A very great, indeed a major part of human energy was sublimated into the religious and the spiritual, and a writer and poet should be the last to complain when this expresses itself in works of art. We may think that these could only be the more necessary to those who imposed lifelong hardship, seclusion, and a meagre diet upon themselves in pursuit of their ideals.

If carried further, it is to be admitted that the contradiction referred to really fulfils itself when the monasteries have become rich and are flowering and blossoming into works of art. It is then, and not where it is a case of hermits living in the Nitrian desert, in caves, or in a particular instance, at Cintra, in cells hewn from the living rock and lined with cork against the rheumatic damp, that the monks are at their most interesting from our point of view. That this degree of desirable attainment is synonymous with some shade of decadence is not to be denied, though it may have been no wickeder than an extra covering at night, or another course or a little wine for dinner. That the adornments and the works of art of ages with which the monasteries and nunneries overflowed were – no more than the stone vessels of their churches – except in very few cases not the work of their own hands, in no way detracts from the total effect or achievement. Any more than, were our subject gardens or country houses, all places were to be debarred where the owners were not their own architects and garden designers, and the contents whether works of art, tapestries, furniture, and so on, or the flowers in the flowerbeds, omitted and not taken into account at all. In short it is impossible not to look upon many of the thousand-year-old monasteries and nunneries of Europe as great estates, huge family houses, or little kingdoms of their own.

This, I think, is the true light in which to treat of them, as though, which is the truth, they were living and corporate bodies, losing, as they aged, some part of their muscular hardness, softening and becoming sedentary, and in the end failing in their will to live. And, if not that, violently taken over and despoiled just because of the accumulation of treasures they contained, with subsequent fate as prison, lunatic asylum, or, more mercifully, museum. It would, I suppose, be an anomaly were there still monks in their hundreds living and swarming in the monasteries; and yet I am not sure of it. In the ideal world there would be no need for the cavalry regiment installed in the halls and corridors of Alcobaça; no reason for the prisoners housed dismally at Cîteaux and at Fontevrault; and no cause for the poor lunatics of Zwiefalten in that inappropriate Rococo setting. The monks, if fewer of them, should be back where it was originally intended that they should be. Let us read again what Edmund Burke had to say when the monasteries of France were abolished during the French Revolution:

The confiscation of the goods of monks and nuns, and abolition of their order does not effect England as a precedent . . . yet it sets justice, the common concern of mankind, at defiance . . . the monks are lazy. Be it so. Suppose them as no otherwise employed than by singing in the choir. They are as usefully employed as those who neither sing nor say. As usefully even as those who sing upon the stage. Why should the expenditure of a great landed property . . . appear intolerable to you and me, when it takes its course through the accumulation of vast libraries, which are the history of the force and weakness of the human mind; through great collections of ancient records, medals and coins, which attest and explain ancient laws and customs; that by imitating nature seem to extend the limits of creation . . .?

Thus, a Protestant and a scholar and a man of letters. But almost in his own words no lover of the arts. Had he been, it is clear that his feelings upon this subject would have been stronger still. The monks were drones; but what, then, are those who inherit titles and estates and money? The argument for their existence is when they improve their properties. But this is precisely what the monks did if they had the opportunity. The addition of a cloister or a lady chapel is no more reprehensible than the building of a ballroom or a new wing with bathrooms. The employment of a great architect, a sculptor, or a painter, far from being wrong in itself is more often than not both a

2

Opposite: Ceiling of church at Steinhausen frescoed by J. B. Zimmermann

self-sacrifice and a fulfilment. But there is even another angle from which the buildings themselves, and not their contents, become clothed and invested with a particular importance in the contemporary world. In the insensate increase in the selling value of works of art, amounting to a cruel and insulting joke played on the artists concerned who would have liked only a tithe of the money in their lifetimes, it is a satisfaction to think that the shell or fabric of the buildings may be almost valueless. Thus do they avenge themselves, increasing in so doing their sentimental and spiritual value to ourselves.

There are experiences to be had of marvellous sort, whether in the ruined fanes or in the living and still functioning body, whether the monks are long gone but are in ghostly presence, or are still there in their twos or threes. One does not know whether to envy most those persons who have loved such things and places all their lives, or have come to it perhaps later with all the shock of a personal discovery. I say this with feeling belonging, as I do, to both classes mentioned. The art historian going round from county to county putting his tag on every building has not diminished the second phase of this enthusiasm. Even those persons who like myself, and to their own sad loss, have no religion must feel the spiritual values imbued into the mere stone by so many generations to whom their religion was all in all and everything. Who is there to deny this, and say it is not true?

Like many Englishmen, and I suspect it is a trait in our national character, my youthful enthusiasm was for abroad and for Italy in particular, and I found more to admire in buildings seen under the Italian sun than, let us say, Amiens Cathedral on a rainy day of which there are enough and to spare in Picardy. This love for the warm South and its buildings, whether on the Mediterranean or further afield, has remained with me, but the great works of art of the Western world are not all Italian, or even French. And it is in this respect that the experiences referred to are to be enjoyed, and that much nearer home; for an Englishman, that is to say, and for many visitors from overseas. At which point let us remember that the monks and nuns are theme of this undertaking and that it is not therefore any and every old church into which we can enter. But of Ely, Lincoln, York, and Durham, those four wonders of the eastern side of England from midland to north, only one is debarred from us, which is Lincoln. All these other minsters or cathedrals are monastic in origin.

It is indeed an advantage in a thousand to be approaching Ely for the first, or fifth, or it could be the hundredth time. For this is a sensation that does not stale. It can be seen from miles away; from a distance that in my experience is only matched when the twin steeples of Chartres rise from ten or fifteen miles in front of you out of the cornlands of La Beauce; or when from a comparable distance over the olive groves you see the huge bulk of the amphitheatre of El Djem. Or there is the Pyramid of Cheops, to mention in the same breath as Ely, but with the proviso that neither amphitheatre nor pyramid are works of art. This, Ely is most emphatically, and at nearer view one might almost add with a vengeance, for there is something militant as of a soldier-minded Prince-Palatine[1] about the castellation of its west tower, and no less so the castellated turret to its side. It would be no surprise to see bowmen or archers on duty and at look-out on those towers. The nave of Ely in severe Norman style is in the same uncompromising mood till we arrive at the soaring octagon which is something unique in cathedral building and one of the aesthetic and engineering marvels of the Early Middle Ages. The petrified stalks of the vaulting, stalks stripped of their leaves, spread wide their symmetrical and open fans into the star vault of the lantern, which is in fact more like a passion-flower or clematis. The choir beyond this is of pointed architecture with, for lighter and later relief, the seething and prick-ling of the stone stalagmites of Bishop Alcock's chantry chapel in chamber-music Perpendicular. Beyond that again to the left-hand side the Lady Chapel, of earlier elaboration, is of rich sub-aqueous effect owing to the green lights in its chalky whiteness, and is the marvellous finish to a morning or an evening that opened in militant spirit and ends at this foretaste of the calm, empty churches of the nearby fens.

But such adventure is the more enjoyable when it is some old abbey which was but a name before, or even unknown to one and unheard of, and I now attempt an instance in either category, East Anglia, by and large, at its full extent into Norfolk, Suffolk, Essex, and the fen-counties of Cambridge and Huntingdon, being an area of study large enough to last a lifetime. I am remembering in the first place a late autumn afternoon when I saw the nave and two towers of Wymondham Abbey looming through the November mists. It looked at that moment like some great vessel washed ashore; turned-turtle, even, with the roof of its nave for keel and the pair of great engine-rooms or power-houses of uncertain purpose floating upside down in the tideless air of dusk. The great tower of Wymondham is in fact octagonal and, sinister thought, it will have been from one of the upper openings in this steeple that William Kett, a leader of the Rebellion of 1549, was hanged in chains. Had one entered the Abbey only a few years ago 'when services were only conducted under great difficulties owing to the

---

[1] Bishop van Mildert, last Prince-Palatine of Durham (d. 1836), is buried in the Cathedral. He continued to the end to wear his own version of a full bottomed, or judge's wig, much to the annoyance of Ernest Augustus, Duke of Cumberland and King of Hanover.

intrusion of wind and rain through cracks and crevices in the fabric', the illusion of entering the hull of a wrecked vessel must have been stronger still. But the angels of the hammer-beam roof still look down on us, most appropriately here at Wymondham, for this special feature of Norfolk and Suffolk churches is more akin to shipbuilding than to mere carpentering; while the double storey of Norman arches that form the nave are of the stern, the quasi-military school of Ely. And we come away from Wymondham looking back at its towers just as the rooks are wheeling in the winter mists.

Binham Priory, also of the Benedictine monks, near Walsingham, is my other instance chosen in all honesty because I had not even heard of it before. There is but the nave of the church still standing, which became the parish church and occupies, it is said, but one-sixth of the area of the original building. The aisles, the cloister, the guest house, are all in ruins. But there is forlorn and masculine splendour in what is left, the more memorable on that fine Sunday morning. There is little or nothing at Binham Priory to interpose between ourselves and the early thirteenth century, which whether we would have liked it or not is present here and not to be gainsaid even by the sudden screech of a jet-bomber overhead.

Such, and but at random, are experiences that could be repeated in nearly every part of England. If I mention but one more of them in this context, and only a single detail of it at that, it is for the reason that this leaves as lasting an impression as any of the wonders of mediaeval monastery churches in France or Spain. And why indeed should it not do so, for there are places and things of the kind in England just as wonderful as any to be seen abroad. It is at Tewkesbury, an old town in Worcestershire, where the Severn and the Avon join one another, which is not without poetic and symbolic significance and portends at least that it is right in the middle of historic England. The abbey here is most beautiful and impressive from all points of view, not least from the tombs in their chantry chapels that stand round the choir. But on the north side of the choir is the Despenser tomb with the kneeling, mailed figure of its long-dead occupant, Sir Edward le Despenser, kneeling with his face towards the altar. It is as effective and shattering in that silence as a trumpet blown from a tower in the dark of night. And, at that, some old cavalry call of the armoured horsemen. The kneeling figure facing the altar is there night and day, year in, year out, down the centuries, and indeed has knelt there for some six hundred years. It is not a lifesize figure, being in fact no more than half-lifesize. But if we walk round the choir so as to get the best view of him, which is from over the roof of the chantry chapel opposite, the effect, almost the sound of it, is as strange and haunting as that first time one hears the muezzin calling from a minaret, and we come out of Tewkesbury Abbey and back into the present enriched by an experience in its little way as marvellous and memorable as any shock of the suddenly revealed past in whatever other land.

For my first chapter, which has for subject the monasteries and nunneries of England, the material is so copious in every part of the kingdom, although the monastic system came early to an arbitrary and abrupt end, that I have set it down in form of an itinerary or hypothetical journey round and round the country, landing, as it were, on the island and returning eventually to the starting point. There seemed to be no other way to avoid the static 'E.E.' 'Dec.' 'Perp.' and other peremptory terms and admonitions necessary in taking the theme as a whole, century by century, all parts of England at the same time. The method devised gives freedom of movement and takes us where we will. It is a vast subject consisting, as it does, of dead things and things living; by which I intend the ruins, Glastonbury, Fountains, and so on, and the living fanes, Gloucester, Durham, and so forth, where the monks were, and which are still used as churches. One emerges from the spoliation of the monasteries with a lively respect for Henry VIII, the maker of Renaissance England, based mainly on the fear of him, but hating him for his rapacity and cruelty. He may have given shape to the country as it came out of the Middle Ages into the modern world, but it was the overflow or superflux of his huge energies. It was not the only, or even the main intention he had in mind, and he helped himself upon the way.

There are still two opinions, two schools of thought upon the monks in England, and perhaps it is possible to illustrate these by two anecdotes that argue the differing points of view. The first recounts how a lonely sportsman rowing his way home from wildfowl shooting on the fens upon a winter evening in the moonlight saw something ahead of him in the water, and as his oar was about to strike it looked with sudden horror at the pallid bloated face of a monk floating there half in the reeds. He saw the tonsured head and the folds of the brown robe, and rowed on not liking to look back again. This ghost story of but mild potency, coming from a part of England which was full of great abbeys 'set on islands and river banks round the edges of the fens', from in fact a monkish paradise, shows one side of the picture. For we are to imagine the apparition as being the ghost of some monk arraigned and, we may be sure, convicted for those vices of which the King's Commissioners were so lavish in accusing others at that time or earlier, for there had been all the centuries before Henry VIII when there were bad monks. And worse and wickeder kings, as well. The other anecdote is of a different kind. It concerns a wood, I think a wood of beech trees, between Stow-on-the-Wold and Winchcomb in Gloucestershire, at Temple Guiting. This is one of the rare woods where lilies of the valley grow wild in England. A country legend tells that the lilies were planted by the monks wherever they stayed for the night upon some journey. Whither, or where from, we are not told. Nor the purpose of the journey. Nor where else the lilies are found growing. The wood must be a lovely sight in May or June, so beautiful indeed that it calls for explanation, and this could be what gave rise to the legend. It speaks well of the monks. Or is it no more than a countryman's tale; like that which says the Milky Way across the heavens led to the shrine at Walsingham? Which the Spaniards, too, saw for their part as it crossed the empyrean and called St James's Way. Either reason or other, it is but a legend about a wood of lilies of the valley.

The chapter following on the English monasteries and nunneries is very different in purpose and intention. This, designedly, for contrast, though the spirit or animus inhabiting these fantastic and uninhibited creations may not be so far removed as we may imagine from certain facets of the mediaeval mind. It has even been argued that the German Rococo is in some aspects a direct continuation of the Middle Ages, and this view of it, if exaggerated, is more convincing than the theory that the mid-Victorian church builders took up Gothic exactly where it had been left off or lain down and carried it to its logical conclusion. Time moved slowly in past centuries. Germany, torn by religious troubles and by the Thirty Years War, was in abeyance and did not recover until the end of the seventeenth century when the generation of Bach and Handel, and of the architects Neumann, Fischer, Zimmermann, was born. Things had not changed much visually; and if it would be an over-simplification to say that the main difference and innovation was that men wore wigs, it is at least the case that there were few new buildings, little other change or alteration in provincial dress, and that the wig at least and at any rate shows a foreign influence from Louis XIV, the arbiter and great man of the age.

The long dormancy of Germany, lasting from 1550 until 1700, over the span of four or five human generations, left behind it a stagnant provincialism which was yet a fertile soil for new ideas. Hence the quick overrunning of Catholic Germany by the Rococo. But it has to be seen as grafted upon the old mediaeval stock. The background of J. S. Bach, of Dominikus Zimmermann, of any and all of those others mentioned, will have been unbelievably old-fashioned even in its time. First to emerge from the chrysalis or the state of dormancy were the Austrians of the Hereditary Dominions, revitalized by the defeat of the Turkish armies and the raising of the siege of Vienna in 1683. Italian architects came to work for the Habsburg Emperors, to be followed by Fischer von Erlach, Lukas von Hildebrandt and their generation, all of them, be it noted, some forty to fifty years older than the Bavarian and Southern German creators of the Rococo. I have not attempted to conceal my preference for the Rococo over the Baroque in this part of Europe. The Italian architects and fresco painters who arrived in Austria, the Carlone family, or the Altomontes, were not first rate of their kind, if better than painters whom the English suffered like Antonio Verrio, and the native architects when they appeared in the next generation had immense opportunities, but their talent failed them. Only at Melk, at St Florian, did they come up to the occasion, though it would be wrong to belittle the Austrian school of fresco painters who are to be seen to advantage in the libraries and the Kaisersaals of monasteries, let alone the churches; but they, too, are sub-Italian, and if more than passable, not phenomenal. There is a dullness as of the Italianate at second-hand even about the great monasteries of the Danube Valley, and it is arguable that the Austrians, secure in their future after the defeat of the Turkish armies, spent a great part of their energies on the recalcitrant and heretical Bohemians. It is for this reason that Prague with its magnificent Baroque palaces and churches is *par excellence* the city of the Counter-Reformation, and in point of architecture is that much more interesting than Vienna.

How are the fantastic elegancies of the Bavarian Rococo to be explained? Only, as to one aspect of it, by reminding ourselves that its ultra-refinement and elegance are not so unique and isolated as one might think. There are unknown and forgotten parallels in other parts of Europe that are now coming back into general acknowledgement and recognition. Lecce, in Apulia, with its churches and palaces, and other towns near by: Noto, in Sicily, with its superb balconies and façades of convents, and not Noto only, but other towns, Modica, Ragusa, and Vittoria; provincial towns like Lucena and Priego in Andalucia; and the huge old monasteries and convents in Northern Portugal to which I have tried to draw attention in the appropriate chapter, for they are indeed remarkable and a little inexplicable; all of these, and others, are part of the same phenomenon.

It is a mystery that resolves itself into one main question. What was their degree of sophistication? Where the Rococo of Bavaria is concerned, were their flights of fantasy in stuccowork, in woodcarving, in fresco painting but a development and a further flowering of the peasant arts in sub-Alpine villages; arts, to put it crudely, of the cuckoo clock and Christmas tree? But this, looking at it from another angle, is no more remarkable than that, say, the son of an inn keeper and butcher should become a great musical composer[1] in a part of the world, though (Moravia), where most of the

[1] Dvořák.

villagers were musicians and there were many village bands. It cannot be ignored that there was the necessary predisposition toward carving, modelling, painting, in the sub-Alpine valleys, and that this must have been the foundation and start of the movement, just as the golden stone of Apulia that hardens after carving explains the graceful lines and the fantastic ornaments of Lecce. But that far extremity of Apulia must always remain remote and in a corner. Bavaria, by contrast, was in the centre of things but half-sleeping, or, after wars and religious struggles, comatose but convalescent.

It lay in a deep trance that had continued from the Middle Ages, and that was safeguarded in its own somnolence by the Holy Roman Empire of which the Seven Electors, though still in full function of their powers, had become as much of a legend and an anachronism as the Seven Sleepers in their grotto or cave at Ephesus.[1] Yet this was the state 'which had existed paramount in Europe longer than any in ancient or modern times, in spite of the dangerous system of elected, instead of hereditary, emperors; whose long line of fifty monarchs exhibits not one tyrant, nor did any of them fall by the fury of the people'. It had been by far the most powerful state in Europe, lasting as it did from the successors of Charlemagne in the ninth century until the Napoleonic Wars. The long slumber of this millenary institution must have been most curious to witness; and nowhere more so than at Regensburg (Ratisbon) where the Imperial Diets were held in latter days, sixty-two of them between 1663 and 1806. Just the lawyers in their long wigs and gowns, and the spectacled scribes who indited legal documents in the mediaeval German lettering upon vellum, will have been a sight that has gone out of the world never to come back again.

It was, need it be added, a state of things in which the monks and nuns proliferated, as they have always done in the stern beginning, and also in the vegetative decay. No condition indeed suited them better than this latter. But in this particular instance they were alive, at least in their building projects, with a new vitality and an elegance ill-matched to the uncouth language spoken. Thus, while certain of the architects, Balthasar Neumann at Vierzehnheiligen, the Court dwarf Cuvilliès at Schäftlarn, Dominikus Zimmermann at Günzburg and Steinhausen, surely J. M. Fischer, too, with his enormous practice – he built more than fifty churches – were to some

---

[1] During the persecution of the Christians in the reign of Diocletian (AD 283 – 304) seven young men with a dog fled to a cave for refuge, and falling asleep did not wake until two hundred years after, though they were not conscious of having slept more than one night. They awoke and went down to the city where they recognized neither people, money, or language; everything was changed and all the city had become Christian. The cave is still shown, and the legend respected by Eastern Christians and Moslems alike.

degree cosmopolitan figures who had worked for Electors and Prince-Bishops, others of the architects and craftsmen of the German Rococo were more earthbound and proletarian. The Asam Brothers, despite their student years in Rome, were of the latter; and Andreas and Caspar Moosbrugger, or Michael and Peter Thumb; their very names bespeak their peasant origin. Yet the latter's Cistercian pilgrimage church of Neu-Birnau, on a hillslope above Lake Constance, yields nothing in fantastic elegance to Cuvilliès' Amalienburg, or J. B. Neumann's Court Chapel in the Residenz at Würzburg, two veritable masterpieces of their kind. From which it is to be assumed that the sophistication was of profound, inborn nature and more than skin deep. But it is apparent that not nearly enough is known yet about these architects and craftsmen, and epistolary material being meagre for the too simple reason that German is a more difficult and intractable language to write in than English, French, Spanish, or Italian, this is a situation that is unlikely ever to be improved upon. It must always remain therefore something of a mystery.

A love of more than forty years' duration for the churches and palaces of German Rococo has made me embrace this opportunity of writing of them probably for the last time. It is only sad for my purpose that the paragon of its kind, the pilgrimage church of Wies, does not qualify for inclusion. The art of façade, of exterior presentation, was not in the Bavarian temperament, while its predominance among the Italians, a part of their Southern eloquence, often made of the exterior a work of art, that lost voice and became muddled and ineffectual in the inside of the building. So it is that the marvel of Wies is its interior which attains to a height of fantasy that, it might be thought, no technique whatever in the arts of decoration could be capable of executing and bringing to successful conclusion. Happily, the pilgrimage church at Steinhausen, another masterwork by Dominikus Zimmermann, being of monastic foundation, falls within my theme. This, and Balthasar Neumann's Vierzehnheiligen, and that incomparable pair Ottobeuren and Zwiefalten, are the wonders of monastic Rococo in Southern Germany. The vast and entire world of monks and nuns, thinking afar and beyond our own frontiers to the lake-gardens and golden screens of Zen monasteries in Kyoto, would be a sadder place without them.

The chapter on Italy has been easier to undertake, for almost everyone who has been to Italy must have seen a monastery. On the other hand they are few who have penetrated to the Certosa di Padula or the Badia Santa Maria in Pomposa, stylistic extremities that are as far apart in intention as they are in distance. I have begun the Italian chapter with a childhood pilgrimage of my own to a monastery outside Florence embarked upon whenever I was taken to Italy for the Easter holidays, an early and wonderful blessing and dispensation in my life; and I have to add that the sight of the Certosa del Galluzzo on its cypressed hill this summer, after I had not seen it for a quarter of a century, and the sensation of the long and hot climb again up to its magical gate that opened onto so many marvels which are not yet exhausted, which are in fact hardly tasted, is something I shall never forget, a thing that rejoins and renews itself in incredible manner with the memories of childhood.

Another experience of the receding but ever present past was the sight of a fanatical, wild-looking figure in a white monk's robe in the street outside a church in Genoa, one of the less pleasant of Italian cities. My eyes can only have caught him for a moment all told that morning when I was nine or ten years old, but I can see now the fury and wildness of his black hair, his eagle nose and his fanatical stare. He seemed to me to be whirled or blown along in a gust of wind, more than it could be said prosaically that he walked or moved away. But he was lost in an instant in the crowd. I asked the sacristan of the church he had just emerged from a minute ago, who this strange figure could be, and his answer was 'a hermit from the hills', and he had seen him before and knew him. And then the sacristan walked away, and would not be bothered with further questioning from a small boy. This hermit, if he was that, became associated in my mind with the figure of Peter the Hermit preaching the First Crusade; and I have no doubt that a lifelong interest in every kind of Gypsy and 'traveller' upon the roads, whether fairground folk or wandering tinkers, and in every form of ascetic from the tramp-monks in Magnasco's paintings to the trident-bearing *saddhus* of Ganges or Brahmaputra, naked and rubbed with ashes, had its origin in the proto-monk of Genoa. I feel his effluence alike in the encampment of Roumanian Coppersmith Gypsies seen in the spring of this year at Recife, in a suburb of the town, a marvellous Callot-like scene of huge low tents with the allurement of a dozen Carmens and their flashing eyes and smiles, and in the monks of the monastery of Petropavlovsk who come later in these pages. Of such is a personal mythology made up, and it lasts and never fades.

At Venice I have lamented the absence of the four great banqueting scenes by Veronese which once adorned the refectories of its chief monasteries. Once they were the sight of Venice, and showed not 'La Serenissima' only but the monks of the religious orders at their height of Renaissance splendour only a generation or so before the decadence of the Republic.

> But chief her shrine where naked Venus keeps,
> And Cupids ride the lion of the deeps;

Where eased of fleets, the Adriatic main
Wafts the smooth eunuch and enamoured swain

and we ask ourselves how these lines of genius came to be written by a poet who had never seen the Bacino di San Marco, nor set foot in Venice.

The monks and friars had their enormous churches, here as in other towns in Italy, built, we may think, in competition with each other, and the nuns employed themselves for their part in teaching the orphans to sing, their musical schools or conservatoires combining indeed something of the screened or latticed gaiety of the convent *parlatorio*, as seen in Francesco Guardi's paintings, with the delights and amenities of the stage door and green room. Particularly was this the case with La Pietà, the church of which almost inevitably in the circumstances has a painted ceiling by Tiepolo. The traveller M de Lalande, writing of this in 1790, praises its 'excellente musique, executée par les filles de la maison', and continues in his chapter on *Les Spectacles de Venise* to tell us there are three other conservatoires of the kind, with a hundred orphans in each, for whom the Doge and Senate pay about a hundred livres a year. 'Elles vont dans les concerts particuliers et viennent dans les campagnes. Il est permis de les voir dans la maison, et de leur faire du bien', which could be rendered: 'they go to private concerts and can be invited (to villas) on the terra firma. One is allowed to see them in the convent and give them presents.' And in the same chapter he continues with the other schools of music; l'Ospedaletto, l'Incurabili, and I Mendicanti, known particularly for its voices, where, 'la musique s'exécute derrière un grillage peu ferré, et l'on a le plaisir d'y voir des musiciennes excellentes toucher les instruments avec délicatesse, avec grace, et avec le force et les sciences des meilleurs maîtres'.[1] And de Lalande remarks again that the *patricien protecteur de la maison* can arrange admission for strangers to hear them sing and play, that the famous La Padovanina was singing there lately, and La Sacchetti and La Pavana only a year or two before, in 1784. But we go back, of predilection, to La Pietà of the Tiepolo ceiling, where the red-haired Vivaldi, *il prete rosso*, was organist and music-master, and where Dr Burney on a visit to Venice saw a young and pretty nun conducting the choir and orchestra of orphan children with a sprig of pomegranate blossom tucked between her coif and hair.

There is the temptation to linger on the terra firma and not go far from Venice with that quatrain by Pope on La Serenissima in her decadence still in mind. But to Verona, at any rate, the second city of the Venetian mainland,

---

[1] 'The music is performed behind a lattice of but thin bars, and one has the pleasure of seeing first rate musicians playing their instruments with delicacy and grace, and with the force and science of the best masters.'

to visit San Zeno Maggiore (whence the monks had removed at the time of de Lalande's visit), if only because of its red marble portal of the twelfth century, wildly romantic of purport, lion-supported, with reliefs of the Arian heretic Theodoric as a wild huntsman, *le chasseur maudit*, speeding headlong to the devil, and because of its marvellous triptych by Mantegna, perhaps the greatest painting extant in any monastery foundation. And writing these lines after having been to Verona again this summer (1964), and after dealing with the monasteries of the Venetian mainland in a later chapter of this present work, there is an overwhelming picture of Venetian magnificence in the *Martyrdom of St George* by Veronese in San Giorgio in Braida, where were Benedictine monks when de Lalande saw it. How could one forget coming into that church on the 'left bank' of the Adige late in the evening behind an old priest and his housekeeper, a middle-aged woman of pleasant appearance wearing a kind of mantilla on her head! While he said his prayers before each altar, too old to kneel but sitting on a bench, she was at her devotions, coming back to him from time to time to look after him and guide his faltering steps. But the light had fused on the great picture behind the high altar, and it was too dark to make it out in detail. Then, wonderfully and unexpectedly, the sacristan mended the light and the picture was lit up in all its splendour; the horseman with the noble head, baton in hand, looking down on the death scene and mounted on a huge horse more than half the height of the whole canvas; the negro page at his saddle-girth in a doublet of green silk; another figure of a horse held by a turban'd Oriental on the left side to balance the composition; and behind that for background a flight of Palladian buildings falling in perspective into the distance, with spectators watching from the balconies. It was a moment ever to be remembered and a picture of the great Venetian Republic in its pride, a magnificence the like of which with its velvets and galleons and pillared palaces the world will never see again.

But the pullulation or swarming of the monks took effect on the warm soil of the south, where sloth and ignorance filled the monasteries, but it would be no more right to censure them for this than to blame any other section of the population for failure to make anything useful out of their lives. In thinking of which I cannot get out of my mind a memory of the opening of a new hotel at Acireale, on the slopes of Etna, in the winter of 1922. At the time I was there, all night long we heard rumbling noises and now and again a loud explosion, seemingly under one's feet, but in fact from one of the craters of the volcano, and the night was lit by the fires of burning streams of lava. The bishop and clergy had gone in solemn progress to hold a service of intercession at the edges of the lava streams, and it was quite a serious eruption. But all was forgotten and gaiety reigned again next morning as the hotel was got ready for its formal opening. The tables in the dining-room were loaded with viands of every kind, and at last towards four o'clock in the afternoon the doors were thrown open. In swarmed the notabilities of Acireale, the mayor and aldermen, the chief of police, and so on, but more numerous and more compact as a body than all the others were some twenty or thirty monks, Capuchin friars to judge from their brown robes, and in five minutes there was not an ice, not *a granita d'arancio*, or *di limone*, or a *cassata siciliana*, to be had. All had been swallowed and gobbled down by the monks, a sight and a sensation that took one back into the Middle Ages, when a pendant scene to this could have been witnessed in any country in Europe while the drones were still in their heyday, before they were expelled and driven away.

The only parallel to this in my own experience was motoring through a remote part of Bohemia, somewhere near Krumau, and stopping just as it got dark at a monastery with a fine Baroque church. The door was open, and we entered the church in the dusk, and then going into the monastery found ourselves in the refectory where a huge feast was preparing. The white-robed monks, they must have been Cistercian, were bustling in and out from the kitchens on their sandalled feet, carrying dishes and putting down plates, and I remember that there was a cold partridge before each place laid at the three long tables. Had the good monks shot the birds themselves in the monastery park? And there were bowls for soup, dishes of fruit with bunches of grapes, and certainly more than one wine glass by the side of every plate. A monk who spoke a few words of French told us it was all for the bishop's arrival who was expected that night in the monastery. And we drove away. This was in 1929, before the *Anschluss* and much else that has happened since, but it is another picture of a mediaeval world that survived in forgotten corners of Europe until the dawning of the atomic age.[1]

From Italy, writing on the monks and nuns, it is an easy and an obvious step to Spain. Here, the convents of Royal foundation are of especial importance and they amount to an unique feature. There is certainly nothing of its kind in Europe to compare with the convent of Las Huelgas, outside Burgos. But there is a Royal convent of only lesser interest in Madrid itself, the interior of which was inaccessible until December 1960, for which reason it is only now written of in this Introduction and not in the body of this present work. It is probably only the dull, unpromising exterior of the

---

[1] As, too, in less pleasant ambience, the Capuchin friars of Mazzarino convicted in the recent Mafia trial in Sicily.

Descalzas Reales that can explain the mystery of its survival 'only a stone's throw from the Gran Via' during the Civil War. The foundress of this convent of Barefoot Franciscan nuns was Doña Juana de Austria, daughter of the Emperor Charles V, sister of Philip II, sister-in-law, therefore, of our Queen Mary I, and mother of Dom Sebastian of Portugal, a personage in fact of rather more than dim importance, on whose genealogical ramifications it is tempting to write at greater length. In the convent church there is the white marble figure of this lady kneeling at her faldstool, by Pompeo Leoni, counterpart to the kneeling bronze statues of her father, brother, and other members of her family by the same sculptor on either side of the high altar at the Escorial. So many widowed Empresses, Queens and Infantas came to live here as nuns that it has been described, not inappropriately, as 'a continuation of the Royal Palace'. In one of the rooms there is a mock-Himalaya, a Kailasa of relics piled on top of one another up to the ceiling. There are superb vestments; royal portraits innumerable of familiar feature, so inbred were the Habsburgs; and any number of extraordinary and touching objects, such as an image of the Infant Jesus in seventeenth-century costume, sitting in an armchair 'in pensive attitude', leaning his head upon his hand; but this is the oddity about it, it is like one of the 'big-head' dolls of baby boys, or *gosho-ningyô* of the doll shops of Kyoto in Japan. Such is a little detail of the Descalzas Reales and its treasures; but the most imposing feature is its painted stair, on climbing which, above the landing on the right-hand wall, there is the sudden vision of Philip IV, his wife Queen Mariana of Austria and the Infanta Margarita looking down from a Royal box or balcony, in counterfeit and exactly as in *Las Meninas* by Velazquez, that miracle of painting; but this is by another and lesser hand, attributed now to Claudio Coello, a most curious supporting or favourable witness to the strange life of Kings.

The curtain of invisibility has been lifted on Las Huelgas and on the convent of the Descalzas Reales, but the Royal nunnery of Sigena, which can have been no less interesting and no less of a survival from the remote past, is a total loss. That there are yet unknown and invisible treasures in Spain will be apparent from the mention of the Royal convents of Tordesillas and Astudillo, and there are stories of Mudéjar ceilings in a convent in Segovia which is still in strict *clausura*. This could seem of little moment in a kingdom which has Poblet and Guadalupe and the Escorial within its borders. Lovers of forgotten fanes can have their fill in the north-east corner of Spain on the road to Santiago, and I have at least mentioned by name some few of the huge old abbeys. They are in a part of the country which eludes the extremes and rigours of the Spanish climate, and in their season nothing could be more beautiful than the green, spring-like setting of these ancient monasteries.

Even so, the descent from them into Northern Portugal, which is not so easy of accomplishment, has some of the effect of arrival in a promised land or Elysian vale. I hope to have proved this part of Portugal was a paradise for monks and nuns. Some ten or a dozen old monasteries and convents offer delights of so unappreciated a sort that experience makes of them a private and personal possession of one's own. I have written before on more than one occasion of the convent church of Santa Clara at Oporto and of the Convent of Jesus at Aveiro, so my admiration for them is declared and will, I hope, be proved contagious. The 'golden' chapels of Portugal that in every instance are of association with monks and nuns, and of which the theory was carried across the Atlantic and re-created in Brazil,[1] are a special and particular feature to which there is no parallel in Spain. Of what there can have been of the sort in Lisbon before the earthquake of 1757 there is no knowing. It was shaken down in golden dust and all destroyed.

Taste, it could be, was more 'correct' in the metropolis of Portugal, but I much doubt it. The few churches in Lisbon that survived the earthquake are sober in mood but that may be only because their decoration was more solid and less brittle. The gilded woodwork of pelmets and organ-cases, which are among the delights of Portugal and carried here to lengths of fantasy attained elsewhere with fan-vaults or painted ceilings, would not need much of a shake or rude shock before it collapsed and crumbled. With her four great monasteries of Belém, Tomar, Alcobaça, and Batalha, it would be true to say that the architectural and the archaeological interest of Portugal lies in her old abbeys to which an exotic flavour is imparted by the Manoelino style and the use made of *azulejos* (tiles). But the districts alone round Braga in the north and Evora in the south of Portugal dazzle and astonish by the number of their monasteries and convents. At least in point of picturesque and pleasurable interest they form one of the very few areas of aesthetic sensation left unknown and untrodden anywhere in Europe.

If somewhat of the same feeling that it is one's own personal and private possession may grow upon us at sites such as Conques or La Charité in France, deriving from their solitude and loneliness, it is the fact that they and their like have been the subject of research and argument for all of a hundred years and more. This is not the case in Portugal where, also, a second or third wind of activity continued almost into the wars of Napoleon. But the force that built great abbeys throughout Europe was largely French in origin, and it is in France that we would hope to find it in its primal

---

[1] Particularly at the 'golden' church of São Francisco at Bahia and the Capela Dourada at Recife.

purity. Would it not be true to say that expectation of an Italy or Spain presupposes some later addition or some ment that purists would qualify as corrupt and in bad o in France, probably because by the time the French had which is one of the results of civilization rebelling against c system had brought about reform within its own body her lived lazily doing nothing at all with the communal their religion seriously, as at La Trappe, to the point of erity. Let us remember that the Benedictines, the Cisterans were French in origin, and the architecture that spread went with the monks to many European countries was as eloquent as the lives they lived or any of their preaching.

As the expression of both a purpose and an ideal there has never been anything in human history to surpass the monastery churches of the eleventh and twelfth centuries in France. There is no such intensity of feeling in the temples of the ancient world; nor are there buildings of this nature in the Far East where the motive force was a passive and not an activist religion. Only in the mosques of the ninth and tenth centuries, as seen in Cairo at Ibn Tulun or Sultan Hassan, or in the Mosque of the Omayyads at Damascus, is there some equivalent to the simplicity in passion of the Cistercian churches, and to their ability to make of a forecourt, an infirmary, or a mere barn, a work of art that combines utility with a grave and serious beauty. Of a certainty there was direct influence from these Muslim buildings as a result of the Crusades, and it is a conscious plagiarism the more understandable if it is conceded that a higher civilization obtained under the Caliphs of Damascus and Córdoba than any in Europe until at least the thirteenth century. That there is this flavour as it were of Saladin (d. 1193) in the pointed arches of the Cistercians is not to be disputed, while it is a compliment to the Saracens that any retro-influence from the Military Orders of Christendom upon their foes has never been suggested. The missionary energies of the French monks from Cluny and Cîteaux, their architecture accompanying them and forming an important part of both their doctrine and their example, has some right to be considered as an expenditure of vital forces not less exhausting than that which crippled Spain and Portugal in the generation after the discovery of the Americas and the voyages to the Indies. The comparative stagnation or vegetative decay of the late Gothic in France, and the ugliness of dress, furniture, ornament, almost everything under the Valois Kings, may have been symptoms of that weakness and fatigue from which France did not recover until the reign of Louis XIV.

At mere mention of the Military Orders a huge theme unfolds itself, for which there has not been space enough within these present pages. How to accommodate Kalat Seman of the Syrian pillar-hermits; Krak des Chevaliers, 'the best preserved and most wholly admirable castle in the world', its cold stone in such good order that the steel-clad garrison could move in again tomorrow; Rhodes of the Knights of St John, and its 'auberges' of golden stone, a street of mediaeval houses that mingles the Levant with the wool-villages of the Cotswolds; Malta, the sea-bastion of Valletta, and its Co-Cathedral of St John's 'with all the chivalry of Europe within its walls', twenty-four tombs of the Grand Masters, and its paving one huge carpet or tapestry of inlaid heraldic floor-slabs of the Knights, but it is indeed a *Totentanz* or Dance of Death, for so many of them include the grinning and prancing figure of a human skeleton! But this is far from all that should be included. There could be Marienburg, the castle of the Grand Masters of the Teutonic Order, who held East Prussia in fief from the Kings of Poland, an enormous brick building, its Summer and Winter Halls with ceilings of intersecting network supported by a single granite column, in fact a brick barracks typical of the eternal Prussian. The Teutonic Order had more castle-strongholds of red brick at Königsberg, and elsewhere in East Prussia, but it would be a pleasanter task to write of their chapels and commanderies in Bohemia and Silesia and other outlying parts of the Habsburg Empire; this in the Baroque age when the rule had been relaxed, there being no more pagan Lithuanians to convert, and when the interests of the Knights had become largely a matter of heraldry to judge from their monuments.

Were the subject carried only a little further it could end at Bayreuth with the chapel and chapter-house of the 'Ordre de la Sincerité', founded by one of the Margraves, where are the arms and shields of the Knights, but later he converted it into the Order of the Red Eagle; or, better still at Ansbach, in the Swan Chapel of the St Gumbertus-Kirche, intended by the Margrave Albert Achilles at its foundation in 1459 to be the capital or headquarters in South Germany of the Knights of the Swan. Here can be seen the 'Swan Altar' with a painting by Wolgemut with portraits of Albert Achilles and his Margravine, and stone monuments of the knights with their hatchments above them, all with swans in view. But this excursion into the realms of Lohengrin takes us outside our bounds; or for their heraldic interest only we could include the stall-plates of Knights of the Garter at St George's Chapel, Windsor. Those are Orders of Chivalry and not monastic orders for they have no religious purpose and their members have not taken vows of celibacy.

Exception, however, could be made for the abbesses of Quedlinburg, in the Harz Mountains, who were Princesses of the Holy Roman Empire,

Opposite: Statue of Sainte-Foy
from Conques

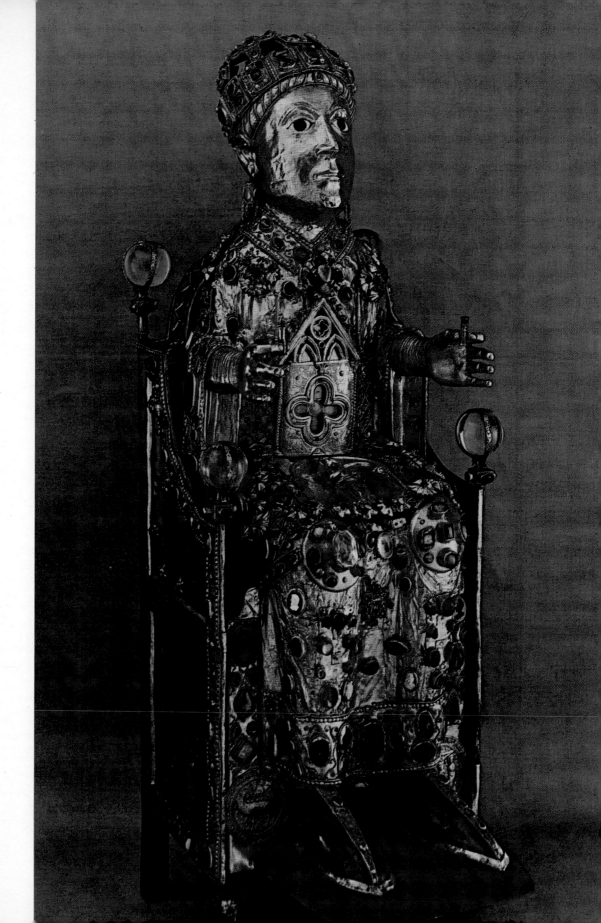

'independant of all spiritual sovereigns save the Pope, having a vote in the German Diet, and a seat on the bench of Rhenish bishops'; a Teutonic pendant in fact, to the abbesses of Remiremont in the mountains of the Vosges. At the Reformation, the abbesses adopted the Lutheran faith, 'lost their feudal sovereignty and most of their estates', and the number of nuns was reduced to five. In its church I have seen the mummified body of the famous beauty Aurora von Königsmarck, mistress of Augustus the Strong of Saxony, mother of the Maréchal de Saxe, and ancestress of George Sand. She was for many years prioress of the nunnery. And having progressed thus far from our conventual frame we should end in Denmark at the lay-convents of Vallø, Gisselfeld, and their like, of which I have written elsewhere. describing how they stand in fine parks like English country houses, and mentioning the portraits of the prioresses, handsome crinolined ladies with powdered hair, crozier in hand, wearing diamond necklaces and earrings.[1]

In the final chapter on monasteries of the Eastern Church I have enlarged the subject a little beyond its usual limits in order to include Roumanian convents such as that of Hurez which offered until only a few years back as living a picture of a nunnery in some outlying province of the Byzantine Empire during the later Middle Ages as any to be gleaned upon the monastery-island of Mount Athos; and a picture perhaps with less of idiosyncrasy and less moribund and dying. I think, also, that the monks of Petropavlovsk in the Danube Delta yielded nothing in picturesque pathos and hopelessness to the monks of the Holy Mountain. When I saw them they were indeed outcasts and rejects from a world that had long passed them and gone by.

They were Russian and not Greek monks it is true; but I suppose that in the minds of even the most ignorant of them the mention of Mount Athos, of the monasteries of Meteora, or of St Catherine of Mount Sinai, would strike some echo, no less, I would like to think, than the names of the Himalayan 'monasteries' of Pashupatinat, Kedranath, or Badrinath to the Hindu *saddhu*, trident in hand, and rubbed with ashes, satisfied as I am while I write this to have seen at least the first named of these shrines. The fame of those mountain-monasteries of the Eastern Church will have reached even to sub-Arctic Solovetsk on its island off Archangel, in the White Sea. Access to mediaeval Russia, not by way of St Petersburg of the rostral columns and classical porticos and colonnades, is had through reading *The Travels of Macarius, Patriarch of Antioch* under whose auspices we arrive in Moscow and visit the monasteries of the Troitsa and the Voskresenski or New Jerusalem, tempered as to the first of these by the Rococo of 'Count'

[1] *cf. Denmark*, Batsford, 1956, pp. 86–9.

Rastrelli. It was a golden age for the monks under the Empress Elizabeth, daughter of Peter the Great, but the philosophizing tastes of the Empress Catherine and her friendship with the French 'encyclopaedists' was less rewarding to them though her astute mind led her to lean on and make use of their ignorance while she lived her life according to her own ideals. It is no less significant that the sinister figure of a monk, or crypto-monk, should loom in the last months of the Russian monarchy, his murder and the reasons for it bringing what was mediaeval in Russia into modern, and no less troubled times.

Aware as I must be of many inadequacies and omissions in this present work, I have to admit that there is not even mention of the many monasteries there were in Poland, the most Catholic of countries, or in Czechoslovakia, the greater portion of which was both showcase and stamping ground for the Counter-Reformation. Thus, a town like Vilna has some ten or a dozen churches of religious Orders, all with convents attached, in a livelier version of late or 'secondary' Baroque than that obtaining in the churches of Warsaw, and a few of them in the local or Vilna variant on the Rococo. It is in fact a city full of fine buildings, a large proportion of which are or were monasteries and convents. The same conditions prevailed, too, only some fifty miles away at Kaunus (Kovno) where there are Baroque convents and churches, the majority of the Lithuanians being Catholic. Over the rest of Poland, incessant invasion by Turks, Tartars, Swedes, and Russians, with more recently two world wars, left the country ravaged and without too many vestiges and remains of its past history. Lwow and Cracow have their old monasteries and convents but without any building that much distinguishes itself or rises above the level of the 'secondary' Baroque. An idea of Warsaw at its apogee during the reign of Stanislas Augustus Poniatowski (1764-95), before the Third Partition of Poland, is to be obtained from the paintings of Bernardo Bellotto, nephew of the great Canaletto, and it is to be seen in them that the churches of Warsaw had classical façades, if unimaginative and lacking in invention, but in sign of study in Rome, or the following of Roman example.

At Prague it is a different matter altogether, for this city can claim to have the most splendid and imposing architecture of any town in Europe after Rome and Venice, due in part to the incomparable siting of churches and palaces, opportunities offered and advantage taken. The huge mass of the Clementinum, a Jesuit congeries of churches and chapels; the Charles Bridge with its Baroque water, or, rather, garden statues of saints; and the still larger and more imposing masses of the Hradchin and the Strahov monastery are the fixed points in a far-reaching panorama of churches and palaces with lesser buildings of many centuries rising from the narrow, winding streets. Kilian Ignaz Dientzenhofer (d. 1750), most talented of his family, was at work in Prague, notably in the Jesuit church of St Nicholas, a magnificent structure in full-throated Baroque, splendid of dome or cupola, and with wonderful interior of running counterpoint compound of paired pilaster and cornice. The Rococo has little place in Prague. Another architect with a touch of original genius, Johann Santin Aichel (d. 1723), who offers himself, because of his Gothicizing Baroque, for comparison with Hawksmoor, worked in Bohemia and Moravia, but mainly on the renovation of old abbey churches, and no great occasion was offered him. The high or 'primary' Baroque continued late in Bohemia, until 1750, and it is perhaps at its best there anywhere outside the Rome of Bernini and of Borromini, in full force indeed during the years that the Amalienburg and Die Wies, the masterpieces of Rococo, were building. But the craftsmen concomitant to this upsurge of activity in Bohemia, some remarkable sculptors and painters among them, are as yet little known outside their native land.

If mediaeval Germany has not been dealt with in these pages, it is for a two-fold reason; a dislike of German Gothic and a desire to write at greater length of the Baroque and Rococo in Austria and Bavaria. Not Cologne and all its churches, nor Nuremberg, nor Rothenburg-ob-der-Tauber, could ever reconcile me to the German Gothic; and if I put against those just the names of Dinkelsbühl of the magpie houses and window boxes of bright zinnias and coloured witchballs, or the abbey church of Rottenbuch, one village church with exquisite Rococo detail and decoration chosen at hazard out of many scores of others, not a few readers may understand my preference. There are more reasons for it than mere personal prejudice or idiosyncrasy. That there were ceiling painters and also sculptors, let alone architects, at work here, who upon a grander scale equalled and surpassed the most finished and famous masters of porcelain is as certain as that in inspiration they were not far behind the master musicians of the period. Have not Ottobeuren or Zwiefalten, weighed in the balance, the equivalent weight of a handful, or more than a handful, of Haydn symphonies? Or of one of Mozart's operas? I think that this is undeniable. The sensation they impart tends certainly to the theatrical, not to say the operatic or the balletic; and an ignored aspect of it is the painted ceilings. These, which are wholly neglected in the histories of painting, are only to be appreciated through ceiling-gazing. They are the enlargement of the Jesuit Padre Pozzo's theories from a single point of perspective into multiple points at which the paintings come to life from different parts of a building, and the painters will have been further stimulated by Tiepolo's frescoes in the Residenz at Würzburg, while in fact the great Venetian master was working in Franconia in their very midst. In short, the ingenuity and theatrical sense of the Italian school of fresco painters has been taken a step further, as we can see by their invention of veritable platforms or gang planks cutting across the corners of the frescoes, on which their painted figures pose with full theatrical effect. Confusing in their multitude, having no sale room value, and almost unwritten of, these frescoed ceilings form the largest body of unappreciated painting that is left to us, and they serve to fill a private and inexpensive *musée imaginaire* of one's own. Typical painters of the school, pursuit of whom into their hiding places would entail a great deal of interior journeying, are J. G. Bergmüller (1688–1762) of Diessen; Matthias Günther (1705–88); J. J. Zeiller of Otto-beuren, and F. J. Spiegler of Zwiefalten, but as well as at those famous abbeys some of the best work of these painters is to be found in country monasteries and small village churches.

And so, having stated the theme in full, the variations now begin. I have not attempted to conceal that it is the splendours and not the miseries of the drones that are my subject. Over many centuries the only chance for those of learned tendency to lead a scholar's life was in the cloister. Outside, all was war or single combat, and the days and nights went down in violence. There were no libraries except in monasteries, and it would only be slight exaggeration to say that their cloisters were the only gardens. Thus, large communities formed which were as palaces exempted from the deaths of kings. Their riches gave them continuity of tenure and of course, in the end, invited seizure. And, as always in such instances, no one was the better for it. Fountains, or Glastonbury, or Poblet, or Las Huelgas, held more treasures in the way of works of art than the royal palaces and castles. Preoccupation with death has been pastime and prerogative of kings since the first Pharaohs built the pyramids, and the only way to secure immortality was at the hands of priests. Thus, the enrichment of the monasteries, in a descending scale beginning with those who could afford to give estates and down to the widow's mite. And who is there to say that this less than parity of nuclear might is not a bargain against death? Thus, the monks and nuns for whom in the early world of the Dark Ages there was all excuse and every necessity. In our world as it shapes now and forms itself anew there is sympathy for their lives of religious conviction and tranquillity, and a curiosity that could become a longing for what is perhaps only latent in us and not lost.

I

Mediaeval Monasteries and Nunneries in England

Two famous and informative works on English monastic life and on Mediaeval Religious Houses in England and Wales[1] end in each case with no fewer
than five maps giving the names and localities of the nine hundred monasteries and nunneries of pre-Reformation England. In addition there is the
Ordnance Survey Map of *Monastic Britain* published in 1950 so that if there
is difficulty in seeing the panorama as a whole it is not because of any lack
of statistical information. The maps, with but minor differences in either
instance, open with Houses of the Black Monks or Benedictines; following
this with Houses of the White Monks, Cistercians, Carthusians, Gilbertines,
and Premonstratensians; the Black Canons or Augustinians coming next;
then the Friars, Dominicans, Franciscans, Carmelites, Austin Friars, and
Friars of the Cross, the so-called Crutched Friars; a map of the English nunneries to follow; ending with Cathedral-Monasteries, Chester, Gloucester,
Peterborough, Westminster, and others; Secular Colleges, Houses of Knights
Hospitallers, Large Hospitals, etc; an enumeration perhaps even more impressive from its being presented in this form on five several maps, than upon
one unfolding sheet as in the map published by the Ordnance Survey.

It is in the Cathedral-Monasteries just named, with such others as Ely and
Durham, or in Minsters like Selby, Beverley, Sherborne, churches that were
taken over directly from the monks and continued as churches, that one can
get some notion of the original vitality of these monastic institutions, it having been remarked of them that 'the abbots of the great monasteries were
patrons of architecture on a larger scale than any of the King's subjects except
great nobles and bishops'. But indeed this qualification almost belittles them
by confining the comparison within this one kingdom. It should embrace,
also, France and Germany, Italy and Spain. Then, with only this little left

---

[1] *Monastic Life in Medieval England*, by J. C. Dickinson, Adam and Charles Black, 1961; *Medieval
Religious Houses: England and Wales*, by Dom David Knowles and R. N. Hadcock, Longmans
Green, 1953.

where for convenience of population a monastery church has been made into a cathedral in some big town, when the ruins of other monasteries and nunneries no less splendid in their day strewn about the countryside in almost every corner of the kingdom, and more particularly in remote places, have been taken in notice and added up into the total, it will emerge that this is a corpus of architecture and a content of lost or destroyed works of art that is unsurpassed in any country of Europe. Let us delay for a moment in order just to mention by name those minsters, abbeys, cathedrals of monastic origin which are still in use and not in ruins. They are Canterbury, Winchester, Westminster, St Alban's, Norwich, Ely, Peterborough, York, Durham, Carlisle, Chester, Gloucester, Worcester, Evesham, Sherborne, Tewkesbury, a list of overwhelming scale when we consider that only Lichfield, Lincoln, Exeter, Hereford, Salisbury are excluded from it because having no monks or friars attached to them, they were priestly, not monastic in establishment.

But whereas the churches just named are still there to be admired and entered, those which are away from the main centres of population and were put there for that very reason, had been deliberately laid in ruins as part of a settled policy at the time of the Suppression under Henry VIII, and since then have been neglected, or no more than maintained in their state of ruin. In general the destruction was immediate, as at Lewes, in Sussex, where a demolition squad of twenty-five men working under an Italian expert brought down with pick and shovel and gunpowder a great church with a vaulted roof rising ninety feet above the high altar, all this destruction accomplished between 20 March and 11 April of 1538 in order to make a house for one of the Cromwell family who writes to say his wife finds it 'so commodious that she thinketh herself to be here right well settylled'; while the same authority from whom we quote remarks on the entire destruction and even virtual disappearance of the Gilbertine monastery (for monks and nuns) at Sempringham with its huge church tower and two cloisters, and mentions the estimate of the Commissioner John Freman that the cost of 'plokying down' all the monastery churches of Lincolnshire would be at least £1,000, with the result that this county which had for its size more religious houses than any other county in England has, comparatively, little left to show after the holocaust.

The deserted fanes are of necessity more mysterious than the cathedrals still in use which have been brought down into later ages by Tudor and seventeenth- to eighteenth-century tombs and wall-tablets with inevitable 'restoration' by anyone and everyone with ideas of his own from Wyatt to Sir G. G. Scott. They may even seem to be no more contingent to each other than a living to a dead body. The ruins are not even the corpses; they are the skeletons, and what little have these to do with the soul and mind inhabiting them when they were alive? So, in England, they come to be heaps of ruins in greater or less preservation in all parts of the kingdom. They are our 'ruins', where other lands have their Angkor, their Abu Simbel, their Uxmal, or their Palenque. They are as dead as those defunct stones, with even less visual evidence as to their builders and inhabitants than is to be deduced from carvings or bas-reliefs in those places named. There, at least, are human beings; whether dancing bayadères, mitred Pharaohs, or feathered astro-nomers and alguacils. But, here, nothing. There is not the silhouette or shadow of a monk or nun in all the ruins, and little more than that in those of the abbeys or priories that were maintained as churches and are still in use. Five centuries, almost, between the Norman Conquest and the Dissolution have had the human element obliterated and removed but for the brass or two of a prior or abbess, and the infrequent and defaced tomb. The stones are there and the great cathedrals, but no sight of the monks and nuns.

Thus, while the abbeys and cathedrals are to be seen, and the ruins sur-veyed though in collapse and dilapidation, life can only be brought back to them through anecdotal means. And there is enough of that, if one looks carefully and is obliged to all the proper researchers and authorities, to bring them to some extent alive. Of similar sources in the instance of those remains in other parts of the world there are no possibilities whatever, with the one extraordinary exception that there should have survived the account of a Chinese traveller who went to Angkor with an embassy from China in 1296–8. In a word, of the Khmers who built Angkor, this one Chinaman apart; of Ancient Egypt; of pre-Columbian America, there are no accounts by contemporary eyewitnesses, but much visual evidence in the way of sculptured figures and bas-reliefs; while of our monks and nuns there are the grand buildings and the empty shells, little or no portrayal of person, but a sufficiency of incident and anecdote, gathered from accounts and wills and from exactly that literary documentation which is absent and lacking from those other civilizations that left behind them great monuments in stone.

It may be that reading into the learned authorities who have made this their life work, and putting ourselves in a very real sense into the shoes of the monks and nuns, their *dramatis personae*, one impression we get is of the apparent size of England and Wales which up till the time of the Dissolution of the Monasteries must have held far corners as remote from each other as the giant redwood glades of California or the cactus plains of Arizona from cities like New York or Boston in the years prior to the American Civil War. There were no roads at all in mediaeval England and only grass tracks, if running at times, as on Watling Street, along the Roman roads. For four or five months of the year travel must have been all but impossible, except between big towns. There would be no getting from, say, Tintern Abbey in Monmouth to its sister house Fountains in Yorkshire, or from Dore in Hereford to Furness in Lancashire, whether on horse or foot, except at walking pace, and a journey of this sort might take some weeks on end.[1] Going from village to village was slow progress, and the patois at one end of the kingdom may well have been incomprehensible at the other. Perhaps England and Wales were made to appear larger still because the scenery changes so quickly and avoids the monotony of large tracts of Germany, France, or Spain. We have no Pomeranian goose plain, future breeding ground for Prussian grenadiers, no Beauce or Orléannais where an old woman spends her senility tending and waiting upon one solitary cow, no tableland of High Castile or Aragón, and the only areas of sameness of landscape upon a large scale are the moors and fens.

This question of comparative distance is both urgent and contingent, it being the policy of some orders of monks to push out into the wilderness and set up their colonies where they could be in solitude and undisturbed. From the earliest years of Christianity in these islands it should be sufficient to mention the Oratory of Gallerus, a mere beehive hut of stone on the Dingle peninsula in Co. Kerry, if, as has been said, 'of the most perfect workmanship in dry rubble masonry . . . excelling anything of its kind to be found in Ireland, or, indeed, elsewhere'; the cells of the Culdee hermits on the Blaskets, most westerly inhabited land in Europe; or the Oratory of St Finan on the Great Skellig, seven miles out in the Atlantic, on a double peak of rock rising to seven hundred feet out of ninety fathoms of ocean, a group of cells reached by a flight of over six hundred steps, enclosed by 'an unmortared wall of perfect construction though on the edge of a dizzy precipice'. To these should be put in addition Holy Island or Lindisfarne, and Iona; the conjectured cells of the Culdees on Tory Island off Donegal, on St Kilda remotest of the Outer Hebrides, even on Rockall, and to certitude still further away in Iceland, and it will be realized that the tweed-coated and trousered, often red-haired and bearded Celtic saints and hermits as we see them portrayed in the Book of Kells sought solitude and achieved it.

In the meantime the Benedictine rule had reached England with the founding of a monastery at Canterbury by St Augustine who had been sent from Rome for this purpose by Pope Gregory the Great. Invasions by the Danes,

---

[1] A picture of this small-scale remoteness is to be had from the beautiful, open octagonal lantern of All Saints, Pavement, in the city of York, where a lamp was kept burning at night to light travellers, who cannot have been more than six to eight miles away, through the forest of Gueldres.

East Anglia and the North of England

Wymondham church, Norfolk, its two towers built in defiant rivalry by the monks and parishioners between whom the church was divided after acrimonious disputes

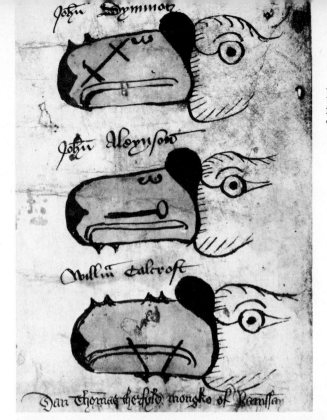

Part of the register of swan owners for 1497–1504, including 'Dan Thomas Therfyld mongke of Ramssay'

West front of Binham priory built by Prior Richard de Parco 1226–44, with one of the earliest tracery windows in England

Double hammer-beam roof (*c.* 1500) of St Wendreda at March in Cambridgeshire alive with angels' wings

Turreted west tower built at the end of the twelfth century at Ely, to be seen from miles away over the surrounding fenland

Terrington St Clement's with detached tower, one of the Norfolk marshland churches between King's Lynn and Spalding

Left: Fleet in Lincolnshire, another of the marshland churches built in rivalry between the East Anglian monasteries. Drawing by F. L. Griggs

Right: Parish church of Heckington, Lincolnshire, perfect example of the decorated style, built about 1345

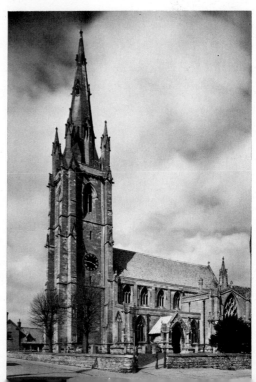

North tower of Cistercian abbey of Fountains in Yorkshire, built by Abbot Marmaduke Huby shortly before the dissolution in 1539

Right: Night-stair in Augustinian priory of Hexham in Northumberland, leading down to the church from the dormitory

Durham Cathedral seen from the west. Founded 1093 by William of St Calais, a Norman monk called to Durham by William the Conqueror

Galilee or Lady Chapel (1170–5) built on to the west end of Durham Cathedral by Hugh de Puiset or Pudsey, who did not want to have women in the eastern parts of his church

who were still heathen in the seventh and eighth centuries, put an end to further activity until the reforming movement of the next century under the Saxon Kings when, and in particular at Winchester, the minor arts found new life especially in the field of illuminated manuscripts. With the Norman Conquest the reformed or Cluniac Benedictines came to England but the emphasis, as could be expected, was upon the securing and administering of large towns. The Black Monks, who were of mixed French and, one surmises, Norse blood, and had come from Norman abbeys at Bec, Caen, Jumièges, Fécamp, had their hand further strengthened by grants of property and tithes in England and Wales, and by the practise of using the chief monastery church in, say, Canterbury or Winchester or other town as the cathedral, with a bishop instead of an abbot and a prior acting under him to run the monastery. Nine cathedral sees were thus settled, all but one of them being of Benedictine foundation, by which time (the end of the eleventh century) the Augustinian or Black Canons, all being priests as well as monks, had begun to appear in England.

The next wave of monasticism to reach England was the arrival of the Cistercian or White Monks, of origin from Cîteaux in Burgundy. While the Benedictine or Black Monks established themselves, as just said, in towns, at York, Worcester, Gloucester, Malmesbury, Tewkesbury, and so on, it was the Cistercians who acted as real colonists and set up in remote places on the fens and in the wolds. There are no cathedrals that were Cistercian abbeys for this very reason that the Cistercians chose sites remote from big centres of population, and it is for the same reason that, first despoiled and then deserted, abbeys like Furness, Fountains, Rievaulx are now heaps of ruins.

The Carthusians, another order of White Monks coming from the Grande Chartreuse in Dauphiné, with a rule based on austerity and solitude, left their mark here more from the devoted martyrdoms of their adherents under Henry VIII than from the number or splendour of their religious houses, a feature of the Carthusian monks that in other lands and later ages demands separate and detailed treatment. The Gilbertines, White Monks and Nuns of an order unique and peculiar to this country will be looked at in more detail when we come to the part of the country they frequented. And the ranks of the White Monks or Canons are completed by the Premonstratensians from Prémontré, near Soissons, who built few monasteries here and not any of great importance.

Last of all to arrive in England were the friars; Dominican or Black Friars, Franciscan or Grey Friars, Carmelite or White Friars, and the miscellany of Austin Friars, Bonshommes, an order peculiar to this country, Trinitarians known, also, as Maturins or Red Friars, and others. Because the Dominicans and Franciscans were, respectively, Spanish and Italian, that is to say, Latin in origin, as opposed to the Cluniacs, Cistercians, Carthusians, who came from France, they seem less in harmony with an English setting, and in any case, being mendicants who wandered about preaching and living on alms, their churches were nearly always built in towns. Even the small memory of them expressed in London street names, Blackfriars, Whitefriars, Crutched Friars, now seems unreal and shadowy beside the deep marks left by the Black and White Monks, Benedictines and Cistercians. The Jesuits, it is hardly necessary to add, did not come to England in time to build churches. Indeed were there Jesuit churches and houses of late sixteenth and seventeenth century date in England it would postulate the entire reversal of our national character and history, everything would be different, Dryden and Pope would not have been Catholic (as they were) for nothing, the art collections of Charles I would have been kept intact to shame the Prado, and the genius of a Vanbrugh been lavished, more appropriately, on huge monasteries and churches than on Castle Howard and Blenheim. This, however, is not to take into account the impossible nature of the Stuarts, Charles II always excepted, and the stature of Henry VIII, for all his cruelty and cupidity the maker of modern England.

But the monks and nuns went. The monasteries and nunneries were dissolved, as we all know. This was accomplished by first of all dissolving the smaller monasteries, those with an income of less than £200 and a community of fewer than twelve monks and a prior or abbot. For this purpose commissioners were sent round the country, Layton and Tregonwell among them who have left remarkable and lively accounts of what they found and saw. The Northern Rising or Pilgrimage of Grace, instigated in Yorkshire and Lincolnshire, counties where monasteries and nunneries crowd thick upon the maps, was in protest against what was to come. The rebellion, which held great danger for King Henry, was skilfully but brutally dealt with by him, as witness his injunction to the Duke of Norfolk that he 'must cause dreadful execution upon a good number of the inhabitants, hanging them on trees, quartering them, and setting their heads and quarters in every town', or, more directly still, and to the same unworthy dispenser of justice, 'you, shall, without pity or circumstance . . . cause all the monks and canons that be in any wise faulty, to be tied up, without further delay or ceremony, to the terrible example of others', while Lord Derby, another instrument of the King's will, was told 'without further delay' to cause the Abbot of Sawley (in Yorkshire) 'and certain of the chief of the monks to be hanged upon long pieces of timber, or otherwise, out of the steeple', which horror, or, at least, the worst part of it, the Abbot escaped for it seems that he was executed not at Sawley, but Lancaster. There followed in 1538–9 the Suppression and Dissolution of the larger houses and of the friars and the driving out and pensioning of those who were acquiescent among the inmates.

That was all. It was quickly accomplished without further trouble, the King, himself, assuming a large part of the revenues. It has been deduced from the *Valor Ecclesiasticus*, or returns of the royal commissioners of 1535, that the total income of monks, canons, nuns, and knights hospitallers came to some £165,000. This estimate covered some 650 religious houses, but does not take account of 187 friaries and hospitals. Undervaluation, more than overvaluation, is likely to have been the rule when the circumstances are considered, and it has been estimated that if the total gross income was nearer £200,000 than the figure named it would represent a value today of some twenty million pounds. The liquidation of the financial resources of the English monasteries was undertaken in wasteful fashion, as is usually the case in such transactions and there was an unseemly rush to take part in the spoils. Typical of this is a letter from Lady Elizabeth Ughtred, a sister of Jane Seymour, asking for 'one of those abbeys, if they go down', and several letters to and from Lord Lisle who could have known better, he was a Plantagenet, and to that extent lucky to be left alive under his royal master, writing to Thomas Cromwell 'beseeking you to help me to some old abbey in mine old days', while his steward writes to him, 'I pray Jesu send you shortly an abbey, with many good new years', and another of his agents writes, 'the abbeys go down as fast as they may' adding, 'I pray God send you one among them to your part'. So the King was not the only despoiler; but the Court of Augmentations which had been set up specially to deal with the business ensuing from the Suppression averaged an income of £140,000 during the eleven years 1536–47, and as the revenue or personal income of the Crown in those years was a mere £100,000 it will be apparent that the King must have much augmented his own revenues.

It is the fact that many of the monasteries had reached their peak of prosperity at an earlier time just before the Black Death, the number of monks being nearly halved in most instances known after this disaster. Nearly always there were double the number of monks in 1250–1350 compared with the number at the surrender in 1538. But, also, there were not as many monasteries since an earlier suppression of foreign or alien priories, of which no fewer than seventy were forced out, chiefly during the reign of Henry V. A typical instance was the priory of Abergavenny, a dependancy of St Vincent of Saumur, in fact an isolated community of Angevin-French monks only half a dozen in number, living in a part of Wales beyond the Black Mountains, who in 1322 had not been visited by a superior of their order for forty years and spent their days and nights in dissipation and worse, 'dicing and gaming', and it would appear from the dog-Latin description, 'entertaining their guests with nocturnal travesties of the Crucifixion'. There may in brief have been 650 religious houses at the Suppression of the Monasteries but there were perhaps nine hundred before the Black Death of 1348-9.

But it is time now to start upon our journey of inspection of the English monasteries and convents, for that would seem to be the only way in which to bring together the items of information that can be gathered and to present them in a form concurrent with the actual remains. For which purpose we are to imagine ourselves as on the road at any and all times between eleven hundred and something and the very morning or eve of the Surrender. It must be taken into consideration, though, that neither strictness of rule and observance, nor abstinence and fasting are what we are coming this long way to see, but, rather, it is the relaxing of the iron or, better, cold stone discipline of the early monks into the luxuries of the arts, while reporting as we go along such anecdote as is telling and picturesque in itself or brings the dead monks and nuns alive. It were better to travel, as did Ingworth, one of the King's Commissioners for the suppression of the friars in 1538, in nearly total ignorance of what we will find next, our destination the next monastery or nunnery 'that I can here off' in his own phrase, enquiring the way, as it were, by word of mouth. The larger houses, Fountains, Ely, Glastonbury, shed their fame for miles around them; but lesser communities like that of Abergavenny and dozens more, if for this part of the journey we take early to the road, will present a picture more like the Middle Ages in the depths of Russia. Let us start off, therefore, with one last reminder that the purport of this journey is to visit the monasteries and view them, wherever possible, as works of art, adding anything helping or contingent to that for detour.

It can begin when we come in sight of the chalk cliffs of Dover, passing a vessel resembling that on the reverse of a gold noble and which has on board Jean II, King of France, going in the contrary direction to ourselves and embarking at Dover for Calais. It is July 1362, he is returning from England where he had been taken prisoner by the Black Prince after the battle of Poitiers. In his list of disbursements there is mention of 'Un homme de Douvres, appelé le rampeur, qui rampa devant le Roy, contremont la roche, devent l'ermitage de Douvres, pour don fait à li par le Roy, 5 nobles, valent 33s 4d'.[1] In fact, the hermit of the Dover cliffs, whose successors were pensioned by Henry IV, awarded an annuity by Richard II, and given alms of four shillings

[1] A man of Dover, called the climber or scrambler, who climbed against the rock before the King's presence, at the hermitage of Dover, for a present made to him by the King, 5 nobles, being the value of thirty-three shillings and fourpence.

and eightpence (iiijs. viijd.) by Henry VIII, while the hermit's cell was rebuilt in 1530 to the charge of the French Ambassador, after which time trouble set in, the hermit was called 'a false French knave', accused of putting a lantern in his chamber to light the King's enemies, was attacked, and in his own words 'knocked with a stone on the mould of the head till I was as dead'.

What exactly is meant by his nickname of 'le rampeur'? Probably we are to understand that his cell was half-way up the cliffs, and that he had to come crawling and scrambling to ask for alms. But at sight of him we delay for a few moments, for lighthouse or light-keeper hermits form a chapter to themselves in the history of ascetics. There were leading lights, in the old meaning of the term, above Ilfracombe, on the Isle of Purbeck, on the South Foreland, and along the North Sea coast, at Hunstanton, at Skegness, and at the mouth of the Humber across from the spire of Patrington – this spire, of closed lantern type, intended to cheer the souls of departing or returning mariners – with sixteen-sided pinnacled arcade from which springs a tapering octagon piercing the fogs or 'sea-rauks' of winter, and making a landmark for much of North Lincolnshire and all of Holderness.

Colleagues to them, it could be said, were the highway and bridge hermits; the ferry hermits, also, who guided across rivers. These were especially useful in marshy districts and in the fens; and the Bishop of Ely in an indulgence of 1458 writes: 'Since our church is surrounded by waters and marshes and the relics of the Holy Virgins lying in it can only be visited over bridges and causeys, requiring daily repair, we commend to your charity William Grene, hermit, who, at our command with consent of the church of Ely, has undertaken the repair of the causeys and bridges of Stuntneys and Some', two villages now calling themselves Soham and Stuntney. Concerning which, more later, when we come to that 'monastic paradise' in the fen lands, if with a a trying climate. But long before we reach that there are the town hermits or recluses of Durham, Leicester, Ely, Colchester, Coventry, Crewkerne, Canterbury, Lydd, Chichester, *inter alia*, hermits living in or just without the town, and often in an enclosed cell attached to the main church. Then, too, there were the solitaries of Crowland, Durham, Westminster, Worcester, and Sherborne, as well as other monasteries, and no small number of hermitresses, among them one who by command of Henry III to the Constable of the Tower received the daily dole of a penny, and every year a new robe, a pension augmented by the King a quarter of a century later to three half pence a day for life.[1]

---

[1] 'There was of course a period in the Middle Ages when practically every (London) City church had its anchorite, the equivalent of a Hindu *saddhu*'. Cf. *Church Brasses*, by A. C. Bouquet, D.D., Batsford, 1956, p. 70 footnote.

Female recluses even when they opened their shutters (there were no glass windows) were hidden by a curtain generally of black with a white cross on it, but details concerning them are by their very nature depressing; as of Matilda de Campden who had herself enclosed in the churchyard at Chipping Campden, or another anchoress who begged for a cell to be built for her within a cemetery. Not satisfied with our normal climatic rigours the anchorites, as in a couple of instances in Norwich churches, had their anchorages (as they should be termed) joined to the north side of the steeple; or, in fact, like the golden eagles they liked their eyries to be facing north. Hermit and hermitress, anchorite and anchoress, alike, suffered torments from the cold, as witness, many gifts of furs; a super tunic of *bifle* left to Dame Lucy, enclosed in the churchyard of Bury St Edmunds; and an anchorite of Holy Trinity, Lincoln, to whom a member of the Scrope family left 20s, a tunic furred with *calaber* with a double hood, and a cloak furred with *gris*. Such must have been most welcome gifts. Anchoresses were enjoined in winter to wear a *pilch*, or garment made of skins, a *pilch* or *pellicea*, being obviously the same as a pellise. It is painful to think of their sufferings, which need be protracted no longer than by mere mention of the anchoress Matilda, of anchorage at Wareham, where she had been enclosed for sixteen years. When her handmaiden, who succeeded her, complained of toothache, Matilda told her 'that she herself had uttered no word or groan even when her jaw had been in such a state of disease that it seemed to be breaking away'. It is an alleviation to read in the *Ancren Riwle*, or thirteenth-century book of rules for hermits: 'Wear no iron, nor haircloth, nor hedgehog skins; and do not beat yourselves therewith, nor with a scourge of leather thongs, nor leaded; and do not with holly nor with briars cause yourselves to bleed without leave of your confessor; and do not, at one time, use too many flagellations.'[1]

But the way is now open over the chalk hills to Canterbury, only rather more than a half day's ride or walk by copses thick with primroses. Hopfields are already in being and oasthouses in embryo, and the quincunxes play among the hop-poles as we go slowly past. It is one of the holy places of England of which in folk memory there are for campanili the pale blue spires of 'Canterbury Bells'. But the sound of bells was louder then than now. The cathedral which rose out of the ashes of the former building and which

---

[1] *The Hermits and Anchorites of England*, by R. M. Clay, Methuen, 1914, gives in her Appendix C a tabulated list of cells occupying 59 pages, and comprising, to my reckoning, 497 names and addresses of hermits and hermitesses, 100 of them in Yorkshire alone. Anchorites, it should be added, were the stricter, or secluded and enclosed improvement upon hermits. *The Ancren Riwle* or *Regulae Inclusarum* was written for the three nuns who settled at Tarrant in Dorset, which later became the richest Cistercian nunnery in England, with an abbess, sub-prioress, and eighteen nuns at the Surrender.

is, in fact, the third church to stand on the same site, is not by personal taste the most exciting or beautiful of English cathedrals. Perhaps because being so typical of them it represents the average or ordinary, remembering always when thinking more of individual persons, that the pattern or archetype can become extreme and exceptional in virtue of that very quality. So Canterbury is the English cathedral *in excelsis* with its Bell Harry Tower rising above the cricket fields of Kent, actual or hypothetical; and with Canterbury cricket week in mind, as close to and as much a part of them as the Moorish Giralda of Seville Cathedral which moved its shadow across the bull-ring during the bull-fights of the Feria. Peculiar to Canterbury is its double set of transepts. The great central tower of Canterbury was added by Prior Goldstone in 1495, a late work comparable to the Perpendicular tower of Fountains, the work there of Abbot Huby, and, like that, one of the glorious church towers of this, our native style or vernacular. The nave, too, of Canterbury is Perpendicular, built under Prior Chillenden (1390–1411), though without fantasy in the form of fan-vaulting or other fanciful excesses. A note of severity, with unfortunate after-effects in mid-Victorian times all the way from Manchester and Liverpool to Sydney and Bombay, is struck by the choir of Canterbury begun by the Frenchman, William of Sens, in 1175 and built of Caen stone shipped from Normandy. But he fell from a scaffolding and was killed only three years later and his plans were completed by William the Englishman who succeeded him as architect.

Flights of steps lead up from the choir to the Trinity Chapel, also the work of William the Englishman, and here stood the shrine of Thomas à Becket, murdered in the cathedral in 1170. The jewels, the vestments, the reliquaries and other works of art accruing to Canterbury owing to his martyrdom are all gone, treasures that accumulated for three centuries after his burial here in 1220, until Erasmus, visiting the shrine in 1512, could write of it that 'gold was the meanest thing to be seen'. We are left with Becket's Crown, the circular chapel or Corona beyond the choir at the far end of the cathedral, which contained a fragment of his skull and still holds the 'Chair of St Augustine' or Archbishop's Chair. And on the east side of the Trinity Chapel we have the tomb of the Black Prince, with his heraldic surcoat, gauntlets, shield, and helmet hanging above in romantic panoply; and things as unique to this country and as English of definition as the fan-vaults in the ceiling of the Angel Steeple, Bell Harry Tower under its other name, a geometrically exact unfolding or opening of no fewer than eight fan-shapes of stone all fitting into the square, as intricate a work as any of Moorish or Mudéjar craftsmen, and a contraption which appears to fold in on itself at any moment with a shutting and a snapping of stone slats.

Canterbury Cathedral Priory was a rich and powerful Benedictine monastery with one of the biggest incomes, nearly £2,400, of any in England and fifty-eight monks at the Surrender, some little idea of the state kept there being the 'iiij monks with bandoggs to kepe the shryne' and more 'monks in everie quarter of the Churche with candills',[1] in other words an all-night watch or vigil over the treasures of the shrine. St Augustine's, also a Benedictine foundation, of which only a few traces are left, was little less important with its one-time eighty monks, reduced to the abbot and thirty monks at the Suppression. But, of course, Christ Church Cathedral Priory was supreme. Were there not fifty privies in its rere dorter; was not its farmery (infirmary) 237 ft. from east to west – and the *necessarium* at Lewes, a Cluniac house, was 158 ft. in length, with seating for 66 – as long as many an abbey church[2]; even if it had not, as had its rival St Augustine's, a flock of 13,730 sheep, precisely numbered, grazing like white clouds on the chalk-edged flat fields of the Isle of Thanet, harbinger of the monastic sheepfolds of the north and west of England!

There could be little of pastoral or bucolic life at metropolitan Westminster, in the midst of mediaeval London. Also, as the place of coronation and royal attendance and as the fane which certain of the Kings and Henry III in particular took into their especial care and protection, to the extent that by 1300 in the words of Dom David Knowles 'its church was probably the most lavishly appointed and gorgeously decorated in England', the fabric, more still the works of art it contained, are less Benedictine than Plantagenet in provenance and origin. Westminster Abbey, as we see it to today, has little of the monks left in it and much of the lay person, royal or commoner. Tombs of Kings and Queens, great nobles, generals, admirals, men of politics, writers, even poets, have only given all the additional weight of tomb and tablet to this direction.

The learned authority just named speaks of the red tower and walls of St Alban's, lending to the ancient abbey something of that distant view of the Alhambra seen from below its hill, which if it gives over-emphasis to the picturesqueness is at least introduction to the men of learning and the treasures, now lost, that it once held. Matthew Paris and his school of sculptors and painters worked here. The high altar of St Alban's was their work, and the shrine of Becket at Canterbury, which may have surpassed all things of

[1] Companion piece to this, and quoted by Dom Knowles, vol. III, p. 271, is the commissioner Layton's account of the Abbot's lodging at Langdon, a house of Premonstratensian canons, also in Kent, which he describes as 'evyn lyke a cony clapper fulle of startynge hoilles', where, when he knocked, 'thabbottes litle doge that within his dore faste lokked beyede and barkede'.

[2] At Furness, in Lancashire, the *necessarium* had the seats set, back to back, with a passage at either side.

Opposite: Fan-vaulted cloister
at Gloucester

its kind except for Byzantine Constantinople. But not a vestige is left. Alike, the work at St Alban's and the shrine of Becket are all perished. The fabric of St Alban's is left, but shorn of its original adornment, in the absence of which it is impossible to judge of their handiwork, and even that of Matthew Paris, his chronicles apart. The Abbey Church is enormous in exterior length, like indeed a great giant's body; early in style as to its interior of Norman-Romanesque, with Roman bricks and tiles from Verulamium, the biggest Roman settlement after York, pressed into service, but marred by the amateur efforts of the mid-Victorian Lord Grimthorpe, who spent his fortune in restoring it and giving it a new wooden ceiling. There are only cold figures that testify to the abbey's importance; expenses of entertainment to Kings and nobles and visitors from abroad; an income of £2,100, among two or three of the largest in England and representing an enormous sum, probably £100,000 in present-day money; an unsurpassed number of satellite priories or smaller monastic houses in different parts of the country, as far away as Belvoir in Leicestershire, Tynemouth in Northumberland, or Pembroke in South Wales; and its complement in later centuries of forty to fifty monks.

But it is time before visiting the monks and nuns in the deep country to take some notice of the rigours of their lives, even if these were in some instances relaxed a little in the course of centuries. It must have been particularly in the early Middle Ages a very hard life and the long winters dreadful indeed. At Canterbury the first service of the day was at 2.30 a.m. when the monks were woken and came down the night stair from the dorter into the church for matins. The night stairs became an architectural feature of a haunting nature. There is a perfect specimen preserved, with worn steps but still with stone parapet in place, at Hexham Priory in Northumberland. Impossible not to people this stone stair with monks – they were Augustinians or Black Canons – coming down it into the dark cold church, though at least the wooden choir stalls, thirty-six in number, argue some screening from the draughts.[1]

Matins were at 2 or 2.30 a.m., Lauds at half past four and Prime at six, with no hot coffee, tea, or cocoa, in between, it must be remembered, and for more than six months of the year this would all be before dawn. The monks then read or walked in the cloister until 8 a.m. Then they changed their shoes (or put off warm slippers?) washed, and went back to church. The Daily Chapter followed, then more church for Sext, High Mass, and None, then, their luncheon about 2 p.m., after which the monks changed into their night shoes again, were allowed a drink in the frater, and then to church once

---

[1] Another night stair, less well preserved, is at Tintern, and a day stair perhaps of happier memory is at Cleeve.

more for Compline, the last service of the day. Lights were out at about 6.30 or 7 p.m., in winter, and at nightfall in summer. Added to all this were the long periods of fasting.

There is a special vocabulary to be learned concerning the monks and nuns. For an example the *minuti* were the monks who were having their seasonal bleeding or *minutio* which took place every few weeks, when they were allowed meat dishes in a special refectory or flesh-frater; salt fish and slices of cake called 'Karpie' at St Alban's, but this is as far back as the eleventh century; and in some houses were even sent away to some monastic grange to be bled, and then recuperate. *Bevers* were the daily drinks of wine before vespers in the *frater*, and the wine surprisingly, perhaps more often than not, was from their own vineyards. A *corrody* was the monk's weekly allowance of bread and beer; a *slype* was a passage, or, more often, a gallery where necessary conversation was allowed; the *coquinarius* was the kitchener; a *corrodian*, someone who on payment by himself or some benefactor obtained life accommodation in a monastery, in fact, a boarder; and a *lavender* (this in nunneries) a laundress. The *calefactorium* was the warming-house of the monks where a fire was kept burning all through winter. *Carrels* were the cubicles for reading set along the cloister. At Durham they were wainscoted and entered by doors, the tops of which were pierced, so that each monk as he worked was under survey. But the most complete set of *carrels* (caroli, i.e. enclosed spaces) in existence is at Gloucester where there are twenty of them, and half as many more at Durham but not so well preserved. It is in the cloister at Gloucester, with its stone winnows or fans forever opening along its ceilings in all the pride of this new invention that the *Scriptorium* of the monks should be seen if, in imagination, we are to add cushions to the stone seats and put in wooden reading desks; as, also, and fan-vaulted, too, the most perfect specimen of a *Lavatorium* with the stone trough for the water and even the stone towel cupboards at the corners. It is to be remarked that the cloisters of England fine as they may be cannot compare with those of Provence, Italy, Portugal or Spain, and the reason is not far to seek. It is the climate. Cloisters in England were built for warmth, not shade, and they lack therefore the particular fantasy that inspired the stone lattices of Indian intricacy at Batalha, or the open arcades of Monreale where all the ornament is on the columns and carved capitals. But, again, chapter houses are among the architectural splendours of England, and unequalled elsewhere, and this may be for the same reason that our difficult climate made it more sensible to keep out of the draughts and be warm indoors. In short, the poetical images evoked by a cloister are quite different here from what they are in other lands.

With the *Refectorium* never far from the cloister perhaps the topic of monastic diet may be carried a little further at this point, though it becomes a
matter of what they ate on feast days, of which there were many, more than
their ordinary daily fare. Thus, better sorts of bread were served on festal
occasions and the pittance, so called, could be wastel bread, spiced with pep-
per, or simnel cakes. Take, for instance, the Lenten store of the nuns of Syon,
the only abbey in England of Brigittines, an order of Swedish origin, and a
foundation immensely favoured by the Kings and Queens of England. Its
income of £1,750 was the largest of any nunnery in England, and at the
Suppression no fewer than fifty-one nuns, four lay-sisters, twelve monks, and
five lay-brothers were given pensions.[1] But their salt store, the one in question, is of an earlier generation. The year is 1481–2, and it includes salt fysshe,
stokfyssh (dried cod like the Portuguese *bacalhau*), white heryng, rede heryng,
muddefissh, lyng, aburden, Scarburgh fysshe, salt samon, salt elys, a barrel
of honey, and figs – with, later in the same year, a kilderkin of good ale, 15
lb of almonds and 39 Essex cheeses. In Lent also they ate dried fruits, particularly almonds, raisins and figs, these latter being made often into little
pies like mince pies called *rischewes*, or russheaulx, the same word, in fact, as
rissoles. That curious word (and confection) of Anglo-Norman invention –
it means less than nothing in French – blancmange makes its appearance.

At the end of Lent, venturing further afield, and leaving the now Adamized
cloister and gallery of Syon for Barking, the nuns of this other great abbey
had, understandably, pancakes or fritters on Shrove Tuesday, but they were
called 'crisps' or 'flawnes' at St Michael's, Stamford; and on Easter Monday,
baked eels with rice and almonds, and wine. Later, on certain feast days, the
cellaress had to provide half a goose for each nun; and 'a lyverey of sowse –
a whole hog's sowse to serve three ladys' at Martinmas. Barking Abbey, we
take this occasion for adding, was a Benedictine nunnery of great antiquity
with an abbess, often of royal blood (three Queens and two princesses were
abbesses of Barking), who took precedence of all other abbesses in England
and was one of four (the others being Wilton, Shaftesbury, and St Mary,
Winchester) who ranked as baronesses.[2]

Syon, that was not so ancient a foundation as these others, had a famous

---

[1] The last abbess Agness Jordayn had the huge pension of £200 per annum, and her sepulchral
brass is not far away in the church of Denham. But most of the nuns of Syon went abroad, first
to Belgium, then to Lisbon where they stayed nearly two hundred years, and are now (since 1861)
at South Brent, Devon, our only living link with the nunneries of pre-Reformation England.

[2] When Barking was surrendered the abbess and thirty nuns were pensioned; the abbess and
thirty-two nuns at Wilton; thirty-two nuns and the abbess at St Mary, Winchester, or Nunminster,
as it was called; and at Shaftesbury, the largest nunnery in England, fifty-six nuns and the abbess.
All four nunneries were Benedictine.

library and a tradition of learning. The nuns, too, came of aristocratic families, Strickland, Scrope, Nevill, Bourchier, Tresham, and it is only for a relief from the tragedy of its fate and extirpation, with the execution of the chief of its priest-monks for refusing to take the oath of supremacy to Henry VIII, that with these nuns in mind, at dinner, young and old, we read of the table of signs drawn up for their convenience. These were to enable them to obtain what they wanted without breaking the rule of silence. Such practice was apparently nothing unusual but obtained in many convents. One who wanted fish would 'wagge her hande displaied sidelynges in manere of a fissh taill', and wanting milk would 'draw her left little fynger in maner of mylking'. For mustard the sign was to 'hold her nose in the uppere part of her righte fiste and rubbe it', and for salt to 'philippe with her right thombe and her forefynger overe the left thombe'. There were over a hundred signs in all in this dumb crambo, and great must have been its humorous openings, both purposeful and accidental. Impossible, indeed, to end this paragraph without quoting from the mediaeval cookery book which tells how to cook herrings:

> The white herring by the bak a brode ye splat him sure,
> Both roe and bones voyded, then may your lord endure to
> eat merily with mustard,

adding, it may be, stewed eels and rice, hog's sowse, rissoles in their early and unfamiliar form, and for envoi quaking blancmange; and so to bed, and lights out, with no more talking until 2 a.m. and the cold night stair!

But we would follow the nuns farther into the country with destination the White Ladies of Grace Dieu in Leicestershire, a priory of Augustinian Canonesses, a journey into bucolic regions of the monks and nuns with halts and stops upon the way. As we get deeper and deeper into the country and into the leafy silence unbroken by engine of any kind, we hear of harvesting and haymaking, and the like, and even of hunting and hawking. Leicester Abbey, where Wolsey came to die; where, so it was said, the sanctuary lamp hung by a plait of the hair of Petronilla, daughter-in-law of Robert de Bellomont, known as le Bossu, Earl of Leicester, founder of this rich monastery of Black Canons in 1143; where Henry VIII's commissioner Layton, finding the abbot and monks difficult and contumacious, proposed to accuse them of the grossest vices in order to induce them to surrender, and succeeded in his object; it was here in this classical land of the chase that there was monastic hunting across the flat fields and over the hedges. The canons started out early, often before daybreak (cubbing?), this was in 1528, and the abbot seldom made an appearance in choir, and when he did, brought his fool with him who made the Black Canons laugh with his jokes and tag-ends of song. The vicar-general of the diocese, visiting them a few years before the Surrender, had tried to improve things by his order in the original dog-Latin that none of the canons should keep 'ultra iii brase de lez grey-hounds et nulli alii canes nisi ii or iii cowple off Spanyells pro le haris'.[1] And at Ulverscroft, founded for Augustinian hermits by Robert Blanchemain, another Earl of Leicester, which even the Commissioners write, 'standith in a wildernesse in the fforeste of Charnewood and refressith many pore people and waye farying people', the priors kept their hounds and hawks, and had a ranger, a huntsman, a falconer, and seven woodmen employed in cutting firewood for the house. It was indeed but a mile or two from the White Ladies of Grace Dieu.

Here, from the account books of one of the nuns, Dame Petronilla, for the years 1414-18, an impression, as of even the sounds of pastoral life so long ago, is to be gathered in. She gives minute details as to the number of calves and pigs or the sale of wattles and hurdles. The villeins, men and women (some Irish among them, who came here for the harvesting), this in 1415 the year of Agincourt, had each a pair of gloves given to them for weeding the barley. The nuns of St Michael's, Stamford, in this same context who always recorded the day 'when we began to reap', gave eight pairs of gloves at a penny-halfpenny each to the hired reapers to shield them from the thistles.

At Grace Dieu, too, with a feeling of the days drawing in, there is the autumn visit of the candlemaker and the buying of tallow and mutton fat for the making of cressets and rush lights. How dismal and dark the long evenings must have been! Made no more cheerful by the age or madness or eccentricity of some of the inmates; the (only) six monks of Owston, an Augustinian priory not far away, where 'relygion is not very duly kepte for lake of numbers and for because one of them is a very aged man and a nother not havying his wytt very well but fantastycall and more than halfe ffrantyke'; or another complaint of a prior, 'aliquando lunatica . . . ideota . . . furiosam . . . decrepita et non abilis ad equitandum'.[2]

At Langley, another Leicestershire nunnery of Benedictines, there are indications in an inventory of 1485 of a whole sacristy full of embroideries, pieces of that *opus Anglicanum* for which the English nuns were famous, though in fact these are of a late date in this art that had greater association with the early Middle Ages. Four altar frontals are listed of green damask powdered with swans and eagles; and three of black powdered with swans

---

[1] 'More than three brace of greyhounds, and no other dogs unless two or three couple of spaniels to hunt the hares.'

[2] 'More or less lunatic . . . idiotic . . . raving . . . decrepit and unable to get on a horse.'

and roses; a vestment of black damask broidered with roses and stars; a complete vestment of white worked with 'rede trewlyps' though, astonishingly, true lovers-knots are intended by this and not, as one might surmise, 'red tulips'. Those had not yet been brought here from Turkey. A great cloth (banner) the inventory goes on, of red powdered with 'bects beds and boturfleys'; a large coverlet of 'blew and better blewe with swans and cocks', and 'a tapet of ye same'; a coverlet of 'ostrych fydyrs'; one of 'grene and yowlowe with vynys and roses'; of red and white with a trellis of birds; of 'grene and yowlowe with eyes and swannys', and so on. Also, in a smaller way, the nuns of Langley Priory made 'blood-bands' or silk bandages to be worn during the *minutio* or blood-letting.

Distraction from their needlework, and other more serious tastes, was occasioned by Lady Audley, widow of a local magnate who, the prioress complains, 'boards in the house, has a great abundance of dogs, insomuch that whenever she comes to church there follow her twelve dogs, who make a great uproar in church, hindering them in their psalmody and the nuns hereby are made terrified'. Other communities of nuns had their interruptions too. At Ankerwyke – what an apt name for a nunnery! – in Buckinghamshire, the Prioress Clemence Medford, this in 1441, is complained of for wearing golden rings and silken veils and for carrying her veil too high above her forehead so that her forehead, being entirely uncovered, can be seen by all – this was considered in very bad taste, as we shall see, and it is complained further that she comes late into chapel and in the manner of a temperamental orchestra conductor stops the service and makes them start all over again; while of another convent, this time in Lincolnshire, the report in Latin which all can understand remarks: 'Item Priorissa rara venit et matutinas aut missas. Domina Katerina Hoghe dicit quod quedam monialls sunt quodammodo sompnolentes, tarde veniando at matutinas et alias horas canonicas.' While, as to those exposed foreheads, at Elstow a Benedictine nunnery in Bedfordshire, a largish convent with twenty-three nuns in it at the Suppression, the bishop fulminates (in modernized spelling): We ordain and by way of injunction command under pain of disobedience from henceforth that no lady nor any religious sister within the said monastery presume to wear their apparel upon their heads under such lay fashion as they have of late done with cornered crests, neither under such manner of height showing their foreheads more like lay people than religious . . .' and he thunders on that 'none of the said religious sisters do use or wear hereafter any such voided shoes, neither crested as they have of late there used, but that they be of such honest fashion as other religious places'. What can these crested shoes have been? And the bishop's trumpet solo ends on the note that 'there gownes and

kyrtells be closse a fore and not so depe voyded at the breste and noo more
to use rede stomachers but other sadder colers in the same'.

From Leicestershire it would be but commonsense to go on to Peterborough where we set foot among the great Benedictine abbeys of the fens,
of which number are Ramsey, Crowland, Spalding, Thorney. The west
front of Peterborough with its triple porches is often extolled as one of the
greatest and most original works of mediaeval architecture, an opinion with
which it is difficult to concur if one admires, as does the writer, the wonders
of Lincoln with its three towers, its marvellous west façade, and the interior
arcading of its Angel Choir. How, moreover, do Ely and Durham, the other
wonders of mediaeval England, compare with Peterborough? As to its
interior there is no fair comment because it was so thoroughly destroyed or
'put to rights' by Cromwell's troops, a privilege it owed to a personal visit
to the city from this second instalment of that, where all or any of the arts
were concerned, pestilential and destroying family. His soldiers tore down
the chapter house and destroyed every monument they could either shoot
at or lay hands upon, including the catafalque of Catherine of Aragon, which
it would have been most curious to see here on the borders of the fens of
England, a tomb covered with the arms of Castile and Aragon, Catherine
being daughter to Ferdinand and Isabella, who drove out the Moors, con-
quered Granada, and united Spain. Cromwell's troops who, as long as they
remained in the town, drilled in the nave of the cathedral, also pulled down
the cloisters, destroyed all the stained glass, burnt all papers and documents,
and broke to pieces the reredos which was of carved stone, painted and
gilded, and inlaid with plates of silver.

The last abbot of Peterborough became the first bishop under Henry VIII,
who by some quirk of kindness in his merciless nature left it as his first wife's
burial place. But it had many associations with the Plantagenet Kings, his
ancestors, and the influence of this great fane, whose abbot in the early Middle
Ages was Legate of Rome all over England, and at the outer gate of which all
and sundry as at some eastern mosque took off their shoes, spread far and
wide into the surrounding country. It was the abbots of Peterborough who
built the village churches along the Nene Valley, churches that were later to
become the paradise and pilgrimage route of the mid-Victorian ecclesiologist.
The church at Stanwick, and more still that at Raunds with its white, white
tower and spire filling the background very much as in a watercolour drawing by William Blake – for it is of the early thirteenth century, and, therefore, of that primitive simplicity which was his birthright and which he had
neither to affect nor learn – these and other churches along that river valley
were under the mother-wing, of that great abbey. And the Nene at that

period it would seem was navigable. Barnack 'rag' was transported along it, and 'thus conveyed easily into the heart of the country', but that was before the draining of the fens when this whole part of England was of another, or, of the same, only more pronounced and accentuated character; this local stone being, it would seem, excuse and *raison d'être* for the spate of building from quarries which have now lain exhausted for many centuries.[1]

We are now at 'the coronal of old English monasteries set on islands and river banks round the edges of the fens', as Dom David Knowles writes of them with love and pride. It is in fact as rich in architectural interest as any part of the world. The building stone being brought everywhere by water, as easily, an old writer remarks, as in the real Marshland, or along the north coast of Norfolk, where in fact there can be most unpleasant seas. But it is true that at intervals along the coast of this part of England from Blythburgh and Southwold in Suffolk to as far as Patrington, aforementioned, on the north bank of the Humber, there are remarkable and beautiful churches, many of them, particularly in Lincolnshire, being monastic in origin.

Whatever the monotony of landscape, mediaeval monks were particularly enamoured of the marshlands and the fens. The same learned, monastic historian extols the 'paradisiacal fertility of the fenland with its lofty timber and blossoming fruit trees, and the sacred isolation of the monasteries'. Other writers praise 'the park-like meadows and beautiful wealth of red and white chestnut bloom, the remains of ancient manors', but it was surely the isolation and the security this conferred which was the attraction. They, also, liked it for its far horizons, pleasant aspect (*risu decora*), and for its eels and wild fowl, a permitted addition to their strict diet.

There was a proliferation of monasteries and their subject churches in the fenlands, Thorney coming next for our purpose by reason of propinquity, this like most of the others being of Benedictine foundation. All that is left of Thorney is that fragment of it which is now the parish church, but Thorney Island, as it then was, having made its debut into the religious life earlier still as Ancarig, 'the island of the anchorite', became under Benedictine auspices the chosen paradise of mediaeval authors. There are ecstatic accounts of it by William of Malmesbury, writing in the thirteenth century, who came from Wiltshire at the other side of England, from what would seem considerably more of a rural paradise than the cold, wet, bleak fens. Thorney Abbey was small in number of inmates, but rich out of all proportion in the fruits of cultivation. He praises the orchards and the improbable vineyards of the monks in his dog-Latin which is so much easier to read than Esperanto.

[1] 'The strangely broken and tossed ground near the village, which marks their site, is known as the "Hills and Holes".' Murray, 1878.

Monasteries of the West Country

Kneeling effigy of Sir Edward le Despenser (d. 1375) in his chantry chapel at
Tewkesbury, Gloucestershire

West front of Tewkesbury, of military aspect, built in the early twelfth century

Rib-vaulting of choir in church of former Benedictine abbey of Pershore

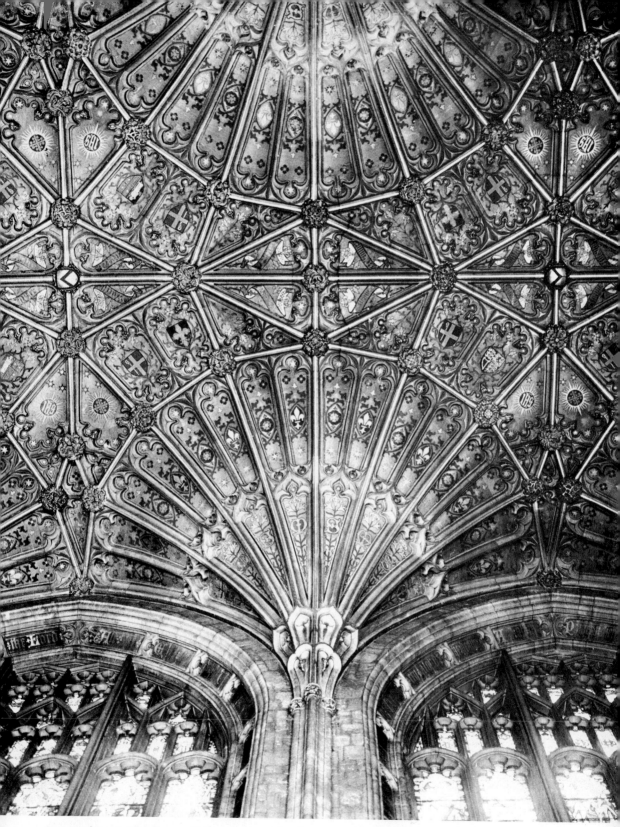

Fan-vaulting in Sherborne Abbey, Dorset. The choir was reconstructed in the fifteenth century under Abbot Bradford

Ruined thirteenth-century church of Tintern Abbey in the Wye valley

Abbot's kitchen at Glastonbury with ruined chapel of St Joseph of Arimethea behind

Barn at Great Coxwell in Berkshire. The porch has a loft in which monks are said to have slept at harvest-time

Above: Unusually constructed barn at Bredon in Worcestershire

Below: Fifteenth-century tithe-barn of monks of Abbotsbury

Collar-beamed tithe-barn (*c.* 1500) at Glastonbury

Three-storeyed Norman nave in Hampshire church of Romsey, which once had many royal abbesses

Below left: Elizabeth Throckmorton (1729) by Nicolas de Largillière. Several members of this English Catholic family were painted by the artist in Dominican habit

Below right: By contrast the prioress of the lay abbey of Vallø in Denmark, Vibeke Margrethe Juel (1734–93), painted by Andreas Brünnicke

'Paradisi simulacrum, quod amoenitate jam coelos ipsos imaginetur ... hic in pomiferas arbores terra se subigit; hic praetexitur ager vineis, quae vel per terram repant, vel per bajulos palos in celsum surgunt.' Does this not mean that the vines creep along the ground, or else are raised on sticks and poles into the air? And he concludes in words that read much like a monkish poem: 'Vere dixerim insulam illam esse castitatis diversorium, honestatis contubernium, divinorum philosophorum gymnasium.'[1]

If the derivation of Crowland is really, as it sounds, 'the land of crows', it would lend colour to the legend of 'lofty timbers' upon the islands of the fenlands. Here was a much richer monastery than Thorney with half as many monks again, and the shrine of St Guthlac; an eighth-century saint who sought refuge here as an anchorite on St Bartholomew's day, in memory of which event little knives were given away on St Bartholomew's feast day, each year, emblematic of his martyrdom by flaying. This custom continued through the Middle Ages until 1476, and these little blades are still occasionally found or dug up. The church of Crowland, as ever, is a melancholy ruin, and shares what little is left of the past with the triangular bridge – a 'dry' bridge for no water runs under it – though once there were three streams – and it is in honour of the Trinity, or else it symbolizes the borders of three counties which meet each other nearby. But the water-history of Crowland is even more visually interesting than the ruin of its once splendid church when we know that Henry VI came by water to Crowland, and that Edward IV embarked at the wharf just below the bridge for Fotheringay, two and twenty miles away by water. Moreover there is even a kind of picturesque memory of its bird life, and of some parallel between it and the young Thames above Windsor where 'swan-upping' still continues among the eyots – it has just begun, and is expected to last for a week or ten days as this is written – when we read of a roll of parchment at the Record office which has a double column of swans' heads, the bills painted in red and showing the names of the different owners for the years 1497–1504, the abbot of Crowland among them, and the monks or the rectors of several churches subject to the monastery.

The swan-marks are in proof of the aqueous lands of the fen monasteries. Crowland is in fact just within the border of Lincolnshire, and the Holland division of that country is full of churches built in rivalry with each other by

---

[1] There are thirty-eight vineyards named in the 'Domesday Book'. According to Edward Hyams, *The Grape Vine in England*, Bodley Head, 1949, Worcestershire was famous for its wine until about 1300, as were also the monks of Ely. But how much of it was wine, and how much, verjuice (unfermented grape juice)? And, again, did they count mulberry trees as vines? Or gooseberries; or red currants?

the abbots of Crowland, Spalding, and Ramsey. They indeed out-rival the churches of the Nene valley built by the abbots of Peterborough and must always in every case have been much too large for the population. The abbots can only have been competing in magnificence. To which of the fenland abbeys was due the church of St Wendreda at March in Cambridgeshire with its 'angel' ceiling of the unique East Anglian kind, a double hammer-beam roof with angels with outspread wings, over a hundred of them in all, in double tiers and along the runway of the ceiling, a roof that flutters and darkens with its rookery of golden wings, in its way as marvellous and poetic a work of art as any in mediaeval Europe?

March, however, is an exception in itself and does not belong to that group of churches in Holland built of Barnack stone 'conveyed by water along the drains'. It belongs more to that group of churches including Whittlesea which were built by the abbots of Thorney and that, famous like Whittlesea for their spires and whether or not due to the abbots of the local monasteries, spread to the south of here across the face of Rutland.

Ramsey Abbey in Huntingdonshire, another of the great Benedictine monasteries, with twenty-nine monks at the Suppression and with an income of £1,700 which puts it among the ten richest monasteries in the kingdom[1] now enters the lists of competition in church building, and many of the village churches in the two counties just named, as rich in this respect as Norfolk and parts of Lincolnshire, but of less repute perhaps only because they are situated in this small and little known county, must be due to the Black Monks of Ramsey.

In this part of England where there is such an incredible wealth of mediaeval building, and so much of it of monastic or coenobitic inspiration, it would seem simpler to repair first to the distant corner of East Anglia and then retrace our steps, beginning at Bury St Edmund's, it being out of context to go back further still as far as Waltham Abbey where we would be only a few miles from London. At Bury there was the shrine of St Edmund who was martyred by the Danes, and here were buried a sister of the Conqueror and a Queen of France, Mary Tudor, sister of Henry VIII. There were fifty to sixty monks here at the Suppression, and the still surviving splendour of the church can only testify to what may have been an even finer building at Ramsey Abbey which we have just left. The monastery had no fewer than four gatehouses;[2] and a gate to its vineyard described as 'ad soladium in-firmorum et amicorum', words which infer a convivial property to the wine

---

[1] The equivalent perhaps of £60,000 a year in modern money.

[2] The Perpendicular 'flushwork' gateway, all that is left of Colchester Abbey, with its flint-panelled and pinnacled turrets, is a beautiful exercise in the local style.

made from its grapes and must point, as is probable, either to special and tried varieties of vine, or to another climate from that which would only produce a thin and sour vinegar in our own day.

But the shrine of St Edmund, deep as was its attraction for pilgrims, was only on the way to Walsingham. One legend is as good as another, and in the Middle Ages the East Anglian countrymen, we have seen, thought the Milky Way in the heavens pointed to the shrine at Walsingham; while in Spain it led to Compostela and was called St James's Way. Of a certainty those molecules of light and huge constellations are moving to some purpose and have direction, and there must be an order in their grand processions and interludes. Shall we call it a nebulous number and leave it to those who would count up the chromosomes in a rose, or look for traffic lights and road signs in the Milky Way? As if it is not enough that the one could be a brook falling lazily through a meadow of daisies, and the rose is a rose.

A path still traceable in places through the countryside is known as 'Walsingham Green Way', or the 'Palmers' Way', though, no doubt, of much older origin than the shrine. Everyone in the villages round knows by heart 'As I went to Walsingham', the pilgrims' song.[1] It is the land of warrens. One warren alone sends forty thousand rabbits in a year to the London of Dick Whittington. There is even a particular warren famous for its rabbits which have valuable silvery-grey fur. This is the district of the 'brecks', wide-open fields mixed with warren and sheep-walk, the haunt of the great bustard. Here, too, are pits of the flint-knappers, which is a pre-historic industry.

The legend of the Green Children tells how as they were watching their father's sheep they heard a loud noise like the ringing of the bells of St Edmund's monastery. And then all at once they found themselves among the reapers in the harvest field at Woolpit, which is some miles away. The children were caught and taken to a cottage 'where for many months they would eat nothing but beans'. They gradually lost their green colour. The boy soon died. The girl survived and married a man of Lynn; but you may look in every churchyard in Lynn, and not find her tomb. And during all the centuries the Milky Way has been crossing the heavens and pointing to Walsingham, forty miles off, but at the far end of the world known to the mediaeval reapers. All of which is but prelude to finding nothing left at all of the shrine and Augustinian monastery which Erasmus visited and wrote of, and which Henry VIII attended as a pilgrim not so very many years before the Dissolution, walking barefoot from Barsham, a memorable sight in itself, in order to hang a chain of gold around the Virgin's neck.

[1] On which song sets of variations were composed by both William Byrd and John Bull, the virtuoso player of his day.

So we return on our path, passing Wymondham where there were Benedictine monks, and where the church, which is of abbatial scale with two
great towers and a hammerbeam roof, is in noble reminder of what it must
have once been. What can be said of it to bring it once more alive, not in its
parochial sense? That Henry I conferred on it the right to all the wrecks along
a stormy section of the Norfolk coast, and to two thousand eels a year from
the parish of Elingey? Norwich, where was another great Benedictine abbey
with its church taken over as the cathedral, still has a Norman air in its nave
and transept with their three tiers or storeys of round arches and their plain
capitals like stone cushions which could have been basket capitals or entwined
palmetto motifs as in San Vitale or Santa Sophia had this church been five
centuries earlier in date and the little space between its bare bones been covered with gold mosaic.

But at Walsingham we were near to Castle Acre and its Cluniac convent
and back again among the monasteries of the fens. Ely is at the far end of
these, if we think of them and their subordinate churches as going from Ely
towards the Wash and on either side of that into Lincolnshire and Norfolk.
The fens must be conceived of in those days as alive with waterfowl of all
sorts, avocets, grebes, godwits, whimbrels, knots, dottrels, yelpers, ruffs and
reeves in their thousands, to but mention what are now the rarest of them;
the peasants had their huge flocks of geese; but the paradise of the monks had
also its ague-stricken inhabitants, known into Victorian times as 'fen-slodgers'
or 'yellow-bellies', when it would be true to say that quite a large proportion
of the population took laudanum to counteract the wet of the climate, and
were in a mild sense opium fiends.

Of all this district Ely was the capital, and does it not look that still now
seen perhaps from fifteen miles away across the heath from near Newmarket?
There is no more wonderful and imposing building in England, varying, as
it does, from the castellan turrets and modulations of its exterior towers to
the fern-frost delicacies of its Lady Chapel, and to the miraculous Octagon,
an engineering feat without parallel in its day – still less in ours when there
is much work of engineers but little art. The whole kingdom was searched
for oaks of scantling or spread enough to give the huge timbers necessary
in its construction; a whole grove was inspected, paid for and cut down, and
the roads and bridges into Ely widened and made strong enough for the sleds
or ox-wagons to bring them in. What else is one to say of the shrine of St
Etheldreda and her sister saints, the Holy Virgins mentioned in the Bishop's
indulgence on an earlier page, since this is not a book on the cathedrals of
England? That here again the monks had vineyards and made wine, which
seems stranger and still more improbable than at Bury? That on the feast of

St Audrey, as she was called in short for Etheldreda, a great fair was held at which silken chains or laces called 'Etheldreda's chains' were sold, as tokens of the pilgrimage, giving occasion for the term 'tawdrey' as derived from those silken cords and other 'flimsy and trivial objects' to be bought from stalls at the fair?

So we leave Ely and make north again towards the Wash in order to strike that line of churches, not in the fens but in the marshland, lying between Spalding and King's Lynn, which were built in rivalry between the abbeys of Crowland, Spalding, and Castle Acre.[1] Here, coming from King's Lynn out of Norfolk towards Lincolnshire, are the marshland churches, Walpole St Peter's, West Walton with a detached tower like an Eastern church, Walsoken, Terrington St Clement's, Wiggenhall St German's, and Wiggenhall St Mary Magdalene with its beautiful carved benches of the fifteenth century. And continuing into Lincolnshire here is the church at Long Sutton, which owes its splendour to its being the property of Castle Acre Priory and which was built in clear rivalry with Whaplode that belonged to Crowland; continuing with Gedney, also in possession by Crowland, Fleet, Holbeach, Moulton, eight churches in all between Long Sutton and Spalding. It is a strange part of the country, completely flat, and where you cannot look in any direction without seeing a church tower or spire, and the most unthinking must be struck by this conviction in building churches at almost every mile. The monasteries must surely have spent their reserves more upon building than upon riotous living.

The maps that give the monasteries and nunneries show a quite extraordinary number of them for Lincolnshire. Not so many Benedictines, but Augustinians in quantity, and Gilbertines, and many nunneries. One cannot in fact remember any comparable number of religious houses within only a fair-sized area of country unless it is in the Pfaffenwinkel, so called, in the south of Bavaria where the abbeys lie as thick as this upon the ground. Certainly there is nothing to compare with it in France. Many of course have disappeared entirely; Bardney, where was a great Benedictine abbey; Barlings; Tupholme (like the hint of sheep farming); a nunnery at Stamfield, and another nunnery at Stixwould. But one must be careful not to attach a

[1] Opinion is not unanimous upon this point. 'It has been stated in several historical notices of the parish that Holbeach church was built by the monks of Crowland Abbey. This was most certainly not the case since monks never built or repaired parish churches unless forced to do . . . The frequently repeated story that the magnificence of the row of churches from Long Sutton to Spalding is due to the rivalry of the monasteries of Spalding, Crowland and Castle Acre is entirely without foundation and is based on a totally false conception of the relationship of religious houses to parish churches.' Kathleen Major, M.A., B.LITT., F.S.A., in a booklet on All Saints Church, Holbeach.

predominant importance to the Lincolnshire monasteries. They may have played a big hand in church building but, as well, there are all the churches they did not build, which built themselves, or were the responsibility of the bishops of Lincoln, churches in fact that were served by secular priests, not monks, though of course the subject churches of the monasteries would have vicars and, again, not monks to serve them. But this exceedingly curious part of England with, as has been said, a church at every mile and a character once again quite different from that of the fenlands of Cambridgeshire and Norfolk has an explanation for this plethora of churches, which is that the division of Holland was the richest part of England according to the poll-tax of 1397, half a century or two generations, be it noted, after the ravages of the Black Death. The many connections of John of Gaunt with Lincolnshire may be proof and illustration of this, and it will be recalled that his son Henry IV was born here. Nor did the spate of church building, whether monastic or not, diminish in other parts of the county, as witness, the line of churches along 'The Cliff', between Honington and Lincoln, Caythorpe, Brant Broughton, Lavenby among them; or going from Boston towards Skegness that other chain of churches which includes Frieston, once a priory, Levinton, Wrangle; or that third group of churches around Sleaford. There are the big town churches of Boston, Stamford, Grantham; and Louth, a bucolic market town which is on the way to nowhere, and even now quite a way away over the wolds on a summer day with larks singing, red poppies in their ragged companies and battalions, and ominous aeroplanes forever overhead – Louth with that giant crocketed spire three hundred feet high rising at an angle as you come to it down the 'somnolent' July street.

By which time we are in Lindsey that third division of Lincolnshire, and in fact have been out upon the wolds where there are far fewer churches than in Holland or Kesteven. Thornton Abbey, of the White Canons, is at the extreme end of this district, and only a few miles from the Humber. More is left of this than of most religious houses in this part of England; the splendid Perpendicular stone gateway, an arch with an oriel window above it, flanked by two pairs of octagonal towers, a bigger and a smaller, like a stone version of the brick gateway to a Cambridge college; and two walls only of what must from its traceries have been a beautiful octagonal chapter house. These both, and the legend of an abbot who was walled up alive, for the abbey seems to have had a sinister reputation, the culprit being one who died in 1385, or another, in 1443. A MS. account of the abbey, now in the Bodleian, says of the former that his record has been mutilated 'to prevent scandal to the church'; and of the other, that 'he died, but by what death I know not. He hath no *obit*, as other abbots have, and the place of his burial hath not been found'. Further to which, Dr William Stukeley, the antiquary (b. 1687), tells of a wall being taken down at Thornton in his time and a sitting skeleton being found inside it, with a lamp.

Coming back once more to Kesteven we must be delayed at Sempringham, near Sleaford, by the Gilbertines, the only Order founded in England, and which was for both monks and nuns. They lived under the same roof, divided by a wall even at mass, and might, as one writer has commented, just as well have been in separate buildings. The Gilbertines, however, who even in St Gilbert of Sempringham's lifetime (he died in 1189 aged, we are to believe, 106!) numbered fifteen hundred nuns and seven hundred canons, the latter in black cassocks with white hoods, and with beards. Black and White Canons, in fact, managed to escape scandal. None of the obvious lurid stories are reported of them. Of Sempringham, the head house of the Order, as has been said already, nothing is left, a high church tower and two cloisters having disappeared entirely. There would seem to have been twelve houses of Gilbertine monks and nuns in Lincolnshire out of some thirty in all, and they and the White Monks and White Canons of Kirkstead Tupholme, and the rest, must surely have owned their share of the flocks of white- or dark-faced sheep that made Holland and Kesteven so rich a part of England.

The monasteries and nunneries were destroyed largely because they had instigated the Lincolnshire Rising or Pilgrimage of Grace of 1536 after which more than one abbot as at Barlings was hanged at his own gate.[1] But non-monastic churches are in multitude, there being probably no comparable area in Europe in quantity of mediaeval remains. It has a quiet beauty of its own, whether of the wolds or marshlands, and effects of which de Wint is master in his watercolours and no less so F. L. Griggs in his pencil drawings of the churches, Spalding, Fleet Church, Algarkirk. He is their ideal delineator. And yet it is a part of the country where few persons would think of spending their holiday in looking at churches. A flatness that only makes the emergence of Lincoln Cathedral upon its hill the more marvellous, poor accommodation, a poorer climate, and an inherent dullness despite beautiful detail, as of spending the holiday with a beautiful but dull friend, may be the reason for this. One of the most lovely of all the churches is at Heckington, a little to the north of Sleaford. This is the perfection of the Decorated style, dating

---

[1] From end to end of England this penalty was inflicted on the abbots or priors of Bridlington, Fountains, Barlings, Kirkstead, Jervaulx, Colchester, Mount Grace, Axholme, Beauvale, and others. Perhaps the culmination of savagery was the burning alive, in 1538, as a relapsed heretic, of the Franciscan monk John Forest, who had been confessor to Catherine of Aragon, after long public argument with Latimer, a wooden image from Llandarvel, 'a noted object of pilgrimage and superstition' being used to make the fire. Could anything be more horrible than this?

from about 1345, its exterior is marvellously and delicately executed as is the interior of Patrington, that other distant and remote church down in the far corner of the East Riding, across the Humber. On the strength of long detours undertaken on two occasions only to see Heckington, the writer would express his admiration for this wonderful work of art, considered in every exterior detail and emerging as almost more of a sculpture to be admired from every angle than as a piece of architecture. Its modest size, and the marvellous reticulation of its buttresses with their receding planes and edges, the beautiful crocketing, the delicate tracery of its seven-light east window, all are admirable at this village church which is one of the beauties, not only of Lincolnshire, but of England. Perhaps this tribute to it will be accepted from one who has admired such a piece of technical virtuosity as the red chapels of Banteai Srei far away in the Cambodian jungles, near to Angkor. And, as there, the problem is who was the architect? Who were the carvers?

The exterior must be due to the master-mason responsible for the delicate stone plinth of the building, the buttresses, and the window traceries of the church at Sleaford. A mason and his men would make their lifework out of two or three nearby churches not many more than that number of miles apart from each other; at Bloxham, Geddington, King's Sutton, in the part of England the writer lives in; and as with the Perpendicular church towers of Somerset which fall into groups, and yet reveal that their designers must have gone from group to group, looking up and taking note, and criticizing. It is the general opinion that Heckington owes this lavish magnificence in detail to its having been taken over by royal licence by the Abbey of Bardney, after which work on it was begun at once and continued over some thirty years. But another reliable authority would not have it so, and describes the monks of Bardney as impoverished and fortunate in this instance to take over a brand new fabric. Thinking over which problem, there will be time to go on to see the church at Ewerby, only two or three miles away, where there is a beautiful spire, the details of light and shade and recession of the exterior have been considered and carved with exquisite care, and throughout there are signs of the master-mason who worked at Heckington.

The transition from Lincolnshire into Yorkshire, where the monasteries and nunneries are concerned, could not bring more difference if it was a question of going from one country to another. For Lincolnshire, although sown, or, rather, strewn with ecclesiastical remains does not exactly qualify as a monkish paradise. The incomparable Lincoln Cathedral and the parish churches predominate over the monastic houses which, although numerous, were mostly on the small side. This smallness and the success of the Gilbertines proves that it was a movement of the people and that most of the inmates were men and women from the Lincolnshire villages and small towns. In Lincolnshire it was the sheep farmers who raised the general level of living, and together with a soil fertile in fruit and vegetables made this into the richest part of England. It could be remarked in passing that this county which should resemble Holland (the real Holland, home of the Dutchmen, and not its own division called Holland) does not in fact, ditches and drains apart, resemble it in the least, this being due probably to the infusion of Danish blood. Between a third and a half of its village names end in Danish terminations. If therefore the big Holland is Germanic, but in its own way, Lincolnshire should more resemble Denmark, which is certainly true of the cornlands of Jutland which are like parts of Lindsey.

But Yorkshire represents another form of colonization altogether, and one in which the monasteries played their part. Owing to its early history, torn between Saxons and Danes, there were but few Benedictine foundations. Whitby and York, Selby, too, which was in a strategic situation just across the, then, bridgeless Humber, among them, which by their very names betray early association. The gaunt appearance of Whitby Abbey on its cliff, as much and as often in the teeth of the wind as its neighbour Scarborough Castle, suggests abandonment long ago, and it comes as a surprise to know that there were monks here until 1539. It has been suggested that the choice of Whitby as a monastic site was due to Northumbrian monks who had known the Scoto-Irish foundations on islands and exposed places like Lindisfarne and Iona. The town of York is another matter. This had been the centre of fertile land whether for crops or grazing in Roman times, which is why they made it their capital. But the huge Benedictine abbey founded here, of which the cathedral-church is now the Minster, represents a deliberate colonizing project on the part of the Norman Conquerors. It was rich indeed, but in matter of income only half as rich as Glastonbury when it was surrendered by the abbot and fifty monks in 1539, having been the seat of an archbishop and primate since the eleventh century. This will explain the enormous scale of the Minster though it is in no way grander in aspiration than Ely, Lincoln, Durham, those wonders of eastern England, to all three of which it ranks lower as a work of art.[1] I find its west front, the tracery of the great west window apart, and its pinnacled pair of towers, unexceptional in this kingdom of beautiful towers, often in mere parish churches; the exterior wings of its transept have become coeval, and not only in dust and dirt, with Street's Law Courts in the Strand; and the reassembled glass of its windows

---

[1] Lincoln has a pair of beautiful rose-windows in its transept; and this is perhaps the place in which to quote a writer's beautiful description of one of them, 'looking from outside like the skeletons of two leaves side by side'.

lacking in their vaunted beauty. Even its octagonal chapter-house must yield in beauty to that of Lincoln which is dodecagonal, and has its place apart, interior and buttressed exterior alike, among English chapter-houses.

It so happened that the colonizing schemes of the Normans where this part of the north of England was concerned coincided with the arrival of Cistercian monks from France, and within a generation of the Conquest they had established themselves at Byland, Fountains, Rievaulx, their chief monasteries in Yorkshire. Within the lifetime, more strictly speaking, of the first generation of children born in England to the Norman Conquerors, say, by 1135. It was the policy of the Cistercians to retire to secluded places chosen for their remoteness and to make them into monkish paradises, though a strict simplicity was inculcated which became relaxed during their four centuries of existence. They chose, too, sites beautiful in themselves, as witness the names of their monasteries not only in England; Clairfontaine, Froidefontaine, being an improvement upon mere Fountains, or 'Fontes' as they called it, with the six springs still rising within its precincts. That it is a beautiful site, none could deny, naturally beautiful, that is to say, without and before any improvement by the hand of man. The eventual plan of the building was brought over from Clairvaux by the third abbot who was a friend of St Bernard, reformer of the Benedictine Order and founder of the Cistercians, and is therefore of direct Cistercian inspiration and a part of their great architectural innovation all over Europe which could be seen more clearly if only, as is so often the case in our country in this respect, there was still a roof on the building and it could be studied in anything better than its bare plan. However, with the aid of that the complete disposition of this twelfth-century monastery can be made out in all kinds of minor detail, such as the long arcaded trough in the cloister near the fratery doorway where the monks washed their hands at mealtimes and combed their beards, and even the special kitchen where more delicate food *cibi subtiliores* was cooked for the infirm monks, and for those who had undergone the periodical bleeding. To give the ruin further life there is the nearly perfect and unruined Perpendicular tower built by Abbot Marmaduke Huby; the refectory can be seen, at least on the ground plan with a row of marble columns down its middle; and there is a good deal more than the foundations of the dormitory where forty monks slept, as at a boys' school, in cells made into partitions by wooden walls. There is even a crypt that may have been the stable where the abbot kept his six white horses. 'Sex equi ad bigam', horses, as we shall know later, of monastic breed. There is no mention of a vineyard, no doubt because this is too far north, which gives more probability to the wine-bearing vines of monasteries in the Severn Valley and other places.

Such was this great religious house, the walled close of which alone held eighty acres, and the boundaries of whose estates extended over an uninterrupted space of thirty miles; while in addition to 'many other wide domains, its lands in Craven held in a ring fence, a hundred square miles, or sixty thousand acres on a moderate computation'.

Other great Cistercian abbeys, Rievaulx, Byland, Jervaulx, Kirkstall, were not far away. Of Byland little is left, though its church was 330 ft long, the length of a cathedral of stone, but of not much more substance now than the strong wind which arose for no reason as late as 1820 when the bones of its Crusader founder Sir Roger de Mowbray were discovered and taken elsewhere for burial, a wind 'raised' by the discovery of his grave. Rievaulx was in its day the largest and most famous monastery in England with 300 monks, and 140 monks and 500 lay-brothers or *conversi* in 1186, but only 21 monks when the abbey was surrendered. The present ruins give little idea of its original size, except for the huge refectory, but Rievaulx lies in an exceedingly beautiful valley which was made the 'theme' of one of the greatest feats of English landscape gardening. Its terrace with a pavilion at either end, laid out by Mr Duncombe about the middle of the eighteenth century, with the garden at Stourhead and the lake and hanging wood in the park at Blenheim, is the supreme achievement of the landscape gardener.[1]

Of Jervaulx there is really nothing left at all, or, at least, nothing that is alive. There is even less in a sense than what 'Old Jenkins', who lived to be 169 (older than Old Parr who was only 152) has to say of it, which is that remembering perfectly well, as he did, the Dissolution of the Monasteries and the mustering before Flodden Field when as a boy of twelve he was sent to Northallerton with a horseload of arrows, he remembered seeing the dole at the gate of Jervaulx, of bread and red and white herrings, to 'poor persons, hermits and children'. And that is all. 'Old Jenkins' has no more to say. The monks of Jervaulx were famous for their cheese which is still made to this day in Wensleydale, and for their white horses. The Commissioners recommended Jervaulx to the King for their horses: 'Surely the breed of Gervaix for horse was the tried breed in the North. I think in no realm should be found the like to them; for there is hardy and high grounds for the summer, and in winter woods and low grounds to fire them.' At Coverham, also, a Premonstratensian abbey a mile or two away, white horses were bred, and probably the white horses of the abbot of Fountains came from there.

---

[1] The pleasure grounds of Studley Royal, laid out by Mr Aislabie, another country gentleman, at the back of Fountains, and not making any play of the ruins, are perhaps equally beautiful, but they belong to another school of gardening, nearer to the fountains and clipped hedge of Beloeil and Versailles.

Kirkstall, near Leeds, a smaller and blackened Fountains, was a fourth Cistercian house; and the roll of the great Yorkshire abbeys is made complete with the addition of Nostell Priory of the Black Canons with twenty-eight priest-monks at the time of the Surrender.

But the monks of this part of England, and the Cistercians in particular, were engaging in new activities. The small slag heaps and the pieces of charcoal still found in the ground at Rievaulx show that iron was worked here. Other monasteries further north in Durham and Lancashire, as we shall see, were coal-owners. But their great wealth was in flocks of sheep. It is here that a pleasant and pastoral picture emerges which, even if it only affected a few of the monks in any one monastery, may be taken in palliation of the undoubted rigours of the Cistercian rule. It entails for one thing the residence of those few of the monks in the monastic granges which would be built near the sheep walks. The shepherding was done in early days by the lay-brothers or *conversi* until the diminishment of their number consequent on the Black Death after which it was the work of hired labourers. There were sheep walks over the Lincolnshire wolds – and one wonders at what date the traditional green smocks of those local farm labourers came in – and, also, there were sheep walks on the flat lands of Holderness along the Humber, and to much greater extent upon the Yorkshire moors. Thus, the wool trade which later in the hands of rich merchants was to produce the 'wool-churches' of the Cotswolds, and churches of the clothiers like Long Melford and Lavenham in Suffolk, was already providing revenue for the Black and the White Monks, and not only in the north of England. The Wiltshire and Dorset and Hampshire downs were white with flocks; the Bishop of Winchester, a Benedictine Cathedral Priory, had 29,000 sheep grazing, more than had Glastonbury, or even Peterborough and Crowland put together. Foreign abbeys owned flocks on the *pré salé* or salt sea marshes of Essex; the nuns of Holy Trinity at Caen had 1,700 sheep on Minchinhampton Common in Gloucestershire, and there were monastic flocks at Strata Florida[1] in Cardigan, and flocks of brown-woolled sheep on the Welsh Hills.

The monks sold the wool and ate the cheeses made from the ewes' milk. Flemish and even Italian merchants from Florence and Lucca came to buy the wool, and two lists for 1280 and 1315 survive, giving the names of the religious houses and the number of sacks of wool delivered, mixed and in bulk by the Benedictine monks, but graded into *bona, grossa et lacei* by Cistercians and Augustinians. It is curious to reflect on a merchant from Florence

[1] How beautiful a name is Whitland or Albalanda, a Cistercian abbey in Carmarthenshire! Valle Crucis in Denbigh has the finest monastic remains in the Principality; and here, at Albalanda and Strata Florida, were novices from the Welsh-speaking, ruling families of Wales.

arriving at Rievaulx or Fountains on an early autumn evening at the season
of the sheep shearing, at about a date which was still twenty years before
Giotto's Tower was built. What would this Italian, who had been through
Lincolnshire on his way, think of these great English abbeys? There was nothing like them in Italy. Just at this time Siena and Lucca were ahead of Florence
which had not quite reached the flowering of its genius. It would have been
interesting to talk to him, and ask if it was not his opinion that this was the
richest land in Europe. Dom David Knowles, who writes with such absorbed
interest of all concerning our religious houses concludes, with a phrase of
which a poet must envy him, that 'the northern houses of monks and nuns
were the best wool-growers save for the small knot of sheepowners in
Shropshire who clipped the finest wool of all – the famed "Lemster ore".'
Other themes no less fruitful come in his pages, as of the abbey of Meaux,
cruelly devastated by the Black Death, which had its sheep walks in Holderness and owned the grange of Croo, 'so named it would seem, from the most
vocal of its tenants, in the open wind-swept country by Beeforth near the
sea'. A thick grove of trees lay round it where nested a large colony of rooks.
The villein who administered the estate, complained of the crying and 'croo-
ing' of the birds, sought the abbot's permission, and cut down every tree on
the place.

But, also, there are the Yorkshire nunneries to be considered and they, too,
dealt in wool. The thirteenth century *Pratica della Mercatura* of Francesco
Pergolotti gives a list of monasteries that sell wool, giving the prices and the
quality, and in the section specially devoted to nunneries, names twenty
houses, all but two of them in Lincolnshire or Yorkshire. Miss Eileen Power
(*Mediaeval English Nunneries*, 1922, p. 111) from whom this is quoted, gives
a picture of an Italian arriving at a nunnery, bargaining for the wool and
riding away with a silken purse, a pair of gloves, or an embroidered blood-
band. There were indeed twenty-seven nunneries in Yorkshire, and it would
seem that their occupants were of aristocratic, not as in Lincolnshire of village origin. Percys, Mowbrays, Fairfaxes were among them, the last-named
family having a particular connection from the fourteenth century onward
with the nunnery of Nun Monkton. How appropriate this name for a convent as, also, that other name of a nunnery, Ankerwyke, with its obvious reference to an anchorite! Moreover, Margaret Fairfax apart, who was prioress
of Nun Monkton in 1397, and of whom it was put in complaint that she
wore expensive furs and silken veils, and (this is confusing) kept company
with John Munkton, who played at 'tables' (a game like backgammon) with
the Prioress and served her with drink, what a beautiful name for a nun is
Joan Blaunkfront, of Moxby Priory, which does apparently really mean what

it sounds to be, that is, with 'a white front or forehead', the forehead, as we have seen before, being a much admired feature in those days, and enjoined for that reason not be shown in public. We are in the north of England near enough to the Border to be harried or even driven out by the Scots, as was the last-named nun, and discipline was lax. If a certain number of nuns, in fact very few of them, had lost their virtue and confessed to having given birth to children, it is possible in several cases that this was before they took their first vows, and was, indeed, the reason for their having entered the convent.

The maps give few monasteries and only three or four nunneries for the whole of Northern England. It was in fact too dangerously near Scotland, though it is to be remarked that the Scots abbeys, Melrose, Dryburgh, and others are much nearer to England than we built our religious houses near to Scotland. Perhaps we were better soldiers when it came to a battle, and the Scots excelled as raiders. In any case but for Blanchland of the night stair, and Hexham where six out of the twenty of the canons had to be hung because of the Pilgrimage of Grace, all is overshadowed in this part of the country by the ancient Benedictine Cathedral Priory at Durham. What more can one say of this wonderful building of 'rocky solidity and indeterminate duration', as Dr Johnson remarked of it, being perhaps the most tremendous work of human hands in the entire kingdom! Mediaeval buildings on this scale have only been matched in the modern world, and then only in scale, not as works of art, by such feats of construction and engineering as the Seagram Tower by Mies van der Rohe and Philip Johnson in New York.

Ely, Lincoln, Durham are the wonders of our mediaeval architecture lying inland from the east coast of England. And having attempted to write of the first named in ineffectual and faint praise in my Introduction, and being debarred from writing of the second because it was not monastic of foundation, I find myself halted before the vast, the tremendous mere strength and bulk of Durham with just the same shock as that of seeing it looming up and above the river for the first time. Lincoln Cathedral, I must allow myself to say in parenthesis, being, I think, the most beautiful in the pleasing sense of all English cathedrals; with the marvellous, visible from afar, almost cumulus-whiteness of its three towers; the running articulation of its west front which is like a worked screen or breastplate of stone, holding in place until the wonders of the interior are ready for one; the beauties of its Angel Choir where such good use is made of Purbeck marble, an unpoetic material but here it has the elegance of an Andalucian patio; and the decagonal, ten-sided chapter-house, inside and out more like a celestial kitchen.

No view of Durham, it is true, could better that seen from the window of

the railway train. Nearer approach but adds to the majesty of the first impression and induces a feeling of respect and awe. All is on the Babylonian,
the Ninevean scale, knowing the while that it far surpasses any building
those satraps of the ancient world could put up of mud or clay that must be
mixed with straw. The central tower of Durham, alone and in itself, is a
stupendous relic surviving out of the ancient night of darkness. When we
know, further to this, that it was the monks of Lindisfarne or Holy Island,
who left their sea-gull'd fastness off the Northumbrian coast for fear of the
Northmen and began the abbey in the tenth century, it but accentuates our
awe and wonder. That this interior with Cyclopean columns of more than
Roman solidity and permanence should result from the sea-serpent haunted
minds of the monks of Lindisfarne, to judge from the snake-finials and
basket-convolutions of their Gospel, is the marvel of Durham which on
opening any atlas we must agree to be the wonder of the north for there is,
in fact, no building on such a scale to the north of it anywhere in Europe or
in Asia. The sternness and grimness are only relieved and carried from the
major into the minor scale at the reredos of the high altar, or 'Neville' screen,
a work of 1380, of lance-like fragility and pointedness, now lacking, of
course, its alabaster figures that were painted and gilded. And another note,
in almost an Oriental scale, sounds from the Galilee Porch, a building of the
late twelfth century which more than one commentator has likened to the
round-arched vessel of a mosque, its purport being to shelter pilgrims from
the wind and rain.

Let us think now of the monastery itself which seems to have been upon
the same scale as the Cathedral Priory, to judge from descriptions in *The
Rites of Durham*, a book by an anonymous sixteenth-century author who may
have been one of the monks.

There was a famouse house of hospitallitie called the geste haule with in the
abbey garth of Durham on the weste syde towards the water . . . ther interteyn-
ment not being inferior to any place in England, both for the goodness of ther
diete, the sweete and daintie furneture of there Lodginges, and generally all
thinges necessarie for traveillers – this haule is a goodly brave place much like into
the body of a church with verey fair pillers supporting yt on ether syde and in
mydest of the haule a most large Raunge for the fyer.

On the right hand as your goe out of the cloysters in to the jermery was the
commone house and a Maister thereof, the house being to this end, to have a fyre
keapt in yt all wynter for the Mounkes to cume and warme them at, being
allowed no fyre but that onely. Except the Maisters and officers of the house who
had there severall fyres. There was belonging to the common house a garding
and a bowlinge allie . . . for the Nouyces Sume tymes to recreat themselves

– no mention of monkish vineyards in this northern clime! – and he concludes with the feast day

when ther Banquett was of figes and reysinghes ails and caikes and thereof no superfluitie or excesse but a scholasticall and moderat congratulacy on amonges them selves.

With which brave words one cannot but contrast the cold days and nights of Durham, where the monks dressed by the light of cressets – bowls filled with oil and floating wicks, and set in hollows in square stones at either end of the dorter. And one fire only at which to warm themselves in the *calefactorium*! But where, on the other hand, the monks were coal-owners; the bursar of Durham spent £7 to winners of coal, '*lucracio carbonarum*', and another sum for '*exasperacione*, i.e. sharpening le pykkes'.

Across at the other side of England on the Irish Sea there were coal-owning monks at Furness in Lancashire, a Cistercian abbey as one might guess from its isolation, and one large enough to have thirty-nine monks and one hundred other inmates, mostly servants, still in it in 1537. They worked iron, or had it worked for them, as well; iron ore found on Walney Island for which the monks put up two furnaces. The abbey, of red sandstone, owned malt-kilns, breweries, fishponds, a private army of twelve hundred including four hundred horse for use against the Scots, an estate as large as the Isle of Man, and presumably the shrimp-sands of Morecambe Bay; and here for four hundred years their abbots reigned in peace and plenty, doing, it must be conceded more good than harm. Carlisle, where the priory of Black Canons is now the cathedral, is so near the Border that the survival of a mediaeval building, particularly with anything so fragile as a large and beautiful east window, is matter for surprise.

That there should be an ancient Benedictine abbey at Chester founded by the first generation of Norman conquerors, on a site which was an administrative centre even in Roman times, and always a border fort against the wild Welsh, is something only to be expected. The building is of red sandstone, an unfortunate material even in the temples of Cambodia, a shortcoming for which the canopied choir stalls and the unusual state of preservation of some parts of the monastery, a perfect example of a slype among them, is little compensation.

But we are now coming to a part of England where, if we can imagine ourselves in the place of Henry VIII's Commissioners, there would be no knowledge at all of what we might find next, it would be a case of enquiring at every village or small town, and proceeding to some religious house with it may be but three or four monks or nuns in it, but who knows what works of art! This would, of course, have been truer still had it been before the Suppression of the alien priories under Henry V.[1] Buildwas in Shropshire with the interesting name is perhaps a case in point. Its name apart we are left now with the bare walls of the church, the chapter house, and little else but the knowledge that it owned nine granges in Salop, besides others, a Savigniac priory in Dublin, the abbey of Basingwerk in Flintshire, that of Dunbrody in Wexford, and a cope worked by the hands of Fair Rosamund. Of Much Wenlock, where was a church four hundred feet long, there are but the ruins; and of Haughenard or Haut Mont, once in its own park, but the triple round-headed Norman arches of its chapter-house and the stone mullions of the abbot's lodging.

And with this let us say to ourselves that we are in the west country, and have arrived at the Severn basin which Dom David Knowles calls 'the richest of all districts in England in great monasteries'. Gloucester, Worcester, Pershore, Evesham, Tewkesbury, Malmesbury, all Benedictine houses, are implied. Gloucester, the cradle of Perpendicular, with its marvellous east window whether or not, but let us have it 'yes', in memory of Crécy, its 'fern-Gothic' canopy for murdered Edward II, and the fan-vaulting of its cloister, rival to any 'apiarist work' of the Alhambra or at Isfahan; Worcester with its cathedral and forty monks to surrender it to the Commissioners, but which to those who have had a surfeit of churches may take on another interest with a quotation from Dom David Knowles of further bucolic details, as of the granges of the abbots of Worcester, and those of Crowle and Grimley in particular which must have been like country houses. A bucolic note is sounded from the start in the arms of Prior Wednesbury, the builder of Grimley, gules, on a Jess sable, between three strawberry branches slipped, with berries proper, as many birds and close, etc: which arms were emblazoned on the windows. There are minute details in Abbot More (the last abbot's) accounts even down to the fish stews. There are the draining of the ponds and moats and the netting of the fish therein, and it is even stated: 'Md. that the Eyghth day of may the Eyre of Swannes within the mott att batnall did ley ix egges v of them wer Addle and iiii of the eggs wer Signetts this year. Item the Swannes in the poole at Grymley did ley vii eggs iiij beying addyl iij of them wer signets.' There are payments to 'the yong men of crowle for syngyng on maii day in the morenyng', and 'to the may-dews of crowle for syngyng an holy rowde day in the morenyng towards

---

[1] Typical of this may have been the White Ladies of Brewood Forest in Shropshire, a Cistercian nunnery founded under Richard I, with the Black Ladies or Benedictine nuns of Brewood, Staffordshire, near by. There were four nuns at the former in 1538, and a prioress and three nuns at the latter. Only the ruins are left of both convents.

our lady light' and Dom David Knowles, the learned author and Regius Professor of Modern History in the University of Cambridge, himself a native of these parts and coming from the Worcestershire-Warwickshire border, finds a mention of payment to 'the moldyer taker for takyng moles' which recalls to him the 'moldiwarps' the gardener talked of when he was a child.

Pershore Abbey is a wonderful relic of the long dead past, and before parts of it were torn down was bigger, and some would say better work than Worcester Cathedral. But it must yield place to Evesham which bears every sign of having been placed among the most fertile and pomiferous orchards in England.[1] Indeed some of the cider apples of the district may date back to monastic days. Yet nothing of it remains, only the feeling of its past, and the Perpendicular bell-tower but just finished before the Suppression, foretaste of other towers in the buttercup fields down to the south – and the two Perpendicular parish churches in the churchyard with their fan-vaulting. Malmesbury is but the nave and aisles of what was once a huge cruciform or cross-shaped building, with a noble and fine Norman church. The grandest and most important of these western monasteries was Tewkesbury which is still overwhelmingly impressive, and an extraordinary instance of the innate military manner of the Norman Conquerors transmuted to other purposes, and this in the meadows and orchards of Gloucestershire, a county which in the Middle Ages was even famous for its monk-made, sweet red wine. That the country house style and tenure of its abbots was not confined to this area, but had spread southwards into Somerset is amplified in the anecdote, in Knowles, of the abbot of Bisham who sold monastery possessions for 'white wyne, sugar, burage leves and seke [sack] whereof he sippes nyghtly in his chamber tyle mydnight'.

From hereabouts it is no great distance, by way of Bath with its abbey of Black Canons, to Glastonbury:

We assure your lordship [this from the Commissioners to Thomas Cromwell] that it is the goodliest house of that sort that ever we have seen . . . a house mete for the kinges majesty and for no man else; which is to our great comfort . . . The house is greate, goodly and so pryncely as we have not seen the lyke; with 4 parkes adjoynyng . . . a great mere well replenished with greate pyke, breme, perche, and roche; 4 faire manour places belonging to the late abbott, the furthest but 3 myles distant, beyng goodly mansions.

[1] Officers and obedientiaries of Evesham in the thirtenth century were the prior, sub-prior, third prior, and other *custodes ordinis*, the precentor, dean of the Christianity of the Vale of Evesham, sacrist, chamberlain, kitchener, two cellarers, infirmarer, almoner, warden of the vineyard and garden, master of the fabric, guest-master, and pittancer.

The end was swift and merciless. Abbot Whiting, accused of hiding treasure and being in possession of treasonable literature against one or other of the King's divorces, was tried and condemned. And dragged on a hurdle with five of his monks from the gate of his abbey through the streets of Glastonbury, and hung on a gibbet on Tor Hill. His severed head was then put above the abbey gate.

Only a few days before this Cromwell writes in his memoranda: 'The plate from Glastonbury, 11,000 oz. and odd, besides gold. The furniture of the house of Glastonbury. In ready money from Glastonbury, £1,100 and odd' (worth perhaps £30,000 to £40,000 in present-day money) 'the rich copes from Glastonbury. The whole year's revenue from Glastonbury'. Who, then, was the robber? And why should it have been Abbot Whiting who was hung on the gallows on Tor Hill? Glastonbury was the most sacred ground in England with a sanctity going back to pre-Christian times, the Apple-Tree Isle or Isle of Avalon of Arthurian legend. The skulls of King Arthur and Queen Guinevere who were buried here, were on occasion put outside the shrine for the devotion of pilgrims. The incalculable treasures it contained disappeared almost overnight; and of monastic buildings, the George Inn apart – the old pilgrims' hostel built by Abbot Selwood with the arms of Edward IV over its gate, supporters the black bull of Clare and the white lion of Mortimer – what is there left which is not a ruin except the Abbot's kitchen, buttressed and lanterned, impressive in scale and ingenious in internal arrangement, for the manner by which the four fireplaces in its angles make the interior into an octagon? How beautiful was the sacred isolation of the Isle of Avalon! The Abbots of Glastonbury had a summer house a little way away at Meare, where is the prehistoric lake village, on an island in a lake variously described as covering five hundred acres, or five miles round. There is, also, the Fish House where lived the abbey fisherman, and a field called Pool-reed where the abbots came by water and their boats were moored. The village could only be reached by a horsepath till Victorian times. The Apple-Tree Isle was in the middle of the reeds.

Athelney and Muchelney, with its abbot's house but only the ground plan of its ruined abbey, were houses of Black monks on islands in the swamp, surrounded by water and by peat bogs, or in dense forests of alders. Of Cleeve Abbey, an ancient Cistercian house, the church is gone but the refectory and other buildings still remain;[1] in direct contrast for instance to Tintern Abbey in Monmouth, across the Bristol Channel, where the church

---

[1] It would be tempting to ascribe some of the Perpendicular church towers for which Somerset is famous to monastic instigation, but this seems impossible except at Bruton where there were Black Canons (and a fine tower) and at Isle Abbots which 'belonged' to Muchelney.

is left but hardly anything of the conventual buildings. If we come back south again, and then turn east along that warmer coast upon the Channel, it is to find Cerne Abbas and Milton Abbas, both of Black Monks, the latter 'improved' by 'picturesque' attention with more of it left than usual in a sequestered abbey, and only ruins left of Tarrant Priory where was an important Cistercian nunnery. Sherborne, an ancient Benedictine abbey is another matter, still in use, and marvellously preserved with the lierne and fan-vaulting of its ceiling.

A beautiful feature of all this west of England are the monastic barns which are found nowhere else in Europe, being especially peculiar to this region, it has been suggested, because of the good building stone, the better climate, and the agriculturally richer monasteries. They are not to be met with in East Anglia or in Lincolnshire or Yorkshire, but only south-west of a line drawn between Birmingham and Brighton; farm buildings as they could be seen through the eyes of a painter of pastorals like Samuel Palmer, or in the woodcuts of pastoral scenes by Edward Calvert, subjects of strict limitation to a particular locality, dialect-pictures, even, of a countryside as of a poet writing in patois. Once seen, one knows them so well with their stone buttresses and stone-tiled roof, their high porches and the glorious 'ships' timbers of their ceilings. They are temples of Ceres of a peculiar and most English poetry inseparable from the landscape, even from the chalk figures on the downs. The monastic barns are scattered so widely over the west of England that it would hardly be possible to know them all; but how beautiful are the fourteenth-century barn at Enstone in Oxon, once belonging to the abbots of Winchcombe; at Great Coxwell, near Faringdon, said to be the finest of all, part of a monastic grange of the monks of Beaulieu; or the great barn of Abbotsbury in Dorset, where the Black Monks owned the swannery and made profitable commerce from quill pens and swan's down.[1]

At Shaftesbury was the largest and biggest of the English nunneries with its abbess and fifty-six nuns at the Surrender, and only the stone foundations left. The abbesses both of Shaftesbury and of Wilton, as mentioned before, took rank as baronesses, with those of Barking and of St Mary Winchester, but are as shadowy now as the twenty-four Benedictine and three Augustinian abbots who were mitred barons of England and had seats in the House

---

[1] Besides the monastic barn at Glastonbury, itself, there are others at Bredon and Middle Littleton in Worcestershire, Frocester and Stanway in Gloucestershire; Doulting, Pilton, and Preston Plucknett in Somerset; Tisbury and Bradford in Wiltshire; Cerne in Dorset; Buckland and Torre in Devon; to which list we put again Abbotsbury, Enstone, and Great Coxwell. The barn at Tisbury, the largest of them all, belonged to the nuns of Shaftesbury.

of Lords. Of Reading Abbey for example, which was an important house of Black Monks with a mitred abbot, 'very little masonry is left, chiefly rubble'. More is to be gathered, in anecdote at least, from the nuns of St Mary's or Nunminster, at Winchester, where before the Surrender were twenty-six nuns, thirty-two servants, five chaplains, three corrodies or life-boarders, thirteen poor sisters, and twenty-six 'chyldren of lordys Knyghttes and gentylmen brought vp yn the sayd monastery', from which what amount to school reports are preserved with much detail concerning one particular child, the Lady Bridget Plantagenet, daughter of Lord Lisle (who was an illegitimate son of Edward IV), as witness a letter from the abbess to the girl's stepmother:

I do perceive your pleasure is to know how mistress Bridget your daughter doth, and what things she lacketh. Madam, thanks be to God, she is in good health, but I assure your ladyship she lacketh convenient apparel, for she hath neither whole gown nor kirtle, but the gown and kirtle that you sent her last. And also she hath not one good parflet to put upon her neck, nor one good coif to put upon her head . . .

Mine singular and special good lady . . . where as your ladyship do write that you sent me an ermine cafe for your daughter, surely I see none. I have sent into you your daughter's black velvet gown; also I have caused kirtles to be made of her old gown, according to your writing . . .

and the abbess concludes with thanks to Lady Lisle for sending a side of venison and two dozen and a half of peewits.

Nunminster is vanished, gone, but there is still Romsey Abbey in Hampshire, a house of Black Nuns, where the Norman church with splendidly masculine choir of triple storeys of rounded arches is still in use; with ninety nuns living in it early in the fourteenth century but only about a third of that number at the Surrender, and the largest of the nuns' churches that survive. It could have been of any of these nunneries, but it was in fact of that of Kington St Michael, his native village in Wiltshire, that John Aubrey writes:

Here . . . the young maids . . . learned needlecraft, the art of confectionery, surgery (for anciently there were no apothecaries or surgeons – the gentlewomen did cure their poor neighbours: their hands are now too fine), physic, writing, drawing, etc:

And in the words, almost, of one who could remember them, he continues:

Old Jacques could see from his house the nuns of the priory come forth into the nymph-hay with their rocks and wheels to spin. He would say that he had told three score and ten, but of nuns there were not so many, but in all, with lay sisters and widows, old maids and young girls, there might be such a number . . .

This was a fine way of breeding up young women, who are led more by example than precept; and a good requirement for widows and grave single women to a civil, virtuous, and holy life.

But let these pastorals continue for a paragraph longer, before the 'nymph-hay' fades from mind! One of the charges brought against the prioress of Arden, in Yorkshire, in 1396, was that 'she compelled three young nuns to go out haymaking very early in the morning and they did not come back before nightfall and so divine service was not yet said'. Or, once more, as in our opening pages, it is the White Ladies of Grace Dieu, in Leicestershire, who, their sub-prioress says: 'sometimes help secular folk in garnering their grain during the autumn season.' And it is complained to the bishop in 1449, concerning Margaret Belers, the cellaress, that 'she goes out to work in autumn alone with Sir Henry (the chaplain), he reaping the harvest and she binding the sheaves, and at evening she comes riding behind him on the same horse. She is over friendly with him and has been since the doings aforesaid'. While at Nuncaton or Nun Cotham in 1440, in Lincolnshire: 'in seed time the nuns clear the crops of weeds in the barns, and there secular folks do come in and unbecoming words are uttered between them and the nuns, where-from, as is feared, there are evil consequences'.

Winchester Cathedral Priory a most venerable and ancient Benedictine foundation, is only not of the order of Durham or Ely, perhaps because of a more salubrious soil or setting away from, alike, the gales of the sea-coast and the mists and dampness of the East Anglian fens. But Winchester is marvellous for length of nave, largely, in the state in which we see it now, the work of the famous Bishop William of Wykeham (1366–1404); for its Perpendicular altar screen; but above all, for its chantry chapels, as English an invention as a fan-vault or a tithe-barn, and which are here in unrivalled number, several of them sited on the feretory or raised platform behind the reredos which was intended for the display of relics. Here are the chantry chapels of Bishop Waynflete and of Cardinal Beaufort, a personage of Shakespearean import who revives in Fuseli's paintings and in romantic plays, and is one of the tinselled figures from the Hoxton drama. Exceptional and wonderful are the carved and painted ceiling-bosses in the nave at Winchester. As minute and intricate as Japanese *netsuke* carvings, and more to be admired than those, they show the arms of Bishop Waynflete and the Beaufort portcullis with much else beside, but are indeed only revealed in their full detail through a pair of opera-glasses.

And these pages approach their end with Christchurch Priory, in Hampshire, a house of White Canons, where for once the whole church was retained for worship, with three storeys of male Norman arches for its nave, and a beautiful chantry chapel; or with Beaulieu Abbey where the church has been made out of the frater or refectory, which would have a reader's pulpit anyway, this being the same abbey of Cistercian monks that built the barn on their farm or grange many miles from here at Great Coxwell. And but a few miles farther, and we are at Battle Abbey, the house of Benedictine monks founded by the Conqueror, of which the gateway, refectory, dormitory are left, but in effect little or nothing of its ancient wonders. How long would it have taken to ride or walk from here to Dover, past Rye and Winchester, through Dungeness and Romney Marsh? In maybe two days we could be back at the chalk hills with the 'homme de Douvres, appelé le rampeur', coming out towards us from his 'anchorage' on the White Cliffs of Dover, having seen this little of some of the wonders of old England and of its splendours which never come second to those of France or Germany, Italy or Spain. This would be true of the relics from only the first half of our history as a kingdom, had we not of our own hands destroyed many of the churches, and most of the monasteries and nunneries herein described.

2

The Eighteenth Century in the
Holy Roman Empire,
Austria and Bavaria

THE deficiency of this age that we are living in is that we need a fluency and an eloquence which have gone out of the world, and not as in the new Coventry Cathedral, a simultaneous stuttering in many different stylistic tongues. It is departed because no one believes in anything, or has faith any more. Not that belief is enough in itself, and all in all, or the mid-Victorian age in England would have been one of the great art epochs of the world. Another approach and a different handling could be the answer. Let us think for a moment, as a prelude to what is to come, of a school of architects and sculptors that has had no equivalent since the Middle Ages. It is of a purpose that we emphasize their rural and bucolic setting.

The churches of the Asam brothers, of Dominikus Zimmermann, and others, chiefly in Bavaria, in their affirmation of living, in their grace and spontaneity, are only approached by such a parallel phenomenon as our mediaeval village churches in parts of England. Johann Michael Fischer, who worked in no less than fifty churches, architect of Osterhofen, Diessen, Berg-am-Lain, Rott-am-Inn, Zwiefalten, and Ottobeuren, and the painters and sculptors who worked with him, were possessed of attributes which in a sister art, that of music, produced a Haydn and a Mozart. If those attributes are universally recognised in the case of the musicians they cannot in fairness be denied to the craftsmen and architects in question who were their equivalents.

The craftsmen of the Middle Ages, and the population for whom they worked, to take only a small corner of England, but one which is significant for just those same qualities, might not be so abashed as we may think at

Opposite: Interior of church
at Einsiedeln

sight of these more recent, maybe final, manifestations of high spirits and ebullience. The carpenters who wrought the double hammer-beams of the roof at St Wendreda's, at March in Cambridgeshire, and made them into a 'rooky wood', but a bright wood of angels, a hundred and twenty of them in all, eight pinions to a wing for every pair of them, in double ranks set one above another, so that the whole roof is aflap and alive with wings; who carved the double hammer-beams of Salle and of Cawston, in Norfolk, with winged angels 'displaying the heavenly hierarchy'; or made the wooden font-cover eighteen feet high, all crockets and pinnacles at Ufford in Suffolk, once gilded and coloured, and articulated so that its three tiers or storeys can slide into and over one another like the parts of a telescope – so fine a work that even the Cromwellian iconoclast and image-breaker Dowsing, writing of it in his diary, 'there is a glorious cover over the font, like a Pope's triple crown, a pelican on the top picking its breast, all gilt over with gold' – even Dowsing spared it and passed by – what would these mediaeval craftsmen have found amiss with the white pilgrimage church of Dominikus Zimmermann at Wies, with its oval interior so gaily painted that it has been called 'the dance-floor of God'?

What would they find wrong in the corals and stalactites of Zwiefalten, marine-motifs as though the pulpits were to be grottoes and the whole church to suffer a sea-change? Would they take objection to the pulpit at Irsee, shaped like a ship's bow with sail raised on the mainmast, and cupids in the ropes and busy in the rigging? Or to the figures of Duke Ottocar and his wife behind the high altar at Osterhofen, he in full armour with the flag of Bavaria in blue and white chequers at his back, and his wife smiling across the altar at him from behind her fan? Least of all, we may think, would they misunderstand Steinhausen, another of Dominikus Zimmermann's pilgrimage churches on an oval plan, so shaped, it has been pointed out, because the congregation to be seated might be small in number, but room was needed for them to process round the walls with their banners – while the craftsmen of the Middle Ages would surely have appreciated what is especial and peculiar to Steinhausen, the stucco birds by the architect's brother who often worked with him, Johann Baptist Zimmermann, perching here and there on capitals, or on the sides of windows. Not too many of them, just one or two, as on any day in the high, empty vessel of a church. A bird like a woodpecker, clinging with little clawed feet to the inner curve or parabola of a Rococo window, and outlined there from far below, pecking with pointed beak and little crested head. Such things are surely in the spirit of the mediaeval builders, and less the eccentricities of an individual than the details in a whole vast movement of unanimity and co-ordination.

This it is, exactly, which is lacking in our time. But, also, development was slower; and in another generation and some half-century after his death they were still under the influence of Bernini, the 'last universal genius of the Renaissance'. Caught in a similar time-lag we would still be in the dog-foot coils of the Art Nouveau of 1900, and indeed by now something might have come from those not altogether inauspicious beginnings.

Up to this point we have been speaking indiscriminately of Rococo churches in Bavaria, whether secular or monastic, and now in the interests of our subject it is necessary to particularize. It will mean that the supreme example of German Rococo, the pilgrimage church at Wies, is debarred from us however tempting the invitation to try to describe it. For Wies was the personal gift or offering of its architect Dominikus Zimmermann. And not only that but the terms of our assignment take us first into Austria – leaving Bavaria till later – into Austria, the magical, easy going Oesterreich of one's youth where nearly everyone goes or tries to go while he is young, and probably for love of Mozart, for which reason this chapter can open in the Mirabell Garden at Salzburg, a garden of statues and espaliered apricot trees; sitting, let us recall, in the café in that garden on an August morning, opposite to a tall, thin young man of indeterminate feature and expression, and of double, or even treble shadow. In the particular sunny light of the morning, as if indeed there are mountains and pine-clad lakes not far away, and with the sound of musical rehearsal from a building near by.

And a few days later we are before the immense, yellowish, sun-washed, even apricot frontage of St Florian which is our introduction into an entirely different and other world from that of previous experience in either Italy or Spain, and which is nothing other than the high Baroque of the Holy Roman Empire. This, in fact, is what it is. That it was a living entity comes to mind whenever we read in old books or letters of 'the Emperor', a shadowy potentate but in his own day of equal importance to the King of France or the King of Spain. He passed by St Florian and up the chain of great monasteries along the Danube on his way to be crowned at Frankfurt with the crown of Charlemagne (in fact that of Conrad II), and to be invested with the coronation robes of the Norman Kings of Sicily that have figures of camels and Arabic inscriptions worked into them, with the pearl-sewn gloves, scarlet stockings and slippers of red silk, and to have the orb and sceptre put into his hand; and there is nothing inherently more bizarre about this ceremony than there is about the coronation of our own Queen in Westminster Abbey.[1] There are State rooms at St Florian to accommodate

[1] There were of old three of these great rituals; the third being the coronation of the Kings of France at Reims.

the Holy Roman Emperor and his suite and a Kaisersaal where local digni-
taries came to pay him homage. Such rooms, however seldom they were
occupied, and in their existing condition they can date from no earlier than
the reign of Karl VI, last of the male line of the Habsburgs and father of
Maria Theresa, bring this shadowy figure and mythical heir of the Romans
before us in a way only paralleled in my experience by the set of rooms
furnished for the Bourbon Kings of Naples at the large octagonal eighteenth-
century Palazzo Badiale below the great pilgrimage shrine of Montevergine.
There, a whole dynasty haunts the shuttered rooms. Here, where the Holy
Roman Emperor, the Römische Kaiser and protagonist of the War of the
Spanish succession – for Karl VI tried to win back the Spanish half of the
Habsburg dominion and then would have been Emperor of half of the New
World, as well – here, where his richly convoluted golden bed is shown,
we must recall that the rebuilding of this great monastery was as a votive
offering after the raising of the siege of Vienna by the Turks. Had it gone
otherwise, their turban'd cavalry would have attained the apple-orchards of
St Florian within a few days, and reached Munich before the week was out.

Nothing could be more typically Austrian than the immense, long façade
of St Florian, shining white now the sun is off it, or than the triple-storeyed
main entrance with its balcony upheld by four slaves, or by Atlantes pre-
tending to be slaves, more pairs of statues standing free above that and a
smaller balcony to top the whole composition, which is in fact a *pièce montée*
thought essential to any important building whether palace or monastery all
over the former Habsburg Empire. Caryatid portals – as seen in palaces in
Vienna or in Prague, become in time more than a little monotonous if only
because so few variations are possible on this awkward theme – as do
caryatid stairs once we have seen the stairway of the Upper Belvedere and
that of the Winter Palace of Prince Eugene in Vienna. But within the court
of St Florian there is the white stairway of Jakob Prandtauer to admire, as
Austrian in essential as the white coats of the old Austrian army (worn till
1866), a double stairway climbing on either side of arches, with iron grilles
on every landing and delightful urns and lamps and cupids along the
balustrade. This leads to the State rooms, including a room painted with
hunting scenes, and to the Kaisersaal or Marmorsaal in red and gold with its
pair of giant fireplaces covered with heraldic achievement; and enough will
have been seen already of St Florian to give its own picture of monastic life.
That this has a luxurious external setting of stairs and libraries, of Marmorsaals and tapestried State bedrooms, is not to imply that the Augustinian
canons – (Black Canons in England) – did not lead lives of regulated austerity
according to their rule. That they lived in an expensive setting is indisputable,

but I cannot believe that anybody seeing this beautiful monastery which so much evokes the serenity of the past in this green land of orchards would grudge it to them. But any misgivings of the sort will be lulled by the church at St Florian which is boring and disappointing because it is Italianate, and therefore neither Austrian nor Italian. In compensation are the glorious wrought-iron screens with their garlands and floriations and flowered urns, and the unexpected presence of Altdorfer's altar painting, 'ombragé par un bois de sapins toujours vert' more than ever any picture by the painter (Delacroix) to whom this line of Baudelaire's poetry was addressed.

Leaving Wilhering and its Cistercian abbey in full Rococo aside for the moment, and keeping it till last for that very reason though it is so near to St Florian, there is Kremsmünster not far away, a Benedictine abbey with a church by another of the Carlone family of architects and stuccoists from Genoa, not therefore in the first flight of Italian art pedigree and dully unimaginative in keeping with that, with none of the flying balconies, opera-boxes, or the fire and exuberance of fancy which we will find in Bavaria, and only the strange discovery of no fewer than five colonnaded fish-tanks opening in perspective out of one another, all kept under lock and key, and each of them adorned with fountain-statues of saints, huntsmen, fishermen, and tritons blowing their conch-shells, or grasping their tridents as though to the sounding of a burglar-alarm. The impression given is that of inspecting the biggest trout-hatchery ever seen; and neither that, nor the unlikely trio of statues of Duke Tassilo, the founder of the monastery and his companions over the main entrance, looking like Vikings or Wagnerian heroes, in plate armour with capes of ermine worn over that, and full blooded *landsknecht* beards below the most florid of crowns, nor even the unusually splendid Kaisersaal, detract from this.

Not a great distance away is another ancient Benedictine abbey, that of Seitenstetten, lying in pastoral country, a large congeries of buildings on a plan ascribed to Josef Munggenast, with a superb palace stair and a fine painted ceiling over it by B. Altomonte, one of the better of the Austrian school of vault and ceiling painters *à l'Italienne* – member, too, of a school whose works can never rocket up to astronomical prices in the saleroom for the reason that they are immovable and therefore unsaleable – but, as well, there are at Seitenstetten the Abbot's Room, a sort of Kaisersaal on private lines, and both here and in the Library there are painted ceilings by Paul Troger (1698–1762), the greatest painter of the school, who worked in monasteries up and down the land, in the Library at Zwettl, at Melk, and Altenburg, and whose considerable level of achievement makes ridiculous the painted stairs and ceilings of Verrio or Laguerre. However, the great curiosity of Seitenstetten is its set of paintings of monastic subjects by Magnasco let into the wall of the Abbot's Room, something the amateur of his pictures may have hoped for but feared impossible to find.[1] Nowhere, it is true, could Magnasco have appeared to greater advantage than in this setting that an admirer might have dreamed of for him.

But it is time now to turn to Melk, second, or some would say first, of the three great Austrian monasteries. How magnificent it looks from the window of the railway train! But better still is the view of it from the road below which allows to the building its full height. I would like to quote on this what I have said before that this very quality of size is used in the most effective manner and is not, as can happen, wasted. The virtuosity of the architect has placed the entrance to the church between the two cupola'd towers of the convent, with an open colonnade in front that looks out over the Danube valley. From this colonnaded walk the two lateral wings stretch away in the two directions of the river-bed, and their hundreds of windows in the flashing white of the two façades make a sight that will never be forgotten by anyone interested in this last of European architectures. One of the pillared pair of projecting pavilions holds the Library, the other the Marmorsaal; both of them with ceiling frescoes by the ubiquitous Paul Troger.

The main gate to Melk flanked by heroic statues on gigantic pedestals, and the tympanum of its archway crowned by reclining statues, are much in Vanbrugh's manner and could be mistaken for an illustration of one of the entrances to Blenheim. Beyond lies the main entrance to the five courts of Melk and its huge complex of buildings from Jakob Prandtauer's plans. Of beautiful design from this provincial architect are the twin pavilions housing the Library and the Marmorsaal with their tall windows and *oeils-de-boeuf* above them bound in with flat pilasters. The blue and gold Library is to be especially admired with its statues and terrestrial globes and rows of backs of vellum bindings, one of a dozen or more monastic libraries in Austria and Bavaria forming a subject to themselves and a strong suit in the architectural beauty of the age. The church at Melk, coming to its door from the little court below the pavilions and looking down once more over the river below from that arcaded terrace, and then up again at the cupola'd ball-towers that are so rich in design with their corner obelisks and bulbous domes of Dürnstein-like pattern, reveals itself as by far the finest monastic church

---

[1] It would appear that there is only a single painting by Alessandro Magnasco (1677–1749) still *in situ* in a church. This is in a village called Campomorto, near Pavia, a macabre subject of a church being broken into by thieves who are frightened away by skeletons rising from their graves; but, then, his paintings of monkish scenes were intended for private purchasers more than for the celibates they not so much satirized as romanticized.

we have seen; with its interior of sombre and unusual colouring, red fluted pilasters lightening to pink and to orange-persimmon, fanciful organ-cases, tentative opera-boxes, not sure yet, we could say, of the performances they are to attend, or the music they are to hear, but a high altar designed (though it appears he did not make the statues) by Antonio Beduzzi, an Italian theatrical engineer. Already, there must have seemed to be nothing incongruous in this idea. Yet, for all this, the interior of Melk like nearly every interior in the Hereditary Dominions of Austria is boring and more than a little disappointing, compared at any rate with what we shall see not many miles away. Perhaps it is just their being the Hereditary Dominions with all that implies, that is to blame for this. Melk is marvellous, though, for its exterior, for its couchant arrogance along the hill above the Danube, for its Library, and in its vast complex there must be lesser and delightful details not always shown, like the Abbot's theatre somewhere in the garden which I believe was opened to the public for the first time only last summer.

Göttweig, another enormous Benedictine abbey on the hills a little farther down the Danube, looks superb from afar but is another disappointment and not worth the trouble of going to but for its staircase, one of the most splendid of its ten or twenty monastic rivals in Central Europe, roofed with a truly enormous cloud and figure fresco, by Paul Troger again, depicting the apotheosis of, precisely, the Römischer Kaiser Karl VI. This stair is part of a huge scheme for the rebuilding of Göttweig from the plans of Johann Lukas von Hildebrandt, and as such takes place with his palace stairs at the Upper Belvedere, and elsewhere in Vienna. On the staircase at Göttweig it is difficult to know whether one is in a palace or a monastery.

There are at least no doubts on this score at Dürnstein, our next place of call, and perhaps the most delightful little town in all Austria, where coming straight from Melk there is something immediately familiar in the church tower because of its being by the same architect Josef Munggenast who remodelled the twin towers of Melk and was cousin and pupil to Prandtauer. And the church at Dürnstein was after all an abbey of Augustinian canons although it may not look like that. What a beautiful little terrace leading to the church, with a balcony looking over the river and up to the tower with its strongly marked volutes and the obelisks at its corners! There is a very splendid porch in the court of the abbey; a frontispiece with columns and obelisks and statues of the Risen Christ and the Four Latin Fathers of the Church, designed, it may be, as one writer suggests, in the form of an altar.[1]

---

[1] *Baroque Churches of Central Europe* by John Bourke, Faber, 1958, p. 206. The same author calls the tower at Dürnstein 'the most beautiful, perhaps anywhere', which could be described as a phrase with holes in it like a sieve, through which the sense runs out.

The church interior is more pleasant than dull, and the monastic amenities included even a little theatre where Passion plays were given.

Before we come to the two other places of the first rank of excellence in Austria, we can summarize what else in Austria of more than passing interest was achieved by monastic orders. At Admont, far up the Enns river and some fifty miles south of Linz, there is the Benedictine abbey with a disappointing church but a fine Library hall, another of the series, this time by J. Hayberger, architect of the Library at St Florian. At Klosterneuburg, just outside Vienna, the abbey of Augustinian canons was an Imperial foundation of Karl VI intended by him as an Escorial or a Mafra, where he proposed to take up residence, but his plans fell through. The Archducal or Electoral caps and Imperial crowns on its gables proclaim this, and it can be seen in sufficient detail from the window of a railway train. Of greater interest is Herzogenburg, near St Pölten, another abbey of Augustinians, with more Ducal hats on its cupolas, and in the interior over a balcony a great organ-case which is a marvellous decorative feature, as beautiful a piece of gilded woodwork as anything of the kind in Portugal, the chosen land of pelmets and gold organ-cases. And at Heiligenkreuz, between Vienna and St Pölten the church of the Cistercian abbey should be seen if only for its ceiling painting by Franz Anton Maulbertsch, if not the most successful certainly the most interesting of the Austrian school, a painter who with curious accents of Caspar Friedrich and even of Fuseli carried further the vein of invention that one would have thought the great Giambattista Tiepolo had exhausted.

This leads the road clear to Altenburg and its Benedictine abbey, a good way inland from the right bank of the Danube, and therefore at one time in the Russian Zone. It has not the situation of Melk, or the apricot and cherry orchards of St Florian, which are extraneous, but they do add beauty to those stairs and landings and great range of buildings; yet in many respects Altenburg is the most interesting of the three. The church perhaps is unexceptional, but it has astonishingly fine frescoes by Paul Troger. His paintings in the dome put him indeed after all but the greatest of Italian names. The abbey was the work of Josef Munggenast; however it is the interior of the monastery itself at Altenburg which is so interesting. The *stucchi* in the various rooms are of superb fantasy; and there is the extraordinary Library. It, again, has ceiling paintings by Troger;[1] and here perhaps more than anywhere else is the art of sham marble or *scagliola* to be studied for certainly at Altenburg

---

[1] A painter whose agreeably busy life took him, also, to Zwettl, not far from Altenburg, where in the Library of the Cistercian abbey are five ceiling paintings by him. He worked, let us recall, in the Library and Marmorsaal at Melk, in that pair of twin pavilions, and in the Library and Abbot's Room at Seitenstetten where the monkish scenes by Magnasco are let into the walls.

it attains that height. The Library occupies three domed rooms, and the pilasters are milky or ice-blue with gilt capitals and porphyry-red entablatures; while the *stucchi* are in green and white and gold, these *stucchi* which are of the highest order of invention, being by a sculptor from the little but, as we shall see, aesthetically important Bavarian village of Wessobrunn. But the most curious feature of this library is the presence, atop four of the milk-blue columns, of stucco figures, of respectively, a pair of leaping horses and a pair of couchant sphinxes, the iconographical import of which even Dr Niklaus Pevsner has been unable to track down and explain. And the crypt under this library has been fresco'd with a Dance of Death, but in fact it is a kind of *singerie* or *chinoiserie* of skeletons mixed up with fountains and water-jets, *putti* with spouting dolphins in their arms, and all manner of grotto decorations. The painter, who is unknown, may have been a monk of morbid but lively fantasy.

The prevailing and comparative interior dullness of most of the High Baroque in Austria – libraries and Kaisersaals and the double open stair of St Florian excepted – now finds contradiction in the church at Wilhering, a Cistercian abbey – and how different from Fountains or Rievaulx! – a few miles from Linz. This is a marvellous example of the elegance and high spirits of the Rococo just at its emergence from the chrysalis of Baroque; the secret being that it is the work almost in entirety of painters and craftsmen who were not, strictly speaking, Austrian. The fresco'd ceilings covering a huge area are by Bartolomeo Altomonte, of origin in the Trentino; while two of the three principal workers in stucco, Johann Georg Üblhör and Johann Michael Feichtmayr, came from the aforementioned Bavarian village of Wessobrunn. The shimmering, flickering colours of this interior, and the incredible grace of its picture frames and door frames, as I have written elsewhere, are no subject for mere prose. The point is that Wilhering is not Austrian: were it so it would tend towards being dull and heavy. But it is an extraordinary and unlikely blend of the sub-Italian and what can only be termed village-Bavarian arising from conditions and circumstances which will be discussed within the next few moments. The placing of the choir organ at Wilhering, and the siting or fixing of the pulpit, are of a needle-point precision and of an elegance one would have thought to be beyond attainment except in dressmaking, until one remembers pelmets and organ-cases as graceful as these in the rustic north of Portugal. But the structure of Wilhering is more informed architecturally; the frescoes are much better – fresco painting hardly existed in this latter country; all in all Wilhering ranks with Ottobeuren and Zwiefalten, and not far below Wies and other churches by Dominikus Zimmermann – who came from Wessobrunn.

Austrian Baroque

Inner court with exterior staircase at St Florian (1706–14)

Wrought-iron screen with garlands and flowered urns in Carlone's Italianate church at St Florian

Audience-hall in royal apartments at St Florian with portrait of Emperor Joseph II. Decorative sculpture (1728) by Leonhard Sattler

Grand portal at St Florian with sculpture by Leonhard Sattler, of a family of sculptors who embellished the monastery

Charlemagne, Emperor Henry II and Duke Tassilo III with a model of the monastery church on main portal (1667) at Kremsmünster

Colonnaded fishponds at Kremsmünster, joint work of Carlone and Prandtauer. Statue of Samson by Andreas Götzinger of Salzburg

View of Melk, planned by Jakob Prandtauer in 1702, from across the Danube

Left: Crypt with *Totentanz* motifs frescoed on walls and vaults at Altenburg

Right: Virgin and Child with saints from centre of stucco Tree of Life (1609–13) by Bartholomäus Steinle above high altar at Stams

Below left: Refectory of the Monks. Painting by Alessandro Magnasco in abbot's room at Seitenstetten

Below: Cistercian monastery of Stams in Tyrol started 1607–9 and completed 1729–32 by Georg Anton Gumpp of Innsbruck

Interior of church of Wilhering designed by Johann Haslinger and the Imperial theatre engineer Andreas Altomonte. Embellished with work of other Altomontes and stuccoists from Wessobrunn

For a final contrast, and in order to get the High Baroque of Austria differentiated once and for all from the Rococo we are coming to, it is only necessary to have seen Stams, another Cistercian abbey about twenty miles to the west of Innsbruck. For Stams belongs to another sub-division. It is in the scarcely existing Baroque of the Tyrol. The whiteness of Stams is dazzling; and the view of its buildings, as one approaches near to it, raises hopes that are not fulfilled. It is heavy in detail; not least the Tree of Life at the high altar, with its red stucco curtain and the tree itself which like any plum or apple tree of autumn is heavy and bowed down with fruit, in over-ripe form of a plenitude of saints and martyrs. Thinking it all over, one is left with the impression that the memorable things in monastic Austria are the open double stair at St Florian, coming to it from the orchard lands outside; Seitenstetten for its Abbot's Room with the Magnasco paintings in their unbelievably suitable setting; the Library at Altenburg for its *scagliola* and its *stucchi*; the marvellous interior at Wilhering; the good fresco painting in so many places; and the first and last views of Melk on its cliffs above the Danube. Even so this is but the beginning. Out of the occasional, but almost occupational stiffness of the Baroque, the marvels of the Rococo are still to come.

That there have been moments in the history of the arts when the hand of man could do no wrong is indisputable, as witness the conditions obtaining in certain districts of England during late mediaeval times as touched upon in the opening paragraphs of this present chapter. That was but a little instance and there have been many that were much greater. They can be manifest, too, in many different directions, when they may become enlarged into a community and not an individual interest. Such a contemporary example is the dance and the music in the isle of Bali; or, for diminuendo, a district anywhere that is particularly rich in folk-song or in peasant costume. 'Arcadian' ages of the farmer and well-to-do peasant have certainly obtained, to name but a few of them, in bucolic parts of the Netherlands, in Zeeland and Friesland; in remote valleys in Switzerland and Austria; in 'peasant' Moravia and Slovakia; in 'costume' villages like Mezökövesd in Hungary and Rucar in Wallachia; or where, too, I have seen them with my own eyes, in Guatemala where nearly every village has its own beautiful and distinctive dress. Such are golden ages *in petto*, particularly when we add to them a village such as Detva, whence both Brahms and Dvořák derived some of their tunes, and where the music tinged with its own Slovak characteristics was itself in reflection of the golden age of music in Vienna. The point of the argument being that Wessobrunn and its school of craftsmen and stucco-workers was just such another instance which had altered its direction.

This village, or, rather, district, south of the Ammer and the Starnberg lakes, once swarmed with monks. Bavaria within its older, much smaller boundaries had fifty-nine abbeys, fifty-five monasteries, and thirty-four convents of nuns; and this of course does not include Franconia, Suabia, or Württemberg. Wessobrunn lay in fact in the Pfaffenwinkel, as the district was called, because of this monastic swarming. That there was nothing even particularly extraordinary in this small district being famous for its stuccoists must, also, be stressed. There was the same specialization in parts of Italy; from the violins and violas of Cremona, the handiwork of Stradivarius, of Guarneri, or Niccolò Amati, down to the plaster figures sold in the streets of Victorian London by itinerant Savoyards, or, till recent times, the organ-grinders who came mostly from Monte Cassino. But the Italian stuccoists were from the shores of the Italian Lakes. *Maestri comacini*, from Como, had been famous for centuries; as had been, too, the craftsmen from the Swiss, Italian-speaking canton of the Tessin, or Ticino.[1] It was the brothers Carbonetti and Francesco Quadri who made the stucco ceilings at Clausholm in Jutland, the veritable palace of the Sleeping Princess; and doubtless it was Italian travelling craftsmen of like provenance who made the ceilings in the old houses ascribed to Daniel Marot at The Hague, in the Russian monasteries round Moscow and, also, before the generation of Irish craftsmen appeared, in the Dublin houses. Occasionally, too, such a school would produce someone more exceptional still, as, for instance, Franz Anton Bustelli, the modeller of the Nymphenburg porcelain figures, who came from near Lugano, in the Ticino.

The art could even be considered as a carrying into *excelsis* of the wood-carving with which the peasants occupied the long winter evenings. Typical families of Wessobrunner stuccoists were the Schmuzers, Johann, Josef, and Franz Xaver; and the Feichtmayrs, Franz Xaver, Johann Michael, and Johann Caspar. They set forth, taking their itinerant workshops with them, but not to far countries like the craftsmen from the Tessin. Their work, in which it is difficult to distinguish one hand from another, was always and particularly in the monasteries laid down minutely for them; where we are concerned,

---

[1] 'Il est bien connu qu'aucune autre contrée de l'Europe a vue autant de stuccateurs fameux que le canton de Tessin. Au XVII et XVIII siécles ils sont partis des petits villages aux bords des lacs et dans les montagnes vertes, et presque partout en Europe on trouve les traces de leur art merveilleux et de leur technique supérieure.' B. J. Grandjean, in an article in *Zeitscrift fur Schweizerische Archaeologie und Kunstgeschichte*, Band 15, 1954, Heft 2, Verlag Birkhauser, Basle, pp. 99–102. 'It is well known that no other country in Europe has so many famous workers in stucco as the canton of Tessin. In the seventeenth and eighteenth centuries they left their little lakeside villages and their green mountains, and almost everywhere in Europe are found the traces of their marvellous art and their superlative technique.'

by some monk-theologian, based more likely than not on Cesare Ripa's *Iconologia*. From such uninspiring sources sprang these figures and patterns of grace. But the local genii, of just this village derivation, were the brothers Dominikus and Johann Baptist Zimmermann; the older brother, architect of Wies and Steinhausen, and the younger brother, first, stuccoist, and then fresco painter. This pairing of names and professions is even the half of the secret of a golden age. For in the case of the younger brother alone, his was the hand that carried out details of the silver stucco work at the Amalienburg, the hunting pavilion outside Munich, and the *stucchi* and the frescoes, also, at the pilgrimage church at Wies, two buildings generally accepted now as the most beautiful of their kind in the world. Like the virtuoso composers of the past, that is to say, like Handel, Bach, and Domenico Scarlatti, like, again, Mozart or Beethoven, Liszt or Chopin, and also Brahms, they both wrote for their instrument and played it.

It may be that in this respect Bernini was first of his kind. How are we to describe him? Was he sculptor or architect, first and foremost? He carved the Apollo and Daphne of the Villa Borghese, the bust of Louis XIV at Versailles, the Ecstasy of St Theresa at Santa Maria della Vittoria, all masterpieces in their kind; it was he who designed the Roman fountains, the fountain in the middle of the Piazza Navona with its figures of the four river gods, of Danube, Ganges, Nile, and Rio de la Plata, and *La Barcaccia* 'in shape of a waterlogged boat leaking in many places' in the Piazza di Spagna, but, then, as well, he designed the bronze tomb of the Barberini Pope Urban VIII in St Peter's; and in addition to this he was architect of the Scala Regia in the Vatican, of the Doric colonnades in front of St Peters, and are we to call him architect or sculptor of the Baldacchino and the Cathedra Petri in the cathedral? – or of the little oval church of Sant' Andrea al Quirinale, built and decorated by him and his pupils, and which was his own favourite among all his works?

It was the Roman influence coming on top of a predisposition and an inherited technique that made possible what we are to witness coming out of dark pinewoods into sub-Alpine meadows, beside the lakes, in the lands of gentian and autumn crocus. It was the effect upon peasant, or, as it were, pilgrim minds of seeing the work of Bernini of Borromini[1] – but to lesser degree, for it went from him with his neophytes, Juvara, Guarini, and Vittone, to other sub-Alpine valleys at Turin – and of 'Fratel' Pozzo, the Jesuit, fresco-painter and perspectivist, himself an emigrant to Rome from his native Trentino, and a figure of comparable importance to his own and the succeeding generation as, say, the inventors of cubism or of abstract painting.

[1] Borromini came from the Ticino and was, therefore, Italian-Swiss.

'Fratel' Pozzo's painted ceiling at Sant' Ignazio, the masterpiece of illusionism and of his doctrine of *sotto in sù*, as, also, his altar of St Ignatius in the Gesù with columns of lapis lazuli and silver statue of the saint, were magnets attracting pilgrims of the kind to Rome. No less so, Borromini's spiral belfry to Sant' Ivo in form of a bee, the emblem of the Barberini pope, or his little San Carlo alle Quatro Fontane, a *capolavoro* of the undulating line; or Baciccia's ceiling at the Gesù, outdoing 'Fratel' Pozzo, but, at least, Baciccia was no architect or engineer; or such another composite genius as Pietro da Cortona who fresco'd ceilings in the Ludovisi and Barberini palaces that are masterpieces of the art, and as well, designed Santa Maria della Pace and Santa Maria in Via Lata, two of the most distinguished of the Roman Baroque churches.

Such were the influences that flowed from Rome, making of the Asam brothers, or of the brothers Zimmermann, joint or combined talents on the lines of those just mentioned, and lifting bands or families of carvers or stucco workers into a virtuosity beyond their ordinary merit, with an occasional figure standing apart and outside of this multiple activity, as with J. M. Fischer, perhaps greatest of these Rococo architects, but who was architect, alone, and nothing else. In this, compared with the two pairs of brothers, and not a few fathers and sons, uncles and nephews, he was exceptional.

Of the brothers Asam, Cosmas Damian and Egid Quirin, born in 1686 and 1692 at Rott-am-Inn, it could be said that both were architects and worked in stucco, while Cosmas Damian was fresco-painter, and Egid Quirin was sculptor and designed the altars which with the Asam brothers are always *coups de théâtre*, intended to catch and hold the imagination. They were in fact less architects than decorators and makers of the *mise en scène*, in which capacity, separately and together, they found much employment. It is fortunate for the purposes of this book that they worked so much in monasteries; and it should be noted at this point that the extreme pietistic *naïveté* of the Asams, peasant-like in its fervency, is more easily understood when we know that another brother was a Jesuit, yet another a Benedictine monk, and that two of Cosmas Damian's daughters were Ursuline nuns in the convent at Straubing where the chapel was the last and most extreme work of the family.

After studying under their father, who was a fresco-painter, they went to Rome in 1712, where one of their masters was the painter and caricaturist Pierleone Ghezzi, and whence they returned home, it can be seen, imbued and intoxicated by Bernini. One of the only churches entirely from their hands is that at Rohr, near Kelheim, in a former college of Augustinian canons, with an interior that I find monotonous and uninteresting because of its lack of colour which I have suggested was due in this instance to the absence of Cosmas Damian who was not here to paint the frescoes. The high altar of the Assumption, which is wholly by Egid Quirin, gives the illusion of an extraordinary act of levitation on the part of the Virgin and two attendant angels who float in air with a green curtain behind them. The group, which must be heavy enough even in stucco, has but an iron bar hidden in a cloud to hold it up, were adverse criticism to be allowed, in best pantomime transformation-scene tradition. The whole grouping is a little jejune, as of figures from a *presepio* enlarged to life size and revealing the peasant hand in Egid Quirin Asam.

The interior at Osterhofen is much more worth seeing. Here, in the Danube valley between Regensburg and Passau, in a chapel of (formerly) Benedictine nuns which is the first and not particularly characteristic work of Johann Michael Fischer, the great builder of monastic churches, the brothers Asam had the decoration entirely in their hands. In the result it is one of the most wonderfully decorated interiors in the world – unless, that is to say, one belongs to that equally convincing school of thought, adumbrated by Adolf Loos and which is the creed of Mies van der Rohe and his followers, that architecture is engineering and that no ornament should be allowed at all. In defiance of which there are six side altars at Osterhofen entered by archways with balconies above them, each altar with the skeleton of a saint below it reclining in a glass case in Spanish court clothes, sewn by the nuns with pearls and semi-precious stones, a sword at his side – their embroidered square-toed shoes a study in themselves – and at the opening of the chancel another pair of superb altars with painted statues, St Anne in her green robe among them, a figure of peasant, Oberammergau intensity leading the eyes to Egid Quirin's high altar in the choir. This has a frontispiece of two pairs of twisting or Salomonic columns, the plinths of which support sculptures that nearly touch the gilded nimbus above them in the coved ceiling. Then our eyes come down to the lifesize figures at the back against the windows of the choir. They are the founders of the convent and their wives, dressed in court costumes and shown as though attending divine service. Duke Odo is in black armour, and his wife carries her prayer book and rosary. Opposite them, Duke Heligo holds the flag of Bavaria in blue and white chequers in one hand, and the plans of the church in the other, while his wife catches the gaze of Duke Odo from across the altar, and smiles back at him from behind her fan. As a whole, Osterhofen is a peasant rendering of Bernini, but by a peasant who had lived and worked in Rome, and a feast of ornament with for dessert the painted ceiling by Cosmas Damian, of perspective and colour that leaves the Bavarian peasant far behind.

Weltenburg, the other masterwork of the Asams and a Benedictine abbey again in the Danube valley, is reached by a narrow road that winds through forests and along the cliff face of the river. Here, the brothers are still more in debt to Bernini, and particularly to his little oval church of Sant' Andrea al Quirinale, but then they worked here directly upon their return to Rome. Cosmas Damian was architect and painted, as well, the ceiling, a pillar'd and cloud-filled hall, peopled with angelic shapes, below and out of which his own stucco figure in fine clothes and periwig looks down into the church.

We go into the church through a vestibule of utmost fantasy in stucco ornament, its overdoors in several shades of gold and silver, in jade green, and in vivid tones of white and coral. The oval body of the church, opening beyond this, glitters across at us like a lit cave or grotto, and projects a gilded crown that fills the circle of the dome as with a cornice. There are magnificent side altars, difficult to take in because of the drama and excitement, as we move in the direction of that grotto towards the scarlet and gold curtain over a projecting balcony that is surely a theatre-box, with another theatre-box and curtain facing it across the chancel, and overdoors below both that are like side entrances onto the stage with a motif above them that is a woman's bust in silver, with a head-dress of silver plumes. The proscenium, itself, is framed in by four very tall Salomonic columns of elegant twisting shape, with gilded capitals, linked together by chains of gilded flowers. They carry a cornice which embodies, and to purpose, a trophy of the coat-of-arms of the Bavarian Order of St George, in chequers again, of blue and white, crowned with the ducal hat, this touching in its turn upon a burst of clouds, and on a host of angelic figures upon a nimbus that vanishes in a blinding glitter of golden rays into the heavens.

Below this, and filling the centre of the stage, the life size figure of St George, a knight in golden armour on a silver stallion, rides out into the light. His high-plumed helmet is like that of the cavaliers in the court masquerades of *Le Roi Soleil*, and with a courtly gesture of his right-hand he despatches the dragon. His lance, like the tournament lances, is given the same Salomonic twist as the twisted pillars upholding the proscenium. The maiden, but it is difficult not to think of her as Andromeda, is dressed like a peasant girl, and holds up her hand before her eyes at this blinding vision. At the side of the pillars, in front of the stage, two saints are commenting upon the stage action. St Martin in golden robes takes off his biretta in homage; and opposite him St Maurus points to the audience, while the golden goose at his feet takes the action from the stage into the church by hissing at the dragon. The ineffable grace of St George's horsemanship, his attitude of arrival to the rescue, are tendered in a wonderful blaze of inspiration, yet with all the intensity of a ghostly vision.

The next Asam church to be described is in a still remoter site some miles from Regensburg. It is the deserted Benedictine abbey of Frauenzell[1] reached by a long narrow road through patches of deep forest. It has a fine Italianate façade of white stone, approached by flights of steps. The interior is of a dazzling whiteness, and is a wide ellipse of great size, the whole church being full of light, which is intensified by accents of a bright green jade in its decoration. Its ceiling is a huge painting by Cosmas Damian of the Assumption which covers the chancel as well. The high altar is simple, but has balconies for the choir to either side, complete opera-boxes that have elaborate *avant scènes* rising above them on the walls of the chancel. And these opera-boxes, which have to be climbed into by separate staircases in the depth of each wall, have their own interior walls painted with a freehand decoration like the most beautiful of Rococo wallpapers. From this vantage, high up, there is a view into all the incident of the fresco'd ceiling, into the body of the church, and over to the fantastic pulpit.

Lastly, there is the little chapel of the Ursuline nuns at Straubing on the right bank of the Danube. Difficult to describe in plan, it takes the form of a Greek cross with arms of equal length out of the body of an ellipse. The four sides of its two lateral arms have grilled and glazed boxes for the nuns high on the walls, over which immense golden crowns are hung. There are Salomonic twisted columns again at the high altar, and a fresco'd ceiling. The pilasters at each end of the central dome have capitals of vivid scarlet, and there are scarlet curtains, inlays of mirror, and accents of pinks, blues, and bright greens. This little chapel is the last work of the Asams; Cosmas Damian died before it was finished. Two of his daughters, as we have seen, were nuns here and must often have looked down into the chapel from one or other of the opera-boxes. In the full tradition of Bernini it was completed in 1738 nearly sixty years after Bernini's death. It was in fact old-fashioned in its time, but so was Bach considered old-fashioned in his day. Or it could be said that with the Asam brothers the last echoes of *Le Roi Soleil* and of Papal Italy have gone, and we are in the full tide of Rococo by now.

The great practitioner of the art where churches were concerned was Johann Michael Fischer who is extolled on his tomb as the architect, in part

[1] Frauenzell has the distinction of having escaped attention and not being mentioned at all in the two books in English on the German Rococo that followed my pioneer effort of 1927 at long interval – to 1958 in the one instance, and 1959 in the other. But I must not complain, I have escaped their notice, too, and am not mentioned by either of them. *Baroque Churches of Central Europe*, by John Bourke, and the 'definitive' *From Baroque to Rococo*, by Nicolas Powell, both books published by Faber & Faber Ltd.

or whole, of thirty-two churches and twenty-two monasteries, a grand total which would have been impossible of achievement had he been, as well, stuccoist or fresco-painter, or anything but architect pure and simple. Fischer is indeed the architect of Bavarian monastic churches *par excellence*, and his confident faith and gaiety on a chord quite different from that of the Asam brothers, left something in the world the like of which will never be seen again. How different, it may be said in passing, are his cheerful interiors from those of what one school of thought would call a later and greater phase in church building, that of mid-Victorian England, which we are told is the direct continuation of the Middle Ages, as though the work was taken up again just where it was left off! The coloured brick interior of St James the Less, in Pimlico, by Street, 'of red brick with much black brick enrichment', or All Saints, Margaret Street, Marylebone, by Butterworth, are a pair of London instances. We are but passing. Let us continue, and pass them by.

It is to be noted that the dates of Johann Michael Fischer (1692–1766) are those almost exactly of G. B. Tiepolo (1696–1770), and that he was of the generation of Handel, Domenico Scarlatti, Johann Sebastian Bach, all three of whom were born in 1685. Even in the minor arts, the same fulness of creation in artists born just at that time appears in the silversmith Paul de Lamerie who was born in 1688. If in his lifetime Johann Michael Fischer was thwarted or misunderstood, there are no signs of it in his buildings, an art in which, if elation can be expressed and is transferable, there can be, as surely, sadness and depression. The most easily accessible of his churches, over which in contradiction to this there was an acrimonious lawsuit, is at Berg-am-Lain, only a mile or two outside Munich. Its builder was Clemens Augustus, Prince Bishop and Elector of Cologne, son of Max Emanuel, Elector of Bavaria, and nephew of the Heiliger Römischer Kaiser Karl VI. It was Clemens Augustus who built the staircase of staircases at Brühl, near Cologne; a prelate whose painted chocolate-cups of Meissen porcelain, sporting-guns inlaid with gold and silver, and appurtenances of life in general were incomparable for expense and elegance. In this respect Berg-am-Lain is even a little disappointing, and in view of its foundation by Clemens Augustus as a collegiate church for a brotherhood, and not as a monastery or nunnery, it is even doubtful whether it should be included here. Its twin-towered exterior is decidedly uninteresting. But the interior, its main feature a rotunda within an octagon, reveals a master hand. The *stucchi* and the frescoes, both by Johann Baptist Zimmermann, and the altars especially, are altogether exceptional; and the person is to be envied, coming perhaps from the Asam brothers' church of St John Nepomuk in Munich, who now has this art in all its fantasy revealed to him for the first time. It is predominantly

Rococo in Bavaria

Egid Quirin Asam's Assumption altar at Rohr (1717–19)

St George and the Dragon lit from the back by hidden windows in the Asam church of Weltenburg

Church of Ottobeuren (completed 1766) designed by J. M. Fischer and stuccoed by
J. M. Feichtmayr

Choir-stalls (1744) at Zwiefalten by
Josef Christian and Martin
Hermann. The gilded reliefs recount
the Life of the Virgin

Organ-case and choir-stalls at
Ottobeuren designed by Feichtmayr and carried out by Christian
and Hermann (1757–64)

Right: Balconies over side altars in
nave at Zwiefalten, designed by
J. M. Fischer

Pulpit at Zwiefalten by J. M. Feichtmayr with figures of Faith, Hope and Charity amid grotto and stalactite motifs

Central altar like a fairy coach at Vierzehnheiligen, designed by Johann Jakob Küchel.
Stuccowork by Feichtmayr and Üblhör

Library hall at Wiblingen completed about 1750

Library at Metten on the Danube
supported by caryatid groups

Death, one of the allegories of the
Four Last Things by Josef Thaddäus
Stammel in the library at Admont
in Styria

Library at Waldsassen decorated in 1724 with caricatures of local characters by the Salzburg wood-carver Franz Stilp

Dominikus Zimmermann's white and gold library at Schussenried with pink *scagliola* columns

Left: Dominikus Zimmermann's exterior of giant proportion at Steinhausen, built between 1727 and 1733

Right: Interior of colonnade at Steinhausen in pale colours and white with no gold. Stuccowork by J. B. Zimmermann

Below: Detail of a capital at Steinhausen, with a magpie on the decoration of the window

Left: Ship-pulpit at Irsee (1725) with cupids manning the rigging and furling the sail

Right: Ship-pulpit at Traunkirchen in Upper Austria (1753) representing the Miraculous Draught of Fishes

Left: Font-cover at Ufford (Suffolk), richly crocketed and beset with finials in six or seven tiers. English craftsmanship comparable to the fantasies of Bavarian rococo

Right: Perspective wrought-iron gates and choir of Caspar Moosbrugger's abbey church at Einsiedeln in Switzerland

Balthasar Neumann's Grand Stair
(*c.* 1720) at Kloster Ebrach

Kaiserstiege (1738) at Göttweig,
part of Johann Lukas von
Hildebrandt's unfinished scheme
for reconstructing the abbey

a white and gold church, with matching pilasters of *scagliola*. The altars at Berg-am-Lain are by J. B. Straub, a woodcarver not a stuccoist, who surpassed himself in fantasy in the side altars at Ettal, another church, and is to be seen here in more restrained mood. But the exuberance in minor detail by other hands is evident in the angel above the pulpit who, no less than as noticed at Osterhofen and at Weltenburg, makes play of the flag of Bavaria and waves its blue and white chequers in his hands.

Those persons allergic to this style of architecture and who cannot see that this and not mid-Victorian England has a direct inheritance from the Middle Ages, will by now have moved away leaving the way clear for us to go to Diessen, a little above the Ammersee, which has to be crossed by steamer if we come there from Munich. And before embarking it is only a short detour to see Andechs, a Benedictine priory with frescoes and *stucchi* of an astonishing elegance, that transform but do not conceal the mediaeval shell of the building, by Johann Baptist Zimmermann. At Andechs, beside his frescoed ceilings, he is to be admired in flower-like golden urns on false balconies, and *trompe l'oeil* windows with red draperies spread on their ledges, and with the bust of a female saint praying as at a *prie dieu*, with a sham window behind her crested with a coat-of-arms. Below this, upon the balustrade, a stucco saint stands rapt in prayer, looking down into the church, with a cupid holding a huge crucifix before his eyes. This corner of Andechs is like the side wing of a sacred theatre built or realized, and given substance.

Diessen, when we get there, is the most beautiful Rococo interior we have seen so far excepting Wilhering. It is in white, white and gold, with details of fantastic invention and lightness all around us. Its interior, unlike Osterhofen, has no galleries, so that it is more open and full of light and gives space to the huge ceiling painting by J. G. Bergmüller, another of this forgotten school of frescoists who make ridiculous the pretensions of a Verrio or a Laguerre. The *stucchi* are by Feichtmayr and Üblhör of the school of Wessobrunn, but far advanced in sophistication from the bumpkin background. It may be at Diessen that the degree of inventiveness lavished upon the Rococo altars dawns upon our minds, and with it the realization that the church is as much a theatre to instruct and interest the spectator as a place of prayer. The altars, again with 'Fratel' Pozzo and his altar of St Ignatius in the Gesù at Rome as model, are conceived of almost as 'drops' or side wings. The painting at the high altar at Diessen is even on a sliding panel so that it can be changed, when necessary. No doubt the Augustinian canons of Diessen knew and had seen the *Theatrum Sacrum* of the Jesuits, while the degree to which they were in touch with the civilized world is shown by their commissioning an altar-painting from Giambattista Tiepolo.

The astonishing whiteness of Diessen, as of a white peacock, or a milk-white steer, the white bull of Europa, remains in memory, and that it should boast this painting by the last 'lion' of Venice.

If Diessen shows this great architect at work with the consummate craftsmen who were to hand in this lesser golden age, then still more is this the case at Ottobeuren, a venerable Benedictine abbey, near Memmingen, which was already only short of a thousand years old when rebuilding was begun. How pleasant to stay in one of the inns further down the village, and have in retrospect and in further anticipation the Rococo wonders of Ottobeuren! The dullness of the exterior with its twin towers is even a heightening of the sensation. The façade as a part or instrument of their art seems never to have occurred to these architects, where in Southern Italy or Spain the façade is not only everything but, often, all or nothing. Nor did they concern themselves with towers or belfries, though Wren and his successors made of these a feature of conspicuous and endless variation in the London City churches. Only at Melk and Dürnstein, and at Vierzehnheiligen, are the bell-towers of real importance in the general scheme. But the moment has come to climb the steps and walk inside.

One envies those persons who during the long years when Ottobeuren was empty of monks found themselves alone in the church but for the local country folk, and could have this huge interior and its fantastic decoration to themselves, unappreciated by others. This would have been at any time last century. But now it swarms, and bus-load after bus-load pours into it. White and gold, various shades of pink and rose, and a little blue are its colours, as we come in. And the huge scale of it only appears a long way up the church when one has reached the crossing, and the arms open before us with their fantastic altars. The fresco'd ceilings all over the church by J. J. Zeiller, a painter seen more to his own advantage at Ettal, do not assert themselves and are but uninhabited and airy nothingness, if full of figures. The pulpit and the font, huge confections of statuary with golden rays and clouds and *amorini*, as mysterious in substance or material as window decorations of a shop like Hermès in the rue St Honoré, are by J. M. Feichtmayr from bucolic Wessobrunn. The pulpit rising from a cloud-base that trails its scudding *cirrhi* upon the wall low enough for our hands to touch, like a box in a theatre or upon a state barge with *amorini* at the corners, has the tasselled canopy of a coronation coach, and towers above that up the wall with statues of saints, and sunrays and more cupids, until it fades in more clouds against the sunrise or sunset tinting of the painted *scagliola* column against which it stands. And now it may have begun to pall a little, and we look from and beyond the font up to the scrolls and volutes of the transept wall where a *trompe l'oeil* window has been contrived with a carpet thrown over its windowledge and perspective arches in trick stucco receding, in illusion, far into the distance. The choir-stalls and organ-cases by J. J. Christian are magnificent indeed, solid in timber with gold ornament. But the conventual buildings at Ottobeuren rouse expectation and let it, not too gently down. The library hall is not to be compared with any of a half-dozen, at least, among these monasteries; the Kaisersaal and its sixteen bronzed, not gilt, wooden statues of Habsburg Emperors does not compare to the Marmorsaals in other monasteries; while the theatre, the prospect of which is quite as fascinating and intriguing as that there should be stages for *Noh* plays in the Zen monasteries of Kyoto, is not interesting though it has the original scenery. Having visited the monastery, one must go once or twice again, or more often, into the church which on closer acquaintance assumes once more and immediately its extraordinary character to the degree that did we not know this was not so, we might think this monastery church must be alone of its sort with nothing else like it in the world.

That there is another church on a par with Ottobeuren, if even more fantastically extraordinary in its detail, can only be known to us if we have seen Zwiefalten, which is about an hour away from Ulm in a deep, wooded valley. This other Benedictine abbey has, too, an uninviting exterior despite the huge coupled columns at its door. Within, it is with Wies, the most beautiful, and decidedly the most fanciful Rococo interior in the world. How much of this effect is due to Johann Michael Fischer, how much to the craftsmen working with him, we cannot tell; but the play at least owes much to its actors. I have been to Wies on a hot autumn afternoon when even the coloured postcards seemed to dance and quiver upon their stalls outside the church; and so it is with photographs of the interior of Zwiefalten. There are four bays to each side of the nave between pairs of *scagliola* columns that support a bow-fronted gallery resembling that at Osterhofen, so that on coming in there is the run of the five bays to either side under rather a low painted ceiling. The interior is long and narrow without arms or transepts, and only a slight widening of the vessel of the church where there should be the crossing, at which point there is a saucer-dome fresco'd like the other compartments of the ceiling by a painter, J. Spiegler, who paints here like one possessed. His frescoes are of rushing, whirling, Pentecostal effect, and like a whole cycle of aerial, but near-to-earth dramas taking place upon that tunnel-vault held up by the five bays and their paired columns. For his ceilings at Zwiefalten, alone, Spiegler should not be forgotten as a painter. Nowhere else are there frescoes in quite his vein of raptness and of whirling frenzy. At the altars, at the pulpits, at the mere stucco scrolls and ornaments, it is as though artists of the morbid sensitivity of a Beardsley, or an Utamaro, had been granted long life and given facility to work just as they wished. The truth, which is the very reverse of this, being that the artists and crafts-men had little liberty of action but had according to their contract to carry out every detail as it was laid down for them to do. All the more astonishing therefore the result which seems to have no restraint upon its fantasy. The stuccowork, as at Ottobeuren, is by Feichtmayr of Wessobrunn; and the side altars that are parades of allegorical fantasy in themselves come to a climax in the astonishing pulpit which is as a raised tribune upon a state barge, tasselled and canopied, with gilded stalactites dripping from its deck rail. Its transformation into a state barge like a grotto, wanting only Neptune and his tritons, was the work, too, of Feichtmayr, from sketches, it has been suggested, by the painter of the ceiling frescoes. The *pièce montée* of the Vision of Ezekiel, opposite, across the chancel, is no less curious with its sunbursts, touches of lacquer, and even coral motifs.

There is certainly nothing to approach the interior of Zwiefalten in fantasy unless it be the truly extraordinary altar in the middle of the nave at Vierzehnheiligen, on the site of the vision of the fourteen 'helpers in need'. In this pilgrimage church, a work of supererogation of the Cistercian monks, we are leaving aside J. M. Fischer for the moment, for its architect was J. B. Neumann of Würzburg fame. This fantastic object rises from its balustraded well on the floor of the church; and if asked in fanciful mood to offer some explanation for this apparition, one could only suggest that like the Eleanor Crosses put up by a sorrowing king wherever the body of his wife had lain for the night, this festal coach on the way to some heavenly nuptial, or not less than fairy ceremonial in the land of Elf hame, has paused here to bait the horses and cannot get on. The miracle is that like the catafalque of some dragonfly princess it is still there in the morning, at once a catafalque and a chrysalis. This masterwork of delicate fantasy, for his name must be given, is by Jakob Michael Küchel with *stucchi* once more by Feichtmayr and Üblhör; and scarcely less marvellous is the pulpit opposite with seven bundles or clusters of sunrays shooting out from its canopy in symbol of the seven gifts of the Holy Ghost. But we must get back to Zwiefalten, and be there in time to see by the failing light the choir-stalls and the ceremonial doorway which is part of them, every bit as marvellous as those at Otto-beuren, and by the same craftsman, J. J. Christian. We have Zwiefalten almost to ourselves; but few persons come here. Of the conventual buildings we see nothing for it has been a lunatic asylum for a hundred and fifty years;[1] and on the first occasion I came here (in 1926) through the windows

---

[1] There is a monastic theatre here, as at Ottobeuren, but it is not shown.

86

one could hear their voices. The monastery has been too long haunted and cannot come back to life, but the church is a thing quite marvellous of its sort and kind.

Only one more of Johann Michael Fischer's churches need be described here. It is at Rott-am-Inn, a small country town, a Benedictine abbey standing at the end of a long and pleasant walk uphill from the railway station. Its octagonal plan puts more emphasis upon the architecture than the decoration which is not so overwhelming in fantasy as at Zwiefalten and Ottobeuren. Here Fischer is in ascendance over his coadjutors. Their fantasy is more restrained, if no less delicate and fanciful of execution. The frescoes in the dome of the church depicting the Benedictine Order in glory are by Matthias Günther, of rare competence if by a hand difficult to distinguish from that of other fresco-painters of the school, while the sculptured figures at the high altar, including the famous sainted Empress Kunigunde, are by Ignaz Günther, though the two Günthers were not related. But Ignaz Günther, the pupil of Johann Baptist Straub, the pulpit and altar specialist of Diessen and Berg-am-Lain, of Schäftlarn and Ettal, was the great sculptor of his age and his statues at Rott-am-Inn alone give eminence to this little country town. Had one not seen Ottobeuren and Zwiefalten, the church at Rott-am-Inn would in itself establish the greatness of the architect who built it, and whom it would be a delight to pursue to the fifteen to twenty other monastery churches for which he was responsible, his other secular churches apart. It is only possible to name Altomünster, his latest work, upon a small scale but since it was for the Brigittines a chapel of double purpose, since neither monks nor nuns must catch sight of each other; to which end Fischer contrived a nave in the form of an octagon, with altars by the aforesaid J. B. Straub, and grilled choir-boxes for mutual incognito. And lastly, Fürstenzell of the Cistercians, an aisleless church with high altar in fantastic vein, once more by J. B. Straub.

The two famous names in German porcelain, J. J. Kändler and Franz Anton Bustelli, of Meissen and of Nymphenburg fame, can perhaps be brought into play in contrasting Johann Michael Fischer, the architect we have been following from church to church, with Dominikus Zimmermann, his near contemporary. There is more of nervous vitality in Zimmermann, as there is in Bustelli. The immense output of J. M. Fischer compares with that of J. J. Kändler, whose 'crinoline' groups, birds and animals of all sorts, Turks and Chinamen, harlequins, perhaps above all his 'swan' service, have the endless invention of J. M. Fischer and are not alien to the world of Zwiefalten and Ottobeuren. On the other hand porcelain figures by Bustelli, which are fewer in number, have a sharper and even more personal idiom to them just as, in this context, instead of nearly fifty – as with J. M. Fischer – there are only four churches wholly by Dominikus Zimmermann; and among those four, the church of Wies which has more personality and more of a personal touch to it, the frescoes and *stucchi* being due to his brother, than any other Rococo church.

Happily, two of the churches of Dominikus Zimmermann are of monastic foundation, and therefore eligible for inclusion here. That at Steinhausen, in the neighbourhood of Ulm and Memmingen, is indubitably a masterpiece and merits a long journey. It is a pilgrimage church built by the Premonstratensians of Schussenried, not far away, where the Library, to be noticed later, is by Zimmermann. Coming to it through the streets of the little town, the gabled roof of the church and its high walls make it look more Dutch than German, till one notices that the interior must be oval, a shape that often inspires, whether in Portugal or in Brazil (the churches of the Minas Gerães), or, nearer home, at St Chad's, Shrewsbury, which is oval in appearance but, more strictly, 'formed by the intersection of two circles', and the Victorian commentator goes on, 'redeemed by a Doric portico and tower, the sole feature which prevents the building being taken for a theatre or exchange'.

The exterior, which is in pleasing shades of red and ochre, becomes interesting with its two flights of windows of elaborate shape, the lower of them high above street level, and the moment of entering this pilgrimage church is unforgettable for a certain compact lightness and an essential concentration of intention not found to the same degree in J. M. Fischer's churches. The fluttering cornices of the free pilasters supporting the oval, and the marvels of gracefulness achieved in stucco by Johann Baptist Zimmermann, the brother of the architect, make of this white interior with its notes of green and orange-persimmon something only little below Wies for happiness and beauty; and it is here, as mentioned earlier, that J. B. Zimmermann, who also frescoed the cloud scenes and fountain'd gardens of the ceiling, has interpolated or, it could be said, 'gagged' the action, putting little birds like woodpeckers in stucco on capitals or on the sides of windows.

Maria-Steinbach, another pilgrimage church of the Premonstratensians, near Memmingen, is in the happy position of being ascribed to this most graceful of architects, without proof positive that it is by him. However, no one who has seen Die Wies and Steinhausen, or the Frauenkirche at Günzburg, which is his other church, could have much doubt of it. Maria-Steinbach is a most beautiful little building, inside and out. Its galleried interior, the *stucchi* by Feichtmayr and Üblhör of Wessobrunn, the bridge-like organloft, all combine into making Maria-Steinbach one of the gems of the whole Rococo age, best seen perhaps late on an evening when it is unexpected and one is not prepared for it. The impression left by this little pilgrimage church in its tree-shaded square is of a quasi-Mexican richness, dissimilar in every detail, but becoming in mind the Bavarian equivalent or companion to the church at Taxco.

The two pilgrimage churches by Dominikus Zimmermann, and the knowledge that his brother worked with him both at Die Wies and at Steinhausen, is enough to rouse a lively interest in other work by the two brothers. We have seen that to Johann Baptist is due much of the astonishing beauty of the rooms at the Amalienburg, also some of the decoration of the golden Reiche Zimmer in the Residenz at Munich. Having started his career as perhaps the most imaginative and graceful artist in stucco there has ever been, after he was fifty years old he took up fresco-painting, and those desirous of following this great ornamentalist through all his career will not mind the recapitulation that it was Johann Baptist Zimmermann who made the silvered *stucchi* upon a blue ground, and silver upon *couleur de citron* or *couleur de paille* in the rooms at the Amalienburg; who was both frescoist and stuccoist at Die Wies; who worked the detail at Steinhausen; and who is to be seen in the old Cistercian nunnery at Landshut in both stucco and fresco, and in both arts again at Weyarn, outside Munich, a house of Augustinian canons.

The inexhaustible gaiety and high spirits of this optimist in the dawning age of reason are to be admired again in yet another monastery church, at Schäftlarn which was built for the Premonstratensians. Here he fresco'd and stucco'd, too; and his *amorini* holding garlands or hoops of roses over the altar in this chapel of monks have more than a little hint in them of the children holding hoops of flowers before the waltz begins in the garden of King Florestan's palace. It is not always a mystery why such or such a tune should come into one's head. The ubiquitous J. B. Straub worked here, too, on the altars and the pulpit, making of the latter a vehicle from which it would have been curious, if impracticable, to hear the thunderings of a mid-Victorian evangelist and preacher.

'Paired' altars by J. B. Straub, to be taken in to right and left like side-wings leading to the high altar in a church shaped as a rotunda, and with the degree of balance and homogeneity between them that unites, and separates, 'paired' sonatas for the harpsichord by Domenico Scarlatti, are to be seen at Ettal, a Benedictine abbey but a mile or two from Oberammergau. In this Italianate domed church by Enrico Zuccalli from the Ticino – its architects and craftsmen worked abroad and left little or nothing in their native canton – there is a whirling ceiling fresco of the Benedictine Order in Glory by the same J. J. Zeiller who painted tamely and in good taste at Ottobeuren. And the aforementioned six side-altars by Straub are works of such complex fantasy, and withal slow and careful execution, that it is no longer a mystery that the second generation of great Paris *ébénistes* should have been less often French than German. There are prodigies of technique below the assurance and free flow of a Straub or Zimmermann.

Kloster Ettal, helped by the lovely mountain country it lies in, is one of the most pleasant of these places. Others, which must be touched on, are well known but disappointing. Among these latter, the immense Weingarten, near the Lake of Constance, an enormous Benedictine foundation, happily unfinished, but with fine architectural frescoes in 'Fratel' Pozzo-like perspective by Cosmos Damian Asam. Weingarten I find dull indeed; as, also, Banz, in spite of its terrace, another enormous Benedictine abbey, across the river valley of the Main from Vierzehnheiligen, and although it is the work of one of the Dientzenhofer dynasty of architects.[1]

The name of another architect of the family is in association with Kloster Ebrach, an old Cistercian foundation not far from Pommersfelden, the most splendid of country houses in all Central Europe, the feature of which is its staircase by a Dientzenhofer. The stair at Kloster Ebrach with its galleries and painted ceiling is only a little smaller than that at Pommersfelden, and must echo oddly to the climbing or the descending of white-cowled figures and the shuffle of square-toed slippered feet. What a contrast, might one say, to the night-stair coming down from the dormitory of the monks into the cold church at Hexham, in Northumberland! The building at Kloster Ebrach was enlarged by J. B. Neumann, *Treppenhaus* specialist and creator of the stairways at Bruchsal, Brühl, and Würzburg – in the true 'welfare' state he or his like would have designed the moving stairs at Oxford or Piccadilly Circus – the church with its ceiling frescoes has 'illusionist', perspective iron screens with heraldic and architectural motifs and armoured Herne-the-Hunter-like figures high in the metal boughs; there are fountains and garden statues; when dissolved in the time of Napoleon the abbey owned 25,000 acres of forest, the best vineyards in Franconia, fifty-four villages, and enjoyed an immense income; this home of Cistercian monks had every amenity except a monastic theatre – and Kloster Ebrach is still, or was for more than a hundred years, a prison!

Kloster Ebrach, being in Franconia and near Bamberg, lies considerably to the north of most of the places so far mentioned, but a few more remain to be considered in the monklands of the south towards the Alps. There is Ochsenhausen, of the Benedictines, near Memmingen, a Baroquized church of immense length, with saints wearing haloes of sun-rays as elegant as any tricorne of the boar-hunt, an extraordinary perspective or cross-section of ornament

---

[1] Their masterpiece being the church of St Nicolaus-Kleinseite, in Prague, by Christopher and Kilian Ignaz Dientzenhofer, one of the glories of the Baroque movement.

for the narrow or ship-like nave, a little heavy-footed perhaps in sophistication with the ox-stalls and the cow-bells of sub-Alpine pastures at the gate; there is Gutenzell, not more than a mile or two away, where the daughter of Dominikus Zimmermann was abbess, a Cistercian nunnery Baroquized; and there is Rottenbuch, near Oberammergau, a former house of Austin Canons, where the stuccoists from Wessobrunn achieved an entity on its own from the disparate elements of Gothic and Rococo, and revealed therein the continuity of the tradition. And there is Rot-an-der-Rot, of the Premonstratensians, which is not the same as Rott-am-Inn. It is another of the abbeys near Memmingen, by an architect from the Vorarlberg, which could be described as the district at the Austrian end of Lake Constance, between Bavaria on one hand and Switzerland on the other. Rot-an-der-Rot is a 'wall-pillar' church of simple design and fine noble proportion, of extraordinary, localized sophistication, if derived of decidedly rustic stock, as witness the names of the Voralberg architects, Caspar Moosbrugger, and two pairs of fathers and sons, Michael and Franz Beer, and Michael and Peter Thumb, the son in each case being more interesting than the father.

It is to be noticed that none of them worked in his native Vorarlberg. All went abroad, to Bavaria, to the Tyrol, or to Switzerland, in which context we should remind ourselves of the ramshackle nature of the Holy Roman Empire which at the end of the seventeenth century contained no fewer than eighteen hundred sovereign rulers, including Kings, Electors, Margraves, Landgraves, Wildgraves, Rhinegraves, monasteries, convents, towns, and even villages. Different dialects were spoken all over the Empire; 'no German idiom was yet accepted as that of the educated', and conditions had altered little, if at all, since the end of mediaeval times. As late as the end of the Napoleonic Wars Germany was made up of an agglomerate of little kingdoms and autonomous duchies, bristling with castles, and preserving even in the Gothic character of its handwriting the imprint of the Middle Ages. Roads were as slow as in the day of Albrecht Dürer; and the flowering of the Rococo in these lands was the first sign of recovery since the Thirty Years War of religion had ended in 1648. It had been a disaster of the magnitude of the Black Death extending over the entire lives of one generation of human beings, and taking as long as two more generations before the effects of it wore off. This cannot but have enhanced the distance and backwardness of the bucolic regions and probably nothing could seem more remote and lost than the sensations of a traveller arriving at Ochsenhausen, at Rottenbuch, at Rot-an-der-Rot, just at the time we are writing of, which yet was in the flowering and burgeoning of new ideas.

The country-sounding Caspar Moosbrugger was architect of Weingarten but, more important still, he was architect of Einsiedeln. This Benedictine abbey, where he was a lay brother, though coming from the Vorarlberg, is a further demonstration of the fluid nature of the frontiers because Einsiedeln is in Switzerland, not very far from Zürich, and was an independent principality of the Holy Roman Empire. I have been three times to Einsiedeln, and on each occasion have been disappointed. Its best feature indeed is the arcaded semi-circular approach to the church, where are the souvenir stalls, and whence looking down to the houses below, which are all hotels and hostels for the pilgrims, the mattresses are to be seen airing on the roofs in true Swiss domestic fashion. Both Asam brothers, Cosmas Damian and Egid Quirin, worked here; all is on a huge scale, there is fine ironwork, and there are whole families of *amorini*, but something has gone wrong. Or perhaps it was never right in the beginning. One factor in this may be that it is kept in too good order, has none of the patina of age, and has in fact in this prime land of the hoteliers a touch of the Ritz Hotel about it, but a Ritz near sanatorium pinewoods and in mountain air.

The other great Benedictine abbey, that of St Gallen is ascribed to Peter Thumb, another of the Vorarlberg architects, and I find that the same strictures can be applied to it; quite empty of emotion, with no distinguishing features, too well cared for as by a brigade of Hoovers, and with areas of painted fresco presenting such a preponderance of painted cloud, particularly in the central rotunda-dome of the ceiling, that one wonders all does not blow away and leave the cathedral of St Gallen roofless. There is, though, another church by Peter Thumb which is one of the delights of the Rococo age and has its place beside Die Wies and Steinhausen, Zwiefalten and Wilhering.[1] This is the Cistercian pilgrimage church of Neu-Birnau on a hillside above Lake Constance. Probably drawing inspiration from the view, Peter Thumb has designed a church tower of some pretension, which apart, there is no other indication of anything exceptional to see. The first impression is of a light-filled vessel with a gallery running all round it, painted heavens, and whole nurseries of *amorini*, these latter due to J. A. Feichtmayr (not to be confused with the Feichtmayrs of Wessobrunn). It is one of the white interiors, touched in with pink and green, and of course, gold. The light-heartedness is continued into the painted ceiling, for standing in the right place on the floor you can look up into a piece of mirror in the hand of one of the angels and see yourself in heaven.

---

[1] The Pfarrkirche at Wilten, a suburb of Innsbruck, has had its praises oversung by one of the two English-speaking *epigoni* of the Baroque in Central Europe. *C.f.* John Bourke, *op. cit.* pp. 234, 235. Despite graceful stuccowork by F. X. Feichtmayr, and a pretty baldachin with overlooking opera-boxes, it is no more interesting than the Stiftskirche at Wilten which stands next door.

But there is a type of mind to which the library halls in some of the monasteries are no less inviting. The same Peter Thumb, architect of St Gallen and of Neu-Birnau, built the library at the former of these two, with an inlaid floor to be skated over in socks or wearing *babouches* as in a mosque. To the writer, at least, it does not compare with other monastery library halls; to the blue and gold library at Melk enhanced by the woodwork and the vellum bindings; to that at Altenburg with its milk-blue *scagliola* pillars and domed and painted ceilings; or to the libraries at Admont, at Vorau, or at Seitenstetten. But these are all at monasteries in Austria; and the best are in Germany.

There is the library at Waldsassen, a suppressed Cistercian monastery, in a remote part of Bavaria near the frontier with Czechoslovakia. Here, the exceedingly curious gallery is held up by wooden caryatids carved by a sculptor from Salzburg, of the name of Stilp. They are caricatures in grotesque style of local characters, all in unpainted wood; beggars, rag-pickers, swine-herds, and so forth, of sinister, slightly unpleasant humour. The library at Metten, a Benedictine abbey between Regensburg and Passau is to be preferred, a series of vaulted rooms upheld by four groups of caryatids, in the manner of those in staircase halls at palaces in Vienna and in Prague. The vaulted ceilings are decorated with subjects *en camaieu* and with fresco and stuccowork.

But the two best library halls are at Wiblingen and Schussenried. Of them both it is possible to prefer the former with gay comings and goings of its balcony supported on *scagliola* columns, its library-statues as though these were in corollary to garden-statues, its stucco scrolls and volutes, and its painted ceiling. Was this latter, I wonder, by Januarius Zick, better known for his *Gartensaal* at Würzburg, who was frescoing ceilings for the Benedictines of Wiblingen in just these years? It is perhaps the most graceful and beautiful library in the world, and certainly learning lies but lightly on its painted columns and gilt capitals. It is almost in the nature of a personal sacrifice to prefer Wiblingen to Schussenried because the latter is by Dominikus Zimmermann. It will be recalled that it was the abbot of this Premonstratensian monastery who commissioned Zimmermann to build the pilgrimage church at Steinhausen, four miles away. The same abbot, we may presume, ordered the library for his home monastery at Schussenried. It is a lighter affair, all white and pink, with a bow-windowed gallery, and sham vellum bindings in the book-cases. There are library-statues and a painted ceiling; but the impression given is of lightness and flimsiness, and although pretty and graceful it is disappointing.

If the most beautiful of the monastery churches, and their staircases,

Kaiserhalls, libraries, have been at least noted and described, it will be realized that there are numberless details such as individual statues that must escape mention altogether. On occasion there is some transcendental effect, as that of the *Gnadenaltar* in the middle of the church at Vierzehnheiligen, and there is another instance of this in the pulpit of the Benedictine church at Amorbach. This extraordinary affair with a double stair in full Rococo leading to it is by J. W. von Auwera, whose delicate hand made the light baldachin and its garlands in the Franciscan church at Brühl. The pulpit itself and its canopy, particularly in that rather narrow, cold, white church is like the body of some golden coach without its wheels; or, if such could be, the flowering, golden body of a gondola, hung on the wall for re-gilding in the gondola-yard. Or, for another instance, the transcendental choir-stalls at Bronnbach, in the Cistercian abbey church, of almost galleon solidity, but monkish-Chippendale in style.

Perhaps even in its highest flights this bucolic Rococo was never far removed from the cuckoo clock and Christmas tree, but with those simplicities made magical and carried to the highest point of fantasy. With at an intermediate stage, inclining towards the folk or peasant art, the 'ship'-pulpits; that at Irsee, of the Premonstratensians, where sermons were preached from a ship's bow, with cupids on a rope-ladder, raising the main-sail and busy in the rigging; or at Traunkirchen, near Salzburg, where the symbolism is a little too earthbound, too near the surface of the lake. There are at least two more 'ship'-pulpits in the village churches, but I have not seen them. These latter in any case are not of monastic origin, and are therefore outside our subject. As is, too, that fine sculptor Raphael Donner's leaden equestrian statue of St Martin in Hungarian costume, dressed as a Hussar, dividing his cloak with the beggar. Now it stands outside the choir of the cathedral in Pressburg. Formerly, as can be seen in old prints, it was above the high altar, in that church where the coronation of the Kings of Hungary took place, and every other person, it would seem from the engravings, was in Hussar uniform. A world in which, coming back to the ship-pulpits, it is only surprising that on high festivals the floor of the church was not flooded so that the vessel and the preacher moved along it, with cupids in the ropes, until it reached port and lowered anchor.

3

Italian Monasteries

An account of Italian monasteries can begin appropriately at the Certosa del Galluzzo; and with no passing descent upon it by motor on the way to Siena or San Gimignano, but for full flavour the journey there along the dusty road by tram. Starting from the Piazza del Duomo in Florence after a wait of about a quarter of an hour, and time to look up at the coloured marbles of Giotto's Tower; and not only at that, but to the black or dark green and white octagon of the Baptistery in the middle of the square, while – no less of an excitement to a boy of nine or ten years old – a black-garbed brother of the Misericordia glides past, black hood over his head, with only slits for eyes.

But 'numero uno' tram has come, and emptied, and we climb inside. And with a grinding, screeching of the wheels I will always remember, we have started and are round the corner and out of the cathedral square. The wheels are screeching and moaning again in their tramlines as we come into Piazza Santa Maria Novella, of other nostalgic memory. For in the street leading out of the far right-hand end of it is the Farmacia or Spezeria of the former Dominican monks. We will come back to that later. It is an April morning, in the month of irises – it is indeed for orris-root that the Spezeria is famed – and I could have sworn the tram went by the Mercato Nuovo or Flower Market where is the bronze statue of the wild boar. I have looked up the route in old guide books but it would seem that I am wrong. Yet I see the roses and carnations of the flower stalls, and perhaps it was not on the way there but on the return journey to the hotel.

Now we come out onto the Arno, and are crossing the river by a modern bridge with the beautiful Ponte Santa Trinità on our left and the houses on the Ponte Vecchio beyond it, and all of Florence – Brunelleschi's dome, the tower of the Palazzo Vecchio, the river, the Lungarno, the nearby hills and cypresses – all in the iris of an eye. But I am wishing we were on the Ponte Santa Trinità with the lovely curve of its arches, knowing the town well enough already to anticipate seeing the grotesque mask where two streets would open before us, and the row of houses between them has this mask facing us at the angle of its end house as in a painted street scene at the theatre.

Such was the quick passing through a city which once was considered so beautiful; but, then, ideals of beauty alter, and beauty fades. It is the only city from which a girl's name has been invented, except for Venetia which is but a shade beside it, so that it must have been loved most exceptionally by foreigners, and by our own countrymen in particular, an affection lasting for some two hundred years or more, and that must have been at the last and final glow of incandescence when I was a child.

And now we are in narrow streets with no room to walk on the pavement, and in a few minutes are at Porta Romana which means we are outside the town. In fact we are on the Via Senese, the road to Siena, which I had heard of, but where I had never been. At the time I am thinking of, except for the Bersaglieri with the cocks' feathers round their hats and their cyclist bugle-bands, a sign of the Sardinian 'usurpation', Italy can have changed little, trains and tramways apart, from the Italy of a hundred years ago. It was still, visually, let us say, the Florence of Raphael and Fra Bartolomeo, of Andrea del Sarto, possibly of Fra Angelico – but not at all of Masaccio, of Piero della Francesca, scarcely, even, of Botticelli. So far as what one saw with one's eyes, coming in and out of the town on the way to or from the Certosa, it was the same Florence before the second list of painters mentioned had been heard of, and while the first lot were the familiar names.

At which moment, still at the Porta Romana, as we go by the start of the Viale dei Colli, creeping along under the stucco wall that seems stained with sunlight in the yellow dust of the road, there come a couple of nuns, brown-robed, with sandall'd feet, and wearing a kind of coif or wimple on their heads under a wide-brimmed, high-crowned hat of Tuscan straw. The poorest order of nuns, who are mendicant and have to beg for their living, Discalced Franciscans, I am presuming, but they can have altered little, if at all, down all the centuries. Their habit is the peasant dress of the early thirteenth century as St Francis of Assisi may have seen it in the Casentino, or indeed in any part of Tuscany or Umbria; of the poorest brown cloth, coiffed against both heat and cold, and shaded with a reaper or grape-picker's hat of plaited straw, such as women wore when working in the fields. Mendicant nuns of seven centuries ago, a hundred years before Giotto or Cimabue, and a ghostly vision of Tuscany before its burgeoning, as it might have been a thousand years ago. Are the begging nuns still to be seen in the streets of Florence? I know not. For in spite of family ties with Florence, more than a quarter of a century has gone by since I was in this city where I lived so much as a child and as a young man.

Meanwhile the tram, too, is gathering speed and going quicker, and although the road is lined with houses we are in the country and among low hills. Where there is a bend in the road we see, facing us above the village roofs, a building like a fortress on a hill covered with cypresses. It is the Certosa, which I was to know so well later from the road that branches to the right just at this point and winds up and down over the hills to Monte-gufoni. From its curves to right or left, going up or coming down, you see not only the tiled roofs but apertures which are the courts and cloisters of the monastery. Once, and once only during the years, I have seen the monks in their white robes taking their weekly walk or *spatiamentum*, two by two, on the slanting hillside among the cypresses and olive trees below the monastery wall. If perhaps most of us hold some place sacred in our personal mythology and in our memory, then such for myself is the Certosa, the more so perhaps because I remember it so well from an impressionable age, and because it is now so long since I have seen it.

But now, with the flank of the Certosa hidden from us by the houses, the tram stops at a gateway and we get out. And while the tram goes on its way to Impruneta we are at the foot of a long steep ascent up to the monastery; an approach to it that, all monasteries of whatever religion being to this extent alike, may remind one of photographs of the way up to the Potala at Lhasa. How exciting the climb up to the Certosa! And at the top there is a covered porch where we wait, with an inner and an outer stair leading up from it through locked wooden gates into the monastery. While we are waiting for the monk to let us in it is intriguing to look in the other direction down long vaulted passages which are dark with mystery.

At last we see him coming to us down the inner stair; a bearded Carthusian monk, a Padre Certosino, in his white habit, with white socks or stockings, and heavy black square-toed monk's shoes. He jangles his bunch of keys, opens the gate, and we climb the outer stair into the Certosa, finding ourselves at the top of it in a very large courtyard paved with red tiles, with the church in front of us which we enter through a side chapel. We go down some steps into the lower church, where are the marble tomb slabs of the Acciaioli, founders of the monastery, one of them, that of the young knight Lorenzo of that family, being now ascribed again to Donatello. It is the greatest work of art in the Certosa, and as the figure of a youthful warrior may come to share a place in one's memory with that of Guido Guidarelli, the young knight whose tomb is at Ravenna, and with the *Doncel* of Sigüenza, far away in Spain. The church, when we come up to it again, is late sixteenth century in date, although the foundation by Niccolò Acciaioli was in 1341. It has carved and inlaid choir-stalls, rich marbles, and frescoes by Bernardo

Poccetti, a Florentine of the time, whose paintings have enough, but only just enough of style and personality to survive. There are smaller cloisters to traverse, but at last we are in the great cloister with the monks' cells round it, enclosing it 'like pinnacles', each cell being indeed a little three-roomed house with its own little piece of garden. For the Carthusian monks eat their fleshless meals in solitude, the food being passed to them by a lay brother through a latch that turns round in the wall. Only on Sundays and on certain feast days do they dine in the refectory, their food even there consisting of cereals and vegetables with a modicum of wine. Probably it is the very solitude of their lives that appeals, in comparison to the horrors of a common dormitory. The meagre diet may have been no stricter than in monasteries of other orders, but the solitude must have been a blessing to anyone not drawn and disposed towards a life in common.

Only too soon we are back again in the outer courtyard and coming down the inner of the twin flights of steps into the gatehouse, where a reprieve comes and the same monk leads us down the long dark passage to the Spezeria. It is somewhere further down those dark vaults that the monks distil the Certosino liqueur, green or yellow, in pale reflection of the original liqueur of the Grande Chartreuse, and conducive in maturer years to thinking that rather fewer ingredients may have gone to its distillation than the hundred and thirty mountain herbs gathered in the mountains of Dauphiné, with 'carnations, absinthium, and the young buds of pine trees', added. It is for sale for better or worse in the Spezeria where other things to be purchased are bits of majolica painted with cinquecento grotesques by one of the monks, and always with the ☫ monogram of the Carthusian order very much in evidence; excellent chocolate, also with the monogram upon its paper wrapper; and soap, bath-size, scented with almond or more elusive marshmallow, and stamped not only with the monogram but with the lion of the Acciaioli and the leopard of the Altoviti. I said 'for sale', but should have written 'were for sale', for now the Certosa del Galluzzo after so many centuries has passed out of Carthusian hands and been taken over by the Cistercians. How this may affect its future I am in no position to judge, but I have tried to give a picture of a monastery in Italy, if of a rare order and of particular appeal to the writer.

It is true that St Bruno, founder of the Carthusians, was a canon of Cologne, but he taught in the schools of Reims and Paris, and he belonged to that early dispensation before Germans were permanently differenced from Frenchmen and when their half-formed tongues, never used in any event by the learned, were more or less interchangeable. Was Charlemagne, then, a Frank or was he German? And how much difference of race was there

Opposite: Monks at Refectory (detail)
by Alessandro Magnasco

between Reims and Aix-la-Chapelle or Aachen? St Bruno, who was to die in 1101 at the second Certosa that he founded in Calabria, chose the mountains of Dauphiné for his Thebaid and was established as early as 1084 in the Grande Chartreuse. The Carthusian monk in his white robe, whether at Galluzzo or any other of the Certosas or Cartujas, be it in Italy or Spain, is wearing the dress of an eleventh-century peasant in Dauphiné. It is even said to derive from the cloaks of the herdsmen on those hills who wore, until not long ago, cloaks of white homespun with a hood or cowl called a *mandrilla*, from the Greek word that means a sheepfold. The Carthusian, like the begging nun, wears the dress of the poor peasant of a thousand years ago, and if in both cases, male and female, it has points of resemblance to what the Moors wear in North Africa, it is because they, too, are to this little extent sartorially the heirs or legatees of ancient Rome. No less is the brown habit of the Franciscan or the black and white of the Dominican the poor dress of its time. But if their dress is humble and their diet austere, their churches, their cloisters, even their refectories, can be of the utmost splendour. The Certosini in particular affected a richness in marble, in inlaid stalls, in lavishness of fresco, whether it be at Galluzzo, at Pavia, at San Martino looking out over Naples, or at Padula in the Basilicata, while what is true of the Italian Certosa applies no less to the Spanish Cartuja, as witness those of Burgos, Jerez, Granada.

In general, because there was no movement of conquest to further, as in England under the Norman Kings, or because there were few tracts of land to make fertile and profit from as in the English fenlands, on the wolds of Lincolnshire and Yorkshire, or down the Severn valley, the tendency in Italy was for the great monasteries and nunneries to be in towns. The Certosas apart, comprising those already named and a few more, there are not many country monasteries. Subiaco, Monte Cassino, Montevergine, Monte Oliveto Maggiore, Casamari, Fossanova – that is about all, as against which it would be easy to name twenty or even thirty English country monasteries of the first importance in their day. But the friars, the Franciscans and Dominicans who never 'caught on' in England, and by their very mendicancy were prevented from leaving monuments behind them to compare with those of the Benedictines and Cistercians, built in rivalry with each other in most Italian towns, as witness Santa Croce and Santa Maria Novella of the Franciscans and Dominicans in Florence, and in the same order, in Venice the Frari and SS Giovanni e Paolo, and in Naples Santa Chiara for Franciscan nuns and San Domenico Maggiore, all those mentioned being establishments upon the largest scale.

This said, there is the difficulty where Italian monasteries are concerned in detailing the enormous quantity of works of art with which they are adorned. There is nothing for instance either specifically Franciscan or Dominican about the wonderful tombs of mediaeval Doges in both churches we have named in Venice, whereas there is some quality that is particularly and incontrovertibly Franciscan about the frescoes in the upper church at Assisi, as there is, too, where it is more in the air than on the walls, at St Francis's retreat in the beech woods of La Verna. How to equate those apparent contradictions is the problem; the only solution seeming to be to treat of those churches or monasteries which are works of art in themselves, only drawing attention to their contents when it is either of particular monastic significance, or a painting or other work of art of such outstanding importance that it cannot be omitted.

For a beginning, what could be more redolent of Florence than Santa Maria Novella! The very façade of its church pleases by association, though whether it be 'the purest and most elegant example of Tuscan Gothic' is open to argument. It is a hybrid style in itself, a manipulation of a form which was not natural to the Florentines and which they did not understand. There is this forced feeling about even Giotto's Tower; and it is as though the Italians working in this style felt it was a falsification of the Gothic and that they should be building in stone and not in coloured marbles. Perhaps it would be true to say that Giotto's Tower is a painter's Gothic more than an architect's, a theory which is borne out more than a hundred years later when the very buildings that would be questionable as real structures look radiant and beautiful in Fra Angelico's paintings. But the façade of Santa Maria Novella is not of the order of slender colonnettes and coloured vaults; moreover its marbles are thickly overlaid with dust, a façade to look up at for preference in blinding heat as one holds up the heavy leather curtain and walks thankfully into the cool inside.

Here, again, the interior is disappointing but for its works of art. It is neither a Gothic church, nor a basilica; alternates between the two of them, and cannot make up its mind. But the interior of Santa Maria Novella is saved by its frescoes, by Ghirlandajo, by Filippino Lippi, though the most beautiful paintings of all are in the 'Spanish' chapel in the cloisters. This frescoed chapter house is the work of Andrea da Firenze, painted about 1370. The two greatest of its wall paintings depict the Church Militant and Triumphant and the Glorification of the Dominican St Thomas Aquinas, the church and monastery of Santa Maria Novella being, as we know, Dominican. In the Church Militant and Triumphant the Pope and the Emperor are enthroned, side by side, with priests and monks and hermits round them. In another corner of the crowded fresco some young men and women are wasting the hours in an orange grove. The strong currents of fanaticism are to be noticed. The black and white dogs, *Domini canes*, for the Dominicans: the hermits, particularly, in the Church Militant and Triumphant; or the strange figure, listening, in the ceiling fresco of the Pentecost. Below the feet of St Thomas Aquinas, in his Glorification, are the three heretics, Arius, Sabellius, and Averrhoes, below them a row of fourteen women, who are the arts and sciences, seated upon thrones that are like choir-stalls, and at their feet, as many male figures chosen from among those famous in science or theology. These are most curious. Practical theology with Peter Lombard; speculative theology with Boethius; mystic and scholastic theologies with St Augustine and St John Damascene; grammar with Priscian; but, above all, music with Tubalcain. This fanatic with his dark beard could be a Gypsy blacksmith, without his anvil, listening to music, and in a rhapsodic trance. Where can Andrea da Firenze have met his prototype? It is a figure that haunts the memory and is for evermore a symbol of one half of music. Behind him, his muse plays a stringed instrument, and he is listening to her. It is wonderful to stand here in hot August, for it is cool and empty in the great chapter house and we can pick out the figures of fanatics and heretics. We see Averrhoes in his turban, and Tubalcain like a wild animal entranced by music. All in all, the 'Spanish' chapel at Santa Maria Novella is the most unforgettable aesthetic experience to be had in Florence.

But the cloister of Santa Maria Novella? No one could admire its architecture overmuch who has seen the cloisters in England, with our unique octagonal chapter-houses opening from them, or the cloisters in Spain or Portugal. Of what more there may once have been in the monastery there can be little left, now there is a cinema in one corner of it, and that most of the rest of it has been a barracks for over a hundred years. It is better to walk to the end of the square, turn to the right, and go into the Spezeria, the already mentioned former Farmacia of the Dominican monks, founded in 1612, and for the last century in private hands. Just the long passage leading to it through doors with blue glass in their windows, and the long succession of painted halls, are inviting. Medicines of monastic origin dating from Medicean times are still on sale. There are mysterious potions, like 'Vermouth di Edinburgo', and a wide range of things scented with orris-foot that is produced from the white *Iris fiorentina*. There could be no more fitting introduction to monastic pharmacies.

The other Florentine convent of Dominicans is San Marco where are the frescoes and paintings by Fra Angelico. The church is uninteresting; but, rather, let us look at the angels' wings in frescoes by Beato Angelico, a thaumaturge among painters, and note how in innocence they attach to the angel shoulders. In his cell in the convent of San Marco he must have had visions in which he felt the rush of wings from angel visitants, wings barred like those of the hoopoe in one of the frescoes in the cells, and as much a part of his earthly experience as the peacock, described by a traveller after an all-night journey in a third-class train in India, as standing on a refuse heap beside the station just as the sun rose for another day of torturing heat, and clapping its wings like a being from another world, an India of marble palaces and lily tanks, where the airs smell of jasmine and of sandalwood, clapping its wings, and as it started to scavenge, lifting up its tiara'd head and uttering a raucous cry. The angel and the peacock are spiritual beings, and it should not detract from them that they feel the needs of nature. Some of the most beautiful and appealing paintings in the world are to be enjoyed at San Marco.

Santa Croce, the huge church and monastery of the Franciscans at the other end of Florence, again shows the discrepancies in the Tuscan Gothic style. Its marble exterior is, truthfully, very ugly indeed, while the conversion of the interior into a national pantheon with the tomb of Rossini, monuments to Dante, Alfieri, Macchiavelli, and so on, has conferred a special and very terrible gloom upon it, only dispelled by finding the hand of Rossellino and even of Donatello among the cenotaphs, and by Giotto's frescoes in the Peruzzi and Bardi chapels, the latter of which Ruskin calls in precise endearment of phrase 'the most interesting and perfect little Gothic chapel in all Italy', but the dust of more than a hundred years has further darkened the chapels since his Florentine mornings were spent here. All this in 'the largest church belonging to any of the mendicant orders in Italy' may seem to have little of the Franciscan spirit about it. But Brunelleschi's Cappella Pazzi has the sweet breath of the Early Renaissance which again is another matter and has nothing to do with the Franciscans, and the two sets of cloisters of Santa Croce are in the same spirit. Where indeed that quasi-pagan feeling nearly accommodates itself to the neo-Christian is in the Badia di Fiesole which is a most beautiful Brunelleschian building of the first blossoming.[1] The airs here are young and sweet away from the noise and narrow pavements of the city, as though there were some healing or renewing quality in the architecture. The airs are indeed as balsamic as in the pinewoods of Monte Senario where there is the old convent of Servites and the stupendous view. But nothing in fact in the way of works of art, for which as a farewell to Florence there is always, or there has been for a thousand years, San Miniato al Monte, a Dominican church happily free from the Tuscan-Gothic, for it is too early for that with its early Romanesque front, and again

[1] The Badia di Fiesole was a convent of Austin Canons.

escaping the Gothic with Rossellino's chapel and monument to the Cardinal of Portugal. San Miniato is a sacred *hortus conclusus* where one can spend a little time in thinking over what are beyond dispute some of the beautiful things of the world of human beings, and of the youthful world of the Renaissance at that, the bas-reliefs and sculptures of the brothers Rossellino, of Mino da Fiesole, of Desiderio da Settignano, of Agostino di Duccio. After which one can come out of San Miniato for a last view of Florence.

The huge churches of the Franciscans and Dominicans in Venice, their works of art apart, are disappointing. Of the Frari, it is impossible not to agree with the opinion of an English architect of a hundred years ago, written in all the enthusiasm of personal discovery when such buildings were, as it were, unknown and new.

One cannot but be impressed with the magnificent size of such a church as the Frari, with its many interesting details and its monuments and woodwork. But in spite of all this, there is something wanting. I had not expected larger churches, but I had imagined that their style would be more pure, and at the same time more unlike what I was accustomed to elsewhere. The impression they left on my mind was decidedly that they were very inferior in almost every respect to churches of the same size and degree of ornament in the North of Europe.[1]

Even the brick of which the Frari is built is lamentably disappointing compared to the rose-petal brick of the Pieterskerk at Leyden, or to brick churches in Northern Germany, and but little trouble can have been taken in the brick-kilns. The interior is simple in plan, and as Street comments, of good effect from the plainness of its twelve circular piers and the simple quadripartite groining of its roof. But unfortunately, like Santa Croce in Florence, it has been made 'the last resting place of many eminent men', which portends the tombs of Canova and of Titian, the latter erected by the semi-imbecile Habsburg Emperor (and King of Lombardy) Ferdinand I. Its icy classicism but makes more bizarre the tomb of the Pesaro Doge with its negro bearers and skeletal camels; while the chief treasure of the Frari, the Madonna with mandolin-playing children, angels, *amorini*, call them what you will, that hangs in the sacristy, a beautiful painting by Giovanni Bellini, is more the affair of the donor than of the Franciscan monks who must have swarmed all over this enormous monastery with dull cloisters, now housing the Venetian archives, 'about fifteen million documents, deposited in 298 apartments'.

The Dominican church of SS Giovanni e Paolo is to be preferred in point of architecture to the Frari, even if it has the adventitious aid of Verrocchio's

---

[1] *Brick and Marble in the Middle Ages: notes of tours in the North of Italy*, by G. E. Street, 1855, p. 176 (1874 ed.). The same author's *Gothic Architecture in Spain*, another voyage of discovery, is much to be commended.

equestrian statue of the *condottiere* Colleoni almost at its door, together with the Scuola di San Marco at its side. The latter is a fifteenth-century building, in spite of which it does not escape censure from the English architect of Victorian times whom we accompanied to the Frari who, mincing, rather than not mincing his words, speaks of it as 'built with coloured marble in a horrible sort of perspective, which is the lowest depth to which architecture ever reached', at which words the Lombardi, father and son, architect and sculptor, are hurried off to execution. Splendid in SS Giovanni e Paolo are the tombs of fifteenth-century Doges, several of them three or even four storeys high. Here, our critic praises the curtained tester, on either side of which guardian angels hold back the curtains, 'and allow us to join them in looking at the figure on the tomb', in Victorian death-bed mood. What would the same person have said could he but come with us to the church of the Gesuati, on the Fondamenta Nuova nearby? For this church has its walls, its pilasters, indeed the whole of its interior surface, of white marble inlaid in a brocade pattern with *verde antico*.

The church of the Gesuati, out on the Zattere at the other side of Venice, he would have probably ignored altogether. The Gesuati were an Order founded by Blessed John Colombini (1300–67) but who were dissolved by Clement IX in 1669, for the principal reason that their whole labour was the distilling of liqueurs and scents.[1] Because of that they had a special nickname. After their suppression the Gesuati became a convent of Dominicans, and it was for the nuns of this Order that Giambattista Tiepolo painted the ceilings and, also, an altar painting. The church is not remarkable for its architecture. It has a façade like a Palladian temple in white Istrian stone; while it even added in a way to the beauty of I Gesuati that it used to shut at nine o'clock in the morning and only open again, if at all, in the dusk of the late evening. The church is on the quay, and but a few paces from the shipping. The *trabaccoli*, the *topi*, the *bragozzi* lie outside. The water chops, chops, against the white stone steps. The smell of ships and seaweed comes in through the open door. But it is time to lift our eyes. The painted ceiling prolongs our feeling of an embarkation. This is because the painter has extended the perspective, has made an entrance into the azure of his sky, by the device of a great flight of steps. There is a stone landing stage at the church door and, on entering, you climb from the stone island straight into the clouds where the Spanish saint, St Dominic, rides in glory. It is the festival of the rosary, with the triumph of St Dominic. Tiepolo's other painting is an altarpiece of the Madonna, seated, holding the infant Jesus. A trio of Dominican nuns is in

[1] A principle inseparable from monachism in Italy. There is a liqueur, 'Gemma d'Abeto', sold by the Servite monks at the top of Monte Senario, *vide* p. 111.

the painting; St Clara caresses the child; another nun holds a crucifix; the third is rapt in meditation. They are like beautiful opera singers.

These pictures by the greatest decorative painter there has ever been, the heir of three hundred years of Venetian painting, recall the splendours of Venice which, the tombs of the Doges excepted, are missing from the two brick churches. We have in mind the great banqueting scenes of Veronese, painted for the refectories of the Venetian monasteries. There were four of these, and they were the sights of Venice. *The Marriage at Cana*, now in the Louvre, came from the refectory of San Giorgio Maggiore; the *Banquet in the House of Simon the Pharisee* came from the refectory of the Servite monks. The first of them was taken to Paris by Napoleon when the last Doge abdicated and La Serenissima had ceased to be; the second was presented by the Republic to Louis XIV, and used to hang in the Salon d'Hercule, at Versailles. It, too, is in the Louvre. The third banquet scene was in the refectory of SS Giovanni e Paolo, but was long ago destroyed by fire. The fourth painting, now at Dresden, was also in a refectory. Venetian splendour found its epitome in these banquet scenes. *The Marriage at Cana*, with its hundred and twenty figures and its scheme of Palladian architecture, must remain the expression of Venetian pride and power, even in its ruin and exile in the Louvre. When this painting and its three companion banquet scenes were the living sights of Venice, still independent and alive, these were Shakespearean dramas always playing, with the curtain ever raised. This was the great Veronese, more than in the Palace of the Doges. In imagination, we would pass the whole day in going from one to other by gondola, comparing their magnificence. And indeed nothing could be more splendid than Palladio's San Giorgio Maggiore with its campanile upon its island quay, a Benedictine foundation till not long ago desecrated idiotically into a barracks, but now cleansed and restored, so that one can enter the refectory from which *The Marriage at Cana* is sadly missing, and admire Longhena's staircase which none had been allowed to see before.

But the *terra firma* of Venice is not remarkable for its monasteries. Country convents on a big scale are lacking. It would be idle, though, to deny the title of one of the more beautiful paintings in the world to the *Baptism of Christ* by Giovanni Bellini, in the Dominican church of Santa Corona at Vicenza. This picture is beautiful enough to take one's breath away, with the very 'blueness' – however inapposite this may sound – of the blue *Baigneuses* by Renoir.[1] Mantua, Padua, other towns on the way to Verona, have little

[1] Not so, when I saw it again this summer (1964), and it was in brown tones owing to the change of light, a very signal instance of the importance stressed in old guide books of seeing the paintings in churches at particular times of day.

to offer in the way of monasteries or convents. But this is not the case at Verona, which must always have been the second city of the Venetian mainland. It has town churches, Sant 'Anastasia of the Dominicans and San Bernardino of the Franciscan friars, and two churches of Benedictine monks, San Fermo Maggiore and across the river Santa Maria in Organo, in the latter of which are choir-stalls with intarsia landscapes by Fra Giovanni da Verona who was a monk here. Neither Bergamo, nor Brescia, can compete with this; nor are there monastic remains of note in Ferrara, Modena, or Cremona; and except for the Convento di San Paolo in Parma where Correggio painted frescoes for the abbess of the Benedictine nuns, there is nothing much until we reach Milan. Spanish rule, from 1535 until the beginning of the eighteenth century, brought with it a swarming or pro-liferation of monks or nuns who were as thick on the ground as in Belgium, or in the province of Quebec. But Santa Maria delle Grazie with its choir and dome by Bramante, and Leonardo's *Last Supper* in the Dominican refectory, date from the Sforza rule.

A sensation of curious sort is to be derived from the Certosa di Pavia, with antidote near at hand at Chiaravalle in the Cistercian abbey, which is on the road to Pavia but in the suburbs of Milan. This is a brick building of the thirteenth century with round-arched octagonal steeple rising in tele-scopic stages in the Lombard-Romanesque style. Its purity of style, if seen after Milan Cathedral which is like a sham Alp, and before the Certosa, is of memorable effect. For the Certosa, through and through, is Milanese – which means carved and inlaid and never left quiet for a moment, like the suits of inlaid armour from Milan, or the carved cabinets of Milanese workmanship. Its huge bulk of brick and terracotta looms up over the Lombard plain, above the receding poplars and the mulberry trees. Coming into the fore-court of the Certosa di Pavia is to some little extent reminiscent of the Tomb of Humayun, or other Mughal monument, and more for the same identical fussiness of detail than simply because the Indian buildings are of pink or red sandstone. A cupola, climbing again in telescopic stages but colonnaded and without the round-arched openings, tallies with the façade of the church which is in 'the Lombard-Romanesque style of graduated church fronts', and the most famous of guide-books goes on to describe it as 'unquestionably the finest example of Renaissance decorative work in North Italy, and perhaps the most masterly creation of its kind of the fifteenth century'. But its 'wonderful and judiciously distributed wealth of ornament' is just exactly what makes it anathema to mid-twentieth century taste. The interior with its blue vaults painted, or 'powdered very richly', as G. E. Street has it, with gold stars and comets, the red brick and terracotta walls, and red and white

Monasteries of Northern Italy

Certosa del Galluzzo near Florence in the Val d'Ema

Padri Certosini of Galluzzo by the sixteenth-century well in the *Chiostro Grande*

Detail from Andrea da Firenze's painting of *The Church Militant and Triumphant* set against a background of Florence Cathedral

Façade of church with high double
stair at Certosa di Calci near Pisa

*St Dominic Blessing a Lay-brother of
his Order* by Giambattista Tiepolo
on ceiling of Gesuati church in
Venice

Marriage at Cana by Paolo Veronese, painted for the refectory of the monastery of San Giorgio Maggiore

Left: Fresco by Signorelli in Monte Oliveto Maggiore showing two monks enjoying forbidden hospitality outside the monastery, attended by women

Right: Monastery of Monte Oliveto Maggiore built in the fourteenth century in the '*Deserto di Accona*'

Engraving of Camaldoli with the *Eremo* on the hill-side and the *Foresteria* and
church below

Retreat of St Francis at La Verna from Moroni's *Descrizione del Sacro Monte della Vernia*

Chiostro Grande with 123 arcades at Certosa di Pavia built in the late fifteenth century

Church at Fossanova probably built by Cistercians from the mother-house of Clairvaux. Consecrated by Innocent III in 1208

Triumph of the Name of Jesus by Baciccia painted 1668–83 on ceiling of the Gesù in Rome

contrasting marbles of the pavement, are in noisy accompaniment to paintings by masters of tertiary order like Borgognone. Tombs of Gian Galeazzo Visconti, the founder, and of the Sforza Lodovico il Moro and his wife Beatrice d'Este, are wonderful in the sound, but no longer when you come to look at them. And the great cloister of the Certosa, with 'its arches exceedingly rich in terracotta ornaments', red, red, against the whitewashed walls where are maisonettes of the white-robed 'religious', makes a red and white vision of this Burghley or Wollaton of the Carthusian monks. As to the anomaly of the recluse life – led at a bare subsistence level so strict is the diet, and with duties confined to prayer, solitary meditation, and the care-taking of this most lavish of monuments – it may be pondered whether it would be any more unlikely to find monks, or, better still, nuns, tending the terraces, the orange and lemon trees, the magnolias and oleanders, where Isola Bella rides like Armida's galleon upon the waters of Lake Maggiore.[1]

The extreme pietistic tendencies of the Dukes of Savoy and Kings of Sardinia – as exemplified at Turin in the chapel of the Santissimo Sudario or Holy Shroud, Guarini's funerary masterpiece in black or dark brown marble with its trio of stepped entrances as in a theatre, two leading up for the public, and one down for the Court processions, and its cupola of trans-cendental execution perhaps influenced by ninth-century Arab cupolas Guarini may have seen in the mosque-cathedral of Cordoba, 'a receding tunnel of curved and stepped arches, their impeccable precision suggesting the carefully laid rings of a bird's nest, while at the end of the tunnel the cupola appears like a glimmering star whose pointed rays issue from the Holy Ghost in a blaze of glory'[2] – such feats might incline one to think there would be exceptional monasteries and nunneries in Piedmont. Especially as architects of the stature of Guarino Guarini and Filippo Juvara were at work there. But it is not the case. Guarini (1624–83), a Theatine monk from Modena, built churches and palaces but nothing of monastic purpose. And Juvara (1685–1735), who came from Messina and was ordained priest, built palaces and churches, but his only monastic work was the convent church of the Superga terraced on a hill above Turin, the votive offering of Vittore Amedeo II, with a huge dome and portico in classical sonata form, a belfry in more original style, and a 'suite of royal apartments' which in the guide-book phrase ('never occupied') provides its own epitaph, all glorious without,

---

[1] The Certosa di Pavia has recently been given up by the Carthusian monks and is occupied by Carmelites.

[2] *Baroque in Italy*, by James Lees-Milne, Batsford, 1959, p. 177. His book includes a chapter on Vittone; for whom, *vide*, also, *Art and Architecture in Italy, 1600–1750*, by Rudolf Wittkower, 1958, pp. 282 ff.

but dull and poor within. Third, and last of these followers of Borromini – a movement covering a long span of time when we consider that Borromini was born in 1599 – was the Piedmontese, Bernardo Vittone (1745-70), as bold in experiment as Guarini, whose memory he revered and whose posthumous *Architettura Civile* he edited and published, a master of dome and semi-dome, 'elliptical, spherical and octagonal' of all shapes and sizes, but unfortunately for our purpose his work is confined to small churches and sanctuary chapels in Turin and the nearby countryside and he built no monasteries.[1] It is indeed no part of the world for nunneries or convents. That is to say, there is no town without its Capuchins, but they are mostly poor monasteries of no interest and not contingent to these pages. Once the mendicant orders swarmed in this part of Italy, as can be deduced from almost any painting by Magnasco, the master of monkish scenes, who was born in Genoa, lived some little time in Florence while the plethora of monks still continued from the reign of Cosmo III, that faithful adherent to Jesuitical principles, but spent most of his life in Milan. In which context it is to be noted that Magnasco does not satirize the monks for their lives of supposed idleness and luxury but, rather, his fantasies are based upon their poverty. It is the desert of rocks, or Thebaid, where his monks are gathered like a gang of tramps or hoboes, and when there is a roof over their heads it is half in ruins. He painted indeed just the sort of monasteries we were mentioning, small convents of Capuchins on the hills above the Italian lakes, anywhere between Milan and Genoa, or along the Italian coast between Ventimiglia and Pisa. There is in fact nothing to detain us in Genoa, a city of churches, but no monasteries.

But neither need we halt again until we are in Pisa, and back in Tuscany, at Santo Stefano dei Cavalieri, a church of celibate knights vowed to warfare against the Turks and corsairs, seldom entered because of the greater attraction of the Cathedral, the Baptistery, and Leaning Tower, despite the marble statue of Cosmo I, founder of the Order, after Giovanni da Bologna, at its door. The church and conventual building where the Knights lived are most interesting Mannerist buildings of the time when genius had left Florence and eccentricity had set in. There should be painted halls in the Palazzo Conventuale, the note of which is sounded by the busts of six Masters of the Order over the windows, but it is a school and is not shown. Both this and the church which are from designs by Vasari could be said to

---

[1] The following are works by this little known architect: Santa Maria della Piazza in Turin; San Bernardino at Chieri; the Assunta at Riva, near Chieri; and the sanctuary church at Vallinotto. All are on a small scale, and the interest is in his juggling with their domes and lanterns. He was the Cinquevalli (famous conjurer) of his kind.

pertain to the world of Jacques Callot and Stefano della Bella, and to their frontispieces for theatrical entertainments of the Medicean princes, whose strange busts including that of the semi-Habsburg Cardinal Leopoldo de Medici, founder of the picture collections at the Pitti and Uffizi, stand at the head of the staircase at the latter and will have haunted and inhabited other childhoods besides my own.[1] The church of the Knights which is exceedingly curious, has Turkish trophies and ceiling paintings of the Battle of Lepanto; with, as it were, an appendix or supplement in the statue of Grand-duke Ferdinand I, himself a former Cardinal, with four chained Turkish galley-slaves with shaved heads, 'I quattro Mori', on the harbour-side at Spezia, a few miles away.

Inland from Pisa at about the same distance is the Certosa di Calci, a Certosa which leaves a most pleasing impression on the memory from the moment of seeing the white bearded monk-doorkeeper, bowed with age, slow moving like a tortoise, and the crowd of old and infirm as in the Middle Ages feeding at the cloister door. The monastery, of mediaeval foundation, was largely rebuilt in the seventeenth century. Its huge white cloister, and the façade of the church with high double stair in front of it, all flashing white, are in a charming provincial Baroque which has nothing in it of the bat-winged volutes of the Tuscan decadence; instead one is reminded of provincial towns like Massa, only a few miles away, which was once an independent Duchy. The church has paintings by Poccetti, who worked at the Certosa del Galluzzo and decorated the Tribuna of the Uffizi, and by Stefano Cassiani, a Carthusian monk from Lucca; the Foresteria Granducale has charming, if meaningless frescoed decoration, Italianate, but as though in some monastery in Austria; while in the refectory the subjects of the frescoes, all by a certain Giarre, are worth noting. They include the Banquets of Herod, the Pharisee, the Prodigal Son, and the Marriage at Cana; and two quasi-secular subjects, Catherine de Medici serving the Carthusian fathers at repast in the Chartreuse at Paris, and the Grand-duke Cosimo III, white-wigged and white-moustached, a practising religious maniac, father of the egregious Gian Gastone, last of the Medici, dining in this very refectory with the monks and making conversation with the prior, while the monks ranged to each side of him their white hoods on their heads and absolved from silence for this festive occasion, held their tongues and would not speak. How beautiful this old monastery was on the two occasions that I have been there! It is only sad that the Certosa di Calci of peaceful and pastoral air has passed out of Carthusian hands.

But we are now in that part of all Italy which is the most fertile for genius

[1] The Medici busts are now downstairs in the Uffizi where their effect is totally lost.

in the arts, where it would be impossible to follow the monks into every corner of their activity. In Siena alone their presence is inextricably involved with the history of all the works of art, whether typified in a little but particular instance, as in the painting by Neroccio of St Dominic and two other saints offering the robe of the Dominican Order to St Catherine, which is one of the most beautiful paintings of the Sienese school; in pictures by Sassetta who was pre-eminently the painter of the Franciscan legend; or in all that has to do with either St Catherine or San Bernardino of Siena. It could amount to nothing less than a deflection into a long account of Sienese painting in which these two saintly figures are of perpetual occurrence.

Such are spiritual, more than material beauties of monasticism. But we leave aside the small monasteries in the country round Siena, whatever paintings they may hold by Sano di Pietro, or Matteo di Giovanni, in order to go further afield to Monte Oliveto Maggiore. This monastery of the Olivetans, who are a branch of the Benedictines founded early in the fourteenth century by Bernardo Tolomei, lies in a wild tormented landscape of volcanic aspect much resembling the Auvergne. It is built of bricks made from the red clay of the surrounding hills that have been worn by wind and rain and then baked by the sun into a strange, wild roughness. Fierce ridges, only a few hundred feet high, are worked into a whole Himalaya of peaks and chains. The road to Monte Oliveto Maggiore leads along one of these ridges towards the isolated peninsula where the monastery stands. It is a great old abbey with all its dependencies, of a kind we have not seen since the Certosa di Pavia, but very different from that. In its great cloister is the series of frescoes by Luca Signorelli, masculine and authoritarian in draughtsmanship and temperamental forerunner of Michelangelo. Only eight of the paintings are by Signorelli, and in these it is quickly apparent that the white-clad Olivetan monks are of less interest to the painter than the knights and young warriors accompanying Totila, King of the Goths, in these scenes from the Legend of St Benedict taken, with monkish additions, from the *Dialogues* of St Gregory the Great.

The warriors in Signorelli's frescoes wear clothes almost exactly of the same date and style as those still worn by the different city wards of Siena not twenty miles away at the celebration of the Palio. His warriors are prinked out in the piebald finery of the day, but are huge Germanic giants taller than any Italian, with long fair hair falling over their shoulders. This is sufficiently indicated in the phrase of a book written by a modern monk of Monte Oliveto Maggiore, who says of them, 'masse di biondi capelli sfuggendo da piccoli barretti cadono sulle loro spalle', words which surely are in no need of translation. A pair of mounted knights in one of the frescoes is most wonderfully portrayed, their mail being painted a cold, watery blue, such as our age, to whom armour is extinct, has never had brought before its eyes. The foot soldiers are no less gorgeous of accoutrement. Their hose is of white, blue, and red, worn in its alternations of each leg so that the tongues or flames of red that flicker at ankle and knee into the white ground of the stocking are answered with their equivalent blue at the knee and ankle of the other leg. Their arms, chests, and backs are plated, and they wear long swords at their waists, while the blue steel of their halberds shines against the rocks above them. The strangeness of the landscape inspired Signorelli and gave him the background for this magpie, piebald finery. These eight panels apart, the rest of the frescoes are by Sodoma, of significant appellation, in talented pastiche of Signorelli, but trailing off into the picture-book style of Pinturicchio. The church at Monte Oliveto Maggiore is uninteresting; and there is not much else except a pharmacy where the white-clad Olivetans make a liqueur from twenty-eight local plants.

A Thebaid of another sort altogether lies on the slopes of the Apennines, in that most pleasing part of Tuscany known as the Casentino. Here are found the hermits of Camaldoli, living in their cells in the high woods. Their foundation by St Romuald, a nobleman of Ravenna, as early as the year 1012, preserves for us the dress of humble persons of the eleventh century, nearly a thousand years ago. It is a white woollen habit, and with the monks of Camaldoli there is an air that is half-Druidical. These Tuscan hermits, each dwelling in his little separate hermitage, are priests of the oak trees and the Vallombrosan shades. For half the year they have to sweep the snow away in order to pass from their cells to the convent chapel. The hood of their white habit is of a different shape from the mediaeval hoods of other orders of monks. It is of an earlier age before the birth of painting. The rebuilt church of Camaldoli, and the Foresteria with customary output of monastic liqueurs including 'Lacrima d'Abeto', a concoction from pine trees, not to be confused with the 'Gemma d'Abeto' of Monte Senario – and which prepares as well 'la vera triaca della ricetta de Andromaco', whatever that may be – is a thousand feet below the Eremo where dwell the hermits in two rows of cells, ten to a side, with a flagged path between them. An eighteenth-century English monk, Dom Ignatius Hugford, painted some of the altar pictures in the church of these rare hermits.[1]

---

[1] Twenty-two in number, including three recluses, according to a recent writer, *Worlds Apart: A Tour of European Monasteries*, by Tudor Edwards, Longmans, Green & Co., 1958, p. 103. But, formerly, there were other monasteries of the order including that of Bielany, near Cracow, of which I have seen and admired the seventeenth-century white Baroque church. There was, also, a convent of these hermit-monks at another Bielany, outside Warsaw.

La Verna, a most sacred spot in the Franciscan legend, only a few miles from Camaldoli, has three chapels with della Robbia plaques in bright colours and the caves or 'luoghi santi' of St Francis hidden in the beech woods and among the balsamic pine trees. The purity of the air in this sacred forest makes the della Robbia plaques the most beautiful in all Tuscany. There exists an old book of very special character which has for subject this Thebaid of La Verna, and its woodcuts reproduce the woods and the rocks of that wilderness as no camera has ever been able to do so that they are indeed the best witness after the personal evidence of one's own eyes.[1] As to the church of St Francis in Assisi, it grows weekly, if not daily, more difficult to appreciate it in any peace of mind owing to the bus-loads of pilgrims, worse still, those persons who enter it and are out again noisily in ten minutes. And the frescoes in both churches by Giotto's pupils, but in the Upper Church in particular, are rapidly approaching the state of Leonardo's *Last Supper* in that appreciation is forced and there is in fact little aesthetic pleasure to be had from them. The church of St Francis is beautiful in idea, and from a distance, but it must always yield both in interest and as a work of art to St Mark's in Venice, or to San Vitale. But, also, it is not in churches or convents of the Franciscan Order that we come to look for works of art, unless, that is to say, they have overstepped their own rules of poverty and simplicity. The Franciscan values are spiritual more than they are aesthetic, and they have not the magnificence in simplicity of the Cistercian structures.

If we leave Tuscany now for the States of the Church in search of great monasteries and convents it will begin and end in disappointment. The old Badia Santa Maria in Pomposa, of fine name, lying out in the marshes between Venice and Ravenna, and made uninhabitable by malaria within a hundred years or so of its foundation, has an eleventh-century basilica and campanile and is inaccessible enough to confer a kind of distinction on those who have been there, which does not include the writer. The small duchies like Ferrara or Urbino claimed by the Papacy as vacant fiefs on the extinction of their reigning families and annexed into the Papal dominions, were never rich enough to build large monasteries, and this state of affairs was not reversed under the Cardinal Legate who later ruled them from Bologna. The second city of the Papal States was a town of priests and churches, not of monks and nuns. But, if a note of personal reminiscence may be allowed to creep in, how well I remember long talks with the lay-brother who showed the church of San Domenico at Bologna in the winter of 1919, but

---

[1] Lino Moroni, *La Descrizione del Sacro Monte della Vernia*, 1612, with twenty woodcuts by Jacopo Ligozzi. In one or two of them, Repton's 'invention' two hundred years later, of lifting a leaf of paper to alter the view, is put into use.

indeed I had known and loved this city long before that, as witness a letter written to my brother from Bologna, under date 14 May 1908.[1] San Domenico is the only considerable monastery in the town, and it is the saint's tomb by Niccolo Pisano with its kneeling angel by Michelangelo that is the famed attraction, though it was the inlaid choir-stalls by his fellow Dominican, Fra Damiano da Bergamo that interested my friend the lay-brother, and over which we pored as in the pages of some huge illuminated missal. He was, he told me, one of only three or four monks in the mon-astery; and in general there are more priests than monks in this city of arcades. Whether it is correct to infer from this that the one order or system of celibates does not encourage the other is an open question, but of a certainty what monasteries there are, are small and unimportant. It is a truism which applies to all those towns, Perugia, Orvieto, Viterbo, which were small provincial centres in the Papal States.

When we arrive at Rome where every monastic order had, we could almost call it diplomatic representation, it is to find this, too, upon a dis-appointing scale. San Paolo fuori le Mura, it is true, is the church of a Benedictine monastery and has a famous twelfth-century cloister but it was devastated by fire more than a century ago and is largely reconstructed. The famous church of the Capuchins in the Via Veneto is typical; altar paintings by Guido Reni and Pietro da Cortona, and four burial vaults down gloomy steps wherein are arranged, more than stacked, the skulls and bones of some four thousand 'departed Capuchins'. It was here, as so often elsewhere, a luxury of bones with the Capuchin friars; and their dramatic representations apart, which also partook of the *Totentanz* or Dance of Death, the luxuries of art are not to be expected of them. It is very different in the instance of the Jesuits, in their churches of Il Gesù and Sant' Ignazio; and perhaps it has been sufficiently stressed already that the ceiling painting by Baciccia and Fratel Pozzo's altar with lapis lazuli columns in the former church, and his ceiling painted in perspective at the latter, are key works in the development of Baroque all over Central Europe. Contributing, also, to the theatrical effect of Sant' Ignazio is the piazza in front of it where Raguzzini, a follower of Borromini, has arranged the houses like the wings of a theatre with the converging streets like the traditional entrances upon a stage.

The searcher after great abbeys, not content with the Sepolti Vivi nuns visited by Augustus Hare,[2] or other stories of austerities, must go far afield from Rome with a first halt perhaps at the Certosa di Trisulti. This is to say

---

[1] Quoted in *The Scarlet Tree*, 1946, pp. 273, 274.

[2] The 'buried alive' nuns mentioned by Augustus Hare in his *Autobiography* existed in Rome until 1876, when they were dissolved.

that neither the three monasteries at Subiaco, however beautiful their mountain setting, nor the monastery of Basilian (Greek) monks at Grottaferrata, which has good frescoes by Domenichino in one of its chapels, entirely qualify for admission as great or remarkable monastic buildings. But, if it is not particularly old, though of ancient foundation, the Certosa di Trisulti at least presents the image of a great monastery. It is near Alatri, in the country of the sandal-wearers or 'ciocciari', about sixty miles south of Rome; 'a vast building on the last edge of a rocky platform', close under the snows, and reached through 'a wood of old oaks carpeted with lilies', and Augustus Hare, no lover of the eighteenth century, says of the Certosa di Trisulti that 'though modernised, its well kept courts and fountains have a beauty of their own'. There is, or was, for now it has been given up by the Carthusians and taken over by Cistercians, something touchingly old and beautiful and unspoilt about this monastery with its church and flowering cloister with a fountain in the middle, and one of the more intriguing of monastic pharmacies, upon the products of which a special cachet was conferred by the monogram of the Carthusians upon every article for sale. Trisulti fills a place in the memory beside so many more Certosas, at Calci, at Galluzzo,[1] at San Martino above Naples, at Burgos, Jerez, and elsewhere in Spain, not forgetting the Grande Chartreuse itself in the mountains of Dauphiné.

But there are other, and older abbeys in the 'ciocciaria'; that of Casamari, in Burgundian-Cistercian style of the early thirteenth century, and therefore unique in Latium except for its sister-abbey of Fossanova. Casamari, which is only a few miles from Trisulti, is the less interesting but it is still a monastery only, while Fossanova has become a school. Augustus Hare says of the church of Casamari that 'the cream-coloured tint of the travertine is as fresh as when it was built', but in the hundred years since his time the interior light has become more golden, perhaps because the panes of alabaster have been put back into the rose and lancet windows. There is a vaulted chapter-house at Casamari, and by this time it would be a disappointment indeed were there no pharmacy. Fossanova, in this same country but nearer to the seashore on the way to Terracina, where St Thomas Aquinas died in 1274, has a refectory and chapter-house of great beauty, an octagonal tower, and a church which could well stand in the Burgundian vineyards; while a recent newspaper article observes that 'the ancient custom, familiar from the miniatures of illuminated manuscripts, of planting hooped briars as orchard hedges' survives still in this countryside.[2]

[1] But those of Galluzzo, of Calci, of Pavia, of Trisulti, are now abandoned by the Carthusian monks. This Order seems to flourish less in Italy than Spain.

[2] *The Times* for Saturday, 29 June 1963.

*Opposite: The Virgin Protecting the Order of
Cîteaux by Jan Provoost*

And now, not without a certain relief, we are in Southern Italy, in the old Kingdom of Naples or the Two Sicilies, where the restraining hand of the Papacy had to be exercised across the frontier, and therefore it was the kingdom without limit of the monks and nuns. Perhaps Monte Cassino, destroyed in the fearful battle, was disappointing just because it was so famous a Benedictine centre and had therefore too great an air of sophistication. It was founded by St Benedict on a mountain-top which had been the site of a temple of Apollo, in fact, as so often was the case, upon pagan foundations, and now it is only possible to describe Monte Cassino as remembered from the past. After the long climb up the hill its arcaded courtyard or forecourt with a fountain in the middle seemed the best part of the monastery. The church had bronze doors made in Byzantium in 1066 and paid for by a merchant of Amalfi, and was rich, too rich in marbles. It had the ceiling of its nave and another huge fresco painted by Luca Giordano; and there were four great pictures by Solimena, probably his best work, in the choir, but somehow, the church at Monte Cassino was neither Roman nor Neapolitan, and certainly other decorations in the abbey, and in particular, frescoes by 'members of the Benedictine Order from the art school of Beuron Abbey in Hohenzollern, under the supervision of *Father Desiderius*, and executed in the delicate but strictly formal style developed at Beuron on Egyptian and early-Christian models', did not dispel this impression. Monte Cassino is almost exactly half-way between Rome and Naples, and it is not long before we are out of the mountains and in the Campania Felix, nearing Capua and Caserta, in that country where the vines are wreathed from tree to tree. What more fitting approach could there be to the city which Dr Burney apostrophizes in his *Musical Tour* (1786) as the capital of music!

But, also, in the sense that there were more of the fraternity of monks and nuns in Naples than in any other city of the world, Rome included, it is their capital as well. And for a picture of the siren city at its height of fame there is no better authority than the *Voyage en Italie* of M de Lalande (Genève, 1790) written at a time when the Neapolitan school of painters, including artists like Solimena, whom Fragonard on his Italian travels did not disdain to copy, were still admired. In 1742 there were in Naples nearly five thousand monks belonging to forty-five different orders, and more than three thousand nuns of thirteen orders. Fifty years later in de Lalande's day their number will have doubled. He described churches of the Augustins Déchaussés (Discalced Augustinians), Franciscans, Capuchins, Carmelites, Cordeliers, Osservanti, Olivetans, Dominicans, Servites, Franciscan nuns, Minori Riformati, Celestins, Theatines, Minims, Carmes, Déchaussés, a mere fourteen of the fifty-eight denominations mentioned, and besides listing all the frescoes and altar paintings by forgotten painters in their churches he gives intriguing details, as, of the Gesù Nuovo[1]: 'Il y avoit aussi une apothicairerie fameuse, qui étoit dirigée en 1765 par un Jésuite François', and of the monastery of Monte Oliveto, one of the most famous in Naples; 'Le bibliothéque du couvent est considérable, aussi-bien que l'apothicairerie, qui donne sur la rue de Tólede, et qui est renommée pour les odeurs, les pommades, et les savons parfumés qu'on y débite.' There is, also, much talk of the 'pompe éclatante' of the religious processions. But, from all this plethora of detail on which there is no space to elaborate, one or two instances must be excepted that show the extraordinary character of the Parthenopean City. I would stress from long knowledge of Naples, the sacristy of San Domenico Maggiore with ceiling painted by Solimena, with its wooden gallery reached by a stair where, piled one on another, are forty-five wooden coffins covered with ragged scarlet or green velvet in which lie the bodies of the princes and princesses of the House of Aragon, rulers of Naples in the late fifteenth and early sixteenth centuries. The sacristan would open two or three of the coffins and show one the mummified bodies in their tattered finery. I would mention, also, San Paolo Maggiore, of the Theatine monks, for the reason that its portico is that of a classical temple of Castor and Pollux, with two of its Corinthian columns and part of the architrave still standing, and because of its sacristy with two great frescoes, white horses conspicuous in them, by Solimena, a sacristy which was one of the curiosities of Naples and which Fragonard drew in part for one of the engravings in the *Voyage Pittoresque* of the Abbé de Saint-Non. But, best of all in this wonderful old city, the cloister of San Paolo Maggiore may be on the site of the theatre in which Nero appeared as actor.

Where nunneries are concerned I would mention the church and convent of San Gregorio Armeno, little known and at one time almost impossible of entry, but it is among the wonders of Southern Italy. The painting and gilding in the church are of the sixteenth century; the nuns' choir, seraglio-screened and latticed, is romantic and beautiful, as is the sight of the nuns in their black and scarlet habits. Many years ago when further entry was forbidden, one used to conjecture what could be in the cloister of this convent. Now it is shown and, also, the marvellous upstairs passage running parallel to the nave of the church along its south side, a corridor for which I do not know

[1] It is the Gesù Nuovo, with its façade of stones cut into diamond points and the fantastic monument or Guglia del Gesù at its door, which has the huge fresco over its entrance of Heliodorus driven out of the Temple, painted by Solimena in his eighteenth year. This fresco, one of the pyrotechnical feats of the school of Naples, has an extraordinary resemblance in handling and execution, to the 'grands sujets' or 'grandes machines' of Delacroix.

the correct name, but seldom, if ever, has one seen anything come down so entire out of the past with the wonderful and inexplicable junk of all kinds ranged down its whole length. And Santa Chiara is left till last which I remember when two of the nun-princesses were still alive who had been in the convent since before the Bourbon Kingdom of Naples fell in 1861. This was in 1920; and an old maid-servant sat all day to answer callers in front of the convent grille in her cap or bonnet of strange shape and dress of early nineteenth century. A Franciscan monk from the Trentino, Padre Clemente, dead long ago, but a friend of mine, showed the church and cloister. This was when the church with Sebastiano Conca's ceiling painting of *David dancing before the Ark* was like a gilded ballroom, and only wanted mirrors on the walls; and Padre Clemente would take one up above the tomb of the Angevin King Robert the Wise (d. 1343) at the high altar and show one the tombs of the Bourbon Kings, which no one ever asked to see, in a gallery over the choir. At a grille behind the high altar one could peer into the choir itself, but the nun-princesses owing to their age could seldom, if ever, take their places.

American airmen who mistook the church and its huge cloister for the main railway station dropped their bombs on Santa Chiara to strange effect, because the church was 'restored' on the instant from the eighteenth to the thirteenth century, and when the dust and rubble were removed revealed itself as a vessel of pure Gothic. The Gothic tombs in Santa Chiara are of extreme interest. The volcanic turbulence of Naples, the strangled cardinal and decapitated princess apart, whose mummied bodies one used to be shown at the Castel Nuovo, through its Renaissance triumphal archway down a dark and winding stair, is exemplified in just one of the tombs. It is that of Raimondo Cabano (1336), the Saracen slave, a major-domo under Robert I, who became Grand Seneschal of the Kingdom, having married Filippa, originally a washerwoman of Catania, who had been raised to the position of a kind of governess to Joanna I. It was he who incited his royal mistress to the murder of her husband Andrea, and for this his wife, who survived him, with her children Robert and Sanchia, were tortured with hot pincers through the streets of Naples, after Charles of Durazzo had entered the city.[1] Other, and beautiful tombs are to titular Emperors and Empresses of Constantinople; and to a young girl who died on her fourteenth birthday, on the day appointed for her wedding. Beyond the church of Santa Chiara is the cloister of the Poor Clares of Naples which, again, is one of the glories of the South. Its walks are trellised with vines and lined with majolica tiles from Capodimonte. The octagonal columns all along are wreathed with

[1] *Cf.* Augustus Hare, *Cities of Southern Italy and Sicily.*

china fruits and flowers, or with spilling cornucopias in blue and yellow; while the benches have views of Vesuvius and the Bay of Naples, classical ruins, and even scenes from popular drama with Pulcinella in black mask and flopping white shirt and trousers. He was there, at least, in 1920, though I could no longer find him in 1957.

The cloisters of Santa Chiara and of San Gregorio Armeno which for their quiet in the midst of all the noise of Naples, and for their inaccessibility through the centuries, are as patches of moonlight in all the roar and clamour of the heat, have their rival in the Certosa di San Martino. It is unforgivable that the monks are no longer here, though on one occasion I caught sight of a monk working in a corner of the garden, and one or two monks are in fact allowed here, though seldom, if ever seen. For the flashing white architecture of Cosimo Fansaga was a background to the white-clad Carthusian fathers; and here, if anywhere, the Neapolitan school of painters is to be appreciated for it has examples of the work of every artist from Cavaliere d'Arpino to Bonito, who died in 1789. And this Certosa is a place of contrasts and conflicting points of view. In the Tesoro or Treasury there are cupboards and presses of inlaid wood on which, it is said, two Carthusian monks spent twelve years of their lives. They show landscapes and empty piazzas, and still lifes as formal as those of the Cubist painters, with piles of books, vases of flowers, and often a guitar lying among them that Picasso might have left there. While above, on a cupola and down the ceiling of the room, there are frescoes by Luca Giordano which he painted on his return from Spain, loaded with honours and seventy-two years old, non-stop, in forty-eight hours. Such are the contrasts of this Certosa, which at the time Sir John Swinburne visited it in 1779, had an income, though reduced, of £130,000 a year. And at the end of a long passage is the Belvedere of the monks, a balcony looking over Naples with an immortal view of the volcano and the bay, and with the sounds coming up from the city below as if but a few feet away. What a contrast, this, from the balcony of the white monks of the Certosa to the vine-shaded, or moonlit cloisters of Santa Chiara and San Gregorio Armeno in all the hubbub and the shouting of the warm South!

The pilgrimage shrine of all Naples and the Compania Felix was the convent on Montevergine, near Avellino about sixty miles from Naples, where the writer went, happily, before the funicular was working. It lies four thousand feet up on the ledge of a mountain where in classical times was a temple of Cybele, and a winding road with a view now and then of the smoking cone of Vesuvius leads to it through woods of chestnut trees. The court of the convent for six months of the year is covered with snow, and it is only in May in time for the Whitsun pilgrims that the abbot comes up to live here. A miraculous picture of the Virgin brought from Byzantium is the attraction, and there are tombs of the Angevin princes of Naples, but all is mountain-cold and grim. The spirit has gone from Montevergine, and no longer is the return of the pilgrims 'often twenty thousand in number, welcomed by crowds taking up position about 5 p.m. in the streets skirting the harbour', a festival on the scale of the Festa di Piedigrotta which was attended by the Royal Family in golden coaches driven by coachmen in full-bottomed wigs, with running footmen making way beside them. Not to be missed at Montevergine is the Palazzo Badiale di Loreto, which is a white octagonal building of the eighteenth century by Giovanni Antonio Vaccaro where the abbot and older monks live most of the year in order to escape the cold. It is here that the Bourbon Kings stayed in rooms still hung with their portraits as though they might be arriving next week, and with Flemish tapestries upon the walls. The monks, though Benedictine, wear white habits as they move about in this white octagon, and not the least of the delights of the Loreto is its well-stocked pharmacy.

The Riviera of Amalfi, which I used to know so well, has its monasteries; its Camaldoli dell' Avvocata, where I have climbed; its nuns, of Maiori, who made a liqueur they called a Concierto out of twenty herbs; and its Benedictine abbey of La Trinità della Cava, now a public school, and it is in fact not worth the climb. But the lodestone that drew one to it from the distance was the Certosa di Padula, a hundred miles south of Naples, long past the temples of Paestum and beyond Monte Alburno, so much beloved by Virgil, deep indeed in the Basilicata, just short of Lagonegro, and seemingly impossible of access. This was in the days when one was told that to be the station-master at Paestum was a death sentence owing to malaria. I really think I and my brother were the first Englishmen to get there since the eighteenth century or at least since the Napoleonic wars. When reached at last the Certosa di Padula was of vast size, with three courts or cloisters, and I distinctly remember the four-poster bedsteads still in some of the monks' cells. But the unique feature at Padula is the Belvedere or double open stair at the far end of the monastery, a masterpiece of its sort by Gaetano Barba, and a development from the open stairs of Ferdinando Sanfelice which are to be seen in several of the palaces at Naples. Wartime conversion into a concentration camp was an unromantic episode in the history of this Certosa in what was of intent a remote part of the world. Only an equal passage of years has elapsed between now and my first visit to the Certosa di Padula, as between then and the time when it could be written of a nearby provincial capital that it 'had the aspect of a small Spanish town, and its male inhabitants, with pointed hats like witches, had a very singular appearance'. In fact, it was still the Calabrian brigand country of Fra Diavolo; and on interminable train journeys in that land from Naples to Reggio, or Reggio to Taranto, and *vice versa*, fellow travellers spoke, as though the cardinal directions were reversed, of going north to Naples for sun, out of the gloomy woods, the malarial plains, and mountains.

It was just such a journey in daytime of eleven or twelve hours that brought my brother and I from Salerno to Brindisi in April or May of 1921 in order to see the churches and palaces of Lecce. With a mountain climb at walking pace and many tunnels before we reached Potenza; then down to Metaponto where was once a Greek city on the Ionian Sea; along the coast to Taranto of which one could see little from the train window; and at last to Brindisi from which it was but an hour more to Lecce. There was a peculiarity about the hotel in Lecce which I think is worth mentioning. We were never allowed to pay for our meals. The restaurant was frequented by the leading inhabitants of the town, and it was their custom to entertain any foreign visitors who came. Yet they never spoke to us, and we never met them. When had this custom begun; and one is tempted to ask how long did it continue? It was a linking with the past of a sort to which I only know one parallel. This was when I was told as a child in Venice that the Caffè Florian in the Piazza had been open night and day since the eighteenth century. A row of strange-looking cabs, 'Berlinas', they were called, was drawn up near the hotel at Lecce and must date, I remember thinking, from the time when 'King Bomba' (Ferdinand II) lay dying here. But when I went to Lecce again from Brindisi six years ago the 'Berlinas' were still waiting.

Our concern with Lecce is with its buildings;[1] and for our special purpose these are Santa Croce of the Celestines, Santa Chiara which was Franciscan, il Carmine of the Carmelites, and Sant' Irena of the Theatines. In fact a city of monks and nuns. Santa Croce is the church of the Celestine convent, which is where 'King Bomba' lay so ill, it having been turned into a royal palace by Murat when he was King of Naples. The Celestines

---

[1] First brought to notice, a cursory mention by Gregorovius apart, by Mr Martin Shaw Briggs' *In the Heel of Italy*, 1910, though two hundred years before this no less a figure than the philosopher, Bishop Berkeley, wrote of the incomparable buildings of which he had never seen the like. I was, also, fired with enthusiasm to see Lecce by my father, one of the few Englishmen to have been there. Bishop Berkeley writes: 'The most beautiful city in Italy lies in the heel. Lecce, the ancient Aletium, is the most luxurious in all ornaments of architecture of any town that I have ever seen. I have not in all Italy seen such fine convents . . . Surely there is not a like rich architecture in the world.' *Bishop Berkeley: His Life, Writings, and Philosophy*, by J. M. Hare and M. M. Rossi, London, 1931, pp. 103, 105, 106. Bishop Berkeley's notes on Sicily are lost, but he visited an Italian poet and philosopher at Modica and so, almost certainly, saw Noto.

were an order founded by Pope Celestine V, whose hermitage was on a
hillside above Sulmona. As to the degree of austerity practised by the
'hermits' there are conflicting opinions. Hermitesses of the Celestine Order
wore a white habit with a pale blue scapulary. Decidedly their monastery at
Leece was no hermitage. It is the work of Zimbalo, one of the two great
Leccese architects, and is the finest building in the town. The rusticated
pilasters of its façade, all of the golden local stone, make a foil for two storeys
of windows which are as the richest of picture or mirror frames of about
1680 date. The façade of Santa Croce, itself, with its balcony and rose-
window is of earlier date but the hand of Zimbalo, too, can be detected in it.
Cino, the pupil of Zimbalo, built Santa Chiara and Sant' Irena; and Zimbalo,
the Rosario, with huge stone bowls of flowers and fruit on its façade at which
birds are pecking, and with a huge cloister which is certainly by him.[1] At
Lecce it is wholly an art of façade. A visit to the interior of one church is
enough; their interiors are all the same; huge altars with twisted pillars
aswarm with *amorini* carved in the friable white pumice-like stone which
hardens, after carving, and turns golden. It can never be stressed too much
that this part of Italy, two hundred and fifty miles from Naples, is another
country altogether from either Rome or Naples, and not in the least, as
has been said, like Spain.

Little towns in the neighbourhood of Lecce, Galatina, Nardo, Copertino,
are full of churches, and among them, nunneries. But there is little else in
the heel of Italy, unless it be at Matera which I have not seen. The great
convent or Certosa of Santo Stefano del Bosco that had been founded by St
Bruno, where he was abbot until his death in 1101, was knocked to pieces by
the earthquake of 1783. It was in the fir-tree forest of the Serra San Bruno
and its splendours, as those of the Dominican convent of San Domenico
Soriano, nearby, also destroyed by earthquake, must be taken on trust for
there are no reliable prints or drawings of them in their prime. It is like an
emergence from another world to come out from the dark forests of Calabria
down to the Straits of Messina where are orange and lemon groves and
brakes of oleander. The airs smell of orange blossom; the town of Reggio
is modern; and Messina is opposite, the destruction of which in the earthquake of 1906 was a loss to architecture, and to the Baroque in particular, for
it had its own school of architects and of painters quite distinct from those
working in Palermo or Catania, and it perished at a time before there was
enough interest in this style of building for it to be photographed. There are

---

[1] It was the pillars from this cloister that my father, ahead of his day, wanted to copy for his
lake pavilion at Renishaw. Its sixteen pillars were to have 'capitals with water lilies at the corners,
as with the quadrangle at Lecce'. *Cf. Laughter in the Next Room*, 1949, p. 266.

only, indeed, stray drawings by travelling painters attracted to it by the picturesque. Messina had narrow, steep streets crowded with churches and convents; and in particular the Salita di San Gregorio which 'by a succession of staircases led to the fantastic conventual church of San Gregorio', built on the site of a temple of Jupiter, 'from ridiculous designs by Andrea Calamech', but Hare who so qualifies it only spurs our interest. San Gregorio had in fact a spiral tower and an interior on the plan of a Greek cross, all worked with *pietre dure*, like, therefore, the chapel in the cathedral at Monreale. The balustraded platform or terrace in front of San Gregorio, looking over the Straits to Italy, must have had one of the great views of the world.

Catania, down the east coast of Sicily, has its huge Benedictine convent of San Nicolò, rebuilt by the monk Fra Giovanni Battista Vaccarini after the earthquake of 1693; in actual dimensions larger than any convent in Europe, the palace-convent of Mafra in Portugal excepted, with two tiers of carved stalls in its church to accommodate two hundred singers, and vast dormitories six hundred feet in length, so long that they finish in a point of light. But the town of Noto, inland and beyond Syracuse, of which I may claim to be the discoverer for I do not believe that anyone of whatever nationality had noticed or paid any attention to its architecture until I went there in 1922, is one of the beauties of Europe and is to be preferred to Lecce. The convents of Noto have the most graceful and splendid of iron grilles. Coming into the town from the railway station there is a convent on the right of the road, with magnificent carved windows, the top flight of which have no rooms behind them, but give direct on to the blue sky. Across the road is another convent of the same type; and though this does not of course apply to convents, Noto is the city of balconies. The bulbous grilles of the convent windows and the higher hedgehog-grilles of the convent towers are among the memories of Noto. Towns further inland, Modica and the two Ragusas, have great churches standing at the heads of huge flights of stone stairs, and many convents, the chief architect being named Sinatra; while, beyond again, are other towns, Vittoria and Comiso, the latter laid out on a spider-web plan with radiating streets where there must be convents of graceful and lovely exterior, if there is nothing much inside.

Of monastic interest at Palermo there is the cloister to the Benedictine monastery at Monreale, a Romanesque cloister to equal Moissac or Santo Domingo de Silos. Those persons who take delight in the stuccowork of Serpotta, which does not come into our subject because the three little Oratorios of Santa Zita, San Lorenzo, and the Compagnia del Rosario that contain his work at Palermo are lay confraternities and not convents, and who are of opinion that his particular genius was appropriate and well suited to

Old Kingdom of the Two Sicilies

Façade of Santa Croce at Lecce (Apulia) started by Francesco Zimbalo in the sixteenth century but completed only about 1700

Street of palaces and convents with bulbous wrought-iron balconies in Noto (Sicily)

Left: Fountain in courtyard of Seminario at Lecce by Giuseppe Cino, pupil of Zimbalo

Twelfth-century cloister in Benedictine monastery of Monreale in Sicily with inlaid columns and carved capitals

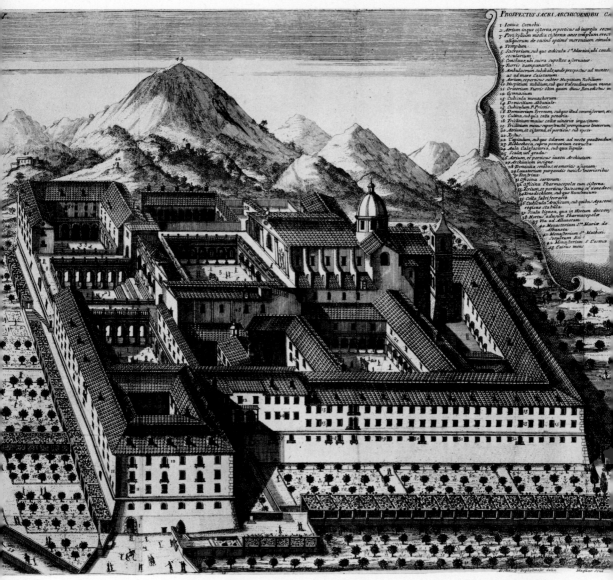

Benedictine abbey of Monte Cassino in the eighteenth century, from Erasmo Gattola's *Historia Abbatiae Cassinensis*

Above right: Garden cloister of Neapolitan convent of San Gregorio Armeno, with Christ and the Woman of Samaria at the Fountain by Matteo Bottiglieri

Right: Vine-trellises and eighteenth-century majolica tiles in cloister of Poor Clares at Santa Chiara, Naples

Detail of double stair by Gaetano Barba at Certosa di San Lorenzo, Padula (Campania)

the nuns, must look for him at Alcamo, fifty miles away, where he is to be seen in Santa Chiara and the octagonal Badia Nuova. But, in general, interest diminishes until it becomes a question of convent sweets and ices, the nuns of Palermo being the real inventors of the *cassata Siciliana*, just as, and it is Salvatore di Giacomo who retails the information, the nuns of Santa Catarina at Palermo were famous for candied pumpkin and blancmange – but it must have been something different from the dreaded blancmange of an English childhood – and he gives instances, some of them with names that give a slight shock, of other sweets and particular dishes supplied for special occasions from the convents of Palermo. In like manner the nuns of Lisbon, and of far away cities such as Lima in Peru, were famed for their sweets and ices. We have travelled in fact a long way from the austere hermits of Camaldoli, but this is Sicily.

4

Monasteries in Spain
and Portugal

THAT tendency of the English, or as many of them who are at all interested in such things, to underrate their own architecture, paintings, or works of literature, in favour of the French who are by nature disposed to agree with them in this matter, is nowhere more manifest than with the mediaeval abbeys which in large preponderance form the subject of these pages. And if, temperamentally, we show the same indulgence towards anything Italian, but find the graceful excesses of the German eighteenth century difficult to stomach, it would perhaps be true to say that our more serious competitor in this field is Spain. For three or four reasons. First, the uninterrupted activity of the Spaniards in abbey building for a thousand years until indeed the generation before the Napoleonic Wars. Second, the impetus given to them as a nation by the union of Castile and Aragón, by the discovery of the New World, and the expulsion of the Moors. From that they became in another generation or two under the Emperor Charles V almost the arbiters of the Old World as well. The Spaniards missed the reformist, ascetic austerities of de Rancé and the Trappists who, while they encouraged no luxury in building for themselves, asserted some sort of moral embargo upon others so that monastic structures in France after the reign of Louis XIII are half-hearted as though the buildings were unconvinced of their right and more than a little ashamed of themselves. The Spaniards, by contrary, ended in a blaze of Southern fantasy and exuberance.

The miracle of Chartres Cathedral apart, it is with Ely, Lincoln, Durham, in mind – two, of the three of them, monastic in origin – that the English look, or should look for rivals in France and be disappointed in their absence. Spain has Burgos, Toledo, Seville, Santiago de Compostela, all of them cathedrals; but, also, Spain has her monasteries as well, and it is in respect of these and their unbroken continuity for some three hundred years after the suppression of the abbeys in England, that Spain occupies an unique position in Europe. If we return to Italy for a moment, where were the best architects and the best painters, the Venetian Republic, *La Serenissima*, with its eyes on commerce was no builder of abbeys; the Pontifical States, governed by priests, were not monk-minded; the other Italian Duchies, Tuscany included, however bigoted, had not the necessary means; and it was only in the Kingdom of Naples whether under Angevin, Aragonese, or Spanish Bourbon, that the monastic orders were uninhibited and could fend and build for themselves unimpeded, though, sadly, it is the part of all Italy where the painters and architects are weakest. Perhaps it is only in the convent of Santa Chiara in the town of Naples itself that these deficiencies are vanquished and overcome. There, we see a town convent such as there is not in Rome or Venice, or, for that matter, in Paris or in any town in France. The Frari, in Venice, its paintings aside, cannot compare with Santa Chiara. Neither is there anything to compare with it in Spain. It is only in England, if we think of those of our cathedrals that were monasteries in origin, Gloucester, Worcester, York, Ely, Durham, Winchester and Westminster, that we realize we have town monasteries in our English cities that have not their equals in any country in the world. And, as well, there were the abbeys in the East Anglian fens, on the Lincolnshire and Yorkshire wolds, in the Severn valley.

It is to these latter that the great convents and monasteries of Spain can be compared. They, again, are a feature we do not find in Italy. A few of the more superb of them are Royal foundations which in a kingdom of such centrifugal force as Spain means much and has its own importance. Among them, and taking its prior place on all accounts, is Las Huelgas, but a mile or two from Burgos. The way thither is along a dusty, tree-lined road. The portico of the convent is a series of arches, and under the colonnade there hang the coats-of-arms of former abbesses with their names and titles. Las Huelgas was a Royal convent of Cistercian nuns, and the abbess was a princess-palatine who possessed the powers of life and death over her serfs, and who yielded in dignity to no one but the Queen. Once there were a hundred nuns here who had to be of noble descent, and brought their dowries with them. Now there are some thirty nuns, still called not *sores* (sisters) but *señoras doñas*. Until a few years ago one was only allowed to step into the huge bare church and look through the grille into the nuns' choir. Now the convent of Las Huelgas has been opened by Papal permission, and it is one of the most magically beautiful places in the world.

On each side of the choir are stone coffins of huge size that hold the bones of kings and queens. Six kings and queens lie buried here, and some thirty princes and princesses. The founder of Las Huelgas, Alfonso VIII of Castile (1187), is here with his queen in a huge double sarcophagus, gilded with lions and castles; she being none other than Eleanor of England, daughter of Henry II and sister to Richard Coeur-de-Lion. Several Infantes and Infantas who were half-Plantagenet through their mothers are here as well. Every one of these tombs excepting that of Fernando de la Cerda was forced open and pillaged by Napoleon's troops. Cracks must have been left in the stone coffins, and the story goes that the sacristan thrust a lighted paper into one of these, not many years ago, and saw some gold object or material glittering from inside. Eventually a commission arrived from the Spanish museums with a permit from the Vatican, and the coffins were opened. There are the dresses and the cushions from the tomb of Richard Coeur-de-Lion's sister; dresses with trains of cloth-of-gold; the surcoats of warriors; the clothes of dead Infantes and Infantas, and the coronets of kings and queens. Objects from the tomb of Fernando de la Cerda are the best preserved of all; there are his sword and spurs, and his belt which has English heraldry upon it. In some of the glass cases there are photographs of the bodies as they were found. It is the most touching spectacle of the crumbling and passing of old glories.

There is no denying that the church of Las Huelgas has an air, not of Spain, but of mediaeval England, and could be the work of an English architect, or, it has been suggested, of an architect from the English Duchy of Anjou. At the high altar are kneeling figures of the founder and his Plantagenet queen; and on the walls of the choir above them hang the red-violet tapestries, stiff with gold, given by Philippe-le-Bel, father of Charles V. There are others, of green silk, hung sometimes in the outer church. Looking through the grilles into the choir one can see the white-robed nuns. But there are other, and interior wonders at Las Huelgas; the chapter house which could be in England, and the cloisters, and little chapels that are Moorish-Andalusian, and the work of Moorish-speaking Moslems in this sacred seraglio of the nuns. How strange to think of Plantagenet princesses here; with others who must have been English-speaking, and were half-Plantagenet through Spanish or Portuguese descent. Neither is this all where England is concerned. Edward I was knighted here before the altar in 1254 by Alfonso el Sabio; and the Black Prince was lodged here in 1367 after the battle of Navarrete. It is an English connection lasting from 1187, the year of foundation, until at least 1367. For an Englishman, or indeed anyone else with imagination, it is impossible not to conjecture what can have been the voices and the accents of these Platagenet or half-Platagenet nuns or noble ladies in the improbable contingency of one's being allowed to speak of them, in some Moorish-looking bower, entered perhaps by a pointed horseshoe arch of brick, with ceiling honeycombed and fringed with stalactites. It occurs to me that the only possible common subject of conversation would be the recent Coronation of our Queen in Westminster Abbey, where there were names that would be familiar and that bridged over the abyss of time. But no less extraordinary were the experiences of the commission who came to open the convent when, according to a personal account that I have been given, a telephone was installed for the first time, and the nuns who had never had the opportunity before spent long hours in telephoning to each other; and a day or two before the commission left and its work was done, a feast was given to them by the abbess and nuns. It took place at some strange hour, three or four o'clock in the morning, recalling accounts of audiences given by the Dowager-Empress of China which were at that hour; and the dishes, I was told, were either of an intolerable nastiness, or else quite exquisite in taste but entirely unfamiliar being from probably thirteenth-century recipes.

It were perhaps best for our narrative to repair straight from Las Huelgas to another royal convent at Sigena, which is between Lérida and Zaragoza, and therefore in Aragón. It was a convent of noble ladies founded in 1188 by Don Alfonso II of Aragón and Doña Sancha of Castile, but its chief interest was that it was the sole surviving relic of the Knights Templar, of, in fact, the Order of St John of Jerusalem. The nuns wore the clothes of ladies of the twelfth century. They had long veils or wimples and head-dresses of extraordinary complexity and elaboration, and wore the red floreated cross of the Order upon their left breasts. There were kings and princesses buried here, and many tombs of abbesses and noble ladies. According to an old authority on the monastic orders there were sixty nuns at Sigena who lived by day in separate apartments but slept together at night in a vast *dortoir* or dormitory; while the Abbess and Princess Palatine, following the custom of Dona Blanca, daughter of Jaime II of Aragón (d. 1336) who had been abbess, had a court about her of seven nuns who were always with her. There was the *Custode*, who received strangers, did the honours, and attended to the private business of the abbess; the *Camerera*, who served her in her chamber; a *Repostera*, or keeper of the wine cellar; a cupbearer, who gave her to drink; and others who served her at table and looked after her person; and the abbesses were always attended by this court in miniature. Divine service was performed with much pomp and majesty; and upon such occasions the nuns wore *rochets* of fine linen and sat in their stalls with silver sceptres in their hands. It was for such occasions and on great festivals that the nuns wore the enormous head-dresses, which, being those of royal princesses of the early fourteenth century, required immense patience and two or three hours in the making. On such days the nuns could be seen at mass in the choir, or walking in the cloister. But, unfortunately, the convent of Sigena was one of the casualties of the Spanish Civil War. It is a total loss. The convent has never been restored; nor has the Order, which was alone of its kind, continued or taken in any new nuns. All are gone. The convent was broken into and destroyed; and the nuns were murdered, many of them having been violated by the communists before they met their end. We may exercise our imagination in thinking of the last day on which this sovereign convent fulfilled its functions, and of the last night on which the nuns of Sigena slept in their *dortoir*, a huge apartment to which the round arched or hooded Romanesque portal to the convent with its no fewer than fifteen concentric ribs or mouldings was contemporary in time. But a little more than nothing was salvaged from the wreckage, though the paintings intended for portraits on the coffin-lids of the noble ladies who were once abbesses have been removed to the Barcelona museum. They could as well have been portraits of the abbesses of Las Huelgas so strong is the Plantagenet influence in their features and their fair hair. An Englishman must be forgiven for wishing that one of our royal nunneries had been preserved, for instance that at Barking; and it is only tragically sad that Sigena which survived till 1935 in all its mediaeval state should have perished utterly and entirely.

But a royal convent and former palace still exists at Tordesillas, which is a few miles from Valladolid. This was the former palace of Alfonso X el Sabio, King of Castile, and was built between 1340 and 1345. It is a Muslim building erected for Christians, the more remarkable therefore as a nunnery, and it has its history. It was here that, in 1494, the Treaty or Line of Demarcation drawn up by the Borgia Pope, Alexander VI was signed, and the New World was divided between Portugal and Spain. Here, also Juana la Loca (Joan the Mad), daughter of Ferdinand and Isabella, wife of Philippe-le-Bel, and heiress of Spain, passed forty-nine years of imprisonment, 'suggested by her father Ferdinand and persevered in by her son, the Emperor Charles V'. Her prison is said to have been a small cell with no windows. Here, too, Pedro the Cruel installed his mistress Maria de la Padilla, heroine of the opera *La Favorita*, and it was their daughter who turned it from a palace into a convent. It has Moorish baths which are still shown, as is the church which still has the organ given by Juana la Loca. Formerly, the patio and cloister could only be seen by special permit from the Pope, or from the King of Spain. Mr Bernard Bevan, who praises the Moorish work at Tordesillas and considers the ceiling of the throne room, that now covers the chancel, 'one of the most sumptous in Spain', calls the

Moorish baths 'in no way inferior to those in the Alhambra of Granada'. Another, and smaller palace built for Maria de Padilla, in the near village of Astudillo, is still in strict *clausura*, and Mr Bevan was only told of the *cosas preciosas* that it contains.

Neither Tordesillas nor Astudillo of the beautiful names have I achieved;[1] nor yet Nájera, with its Benedictine church of Santa Maria la Real, where lie thirty-five bodies of the royal families of Castile and Navarre. This monastery was one of the hospices or resting places upon the pilgrims' road to Compostela. St Ferdinand, who drove the Moors from Seville in 1248, was crowned at Nájera, which is between Logroño and Burgos. Nor have I been, near there, to San Millán de la Cogolla, a Benedictine abbey and 'a sort of Escorial', though this is minimized when it is called the 'Escorial de la Rioja'. It is, at least, not a royal monastery like Nájera.

Far from here, down near to the Mediterranean shore, are the Cistercian abbeys of Poblet and Santas Creus, both of them royal foundations in successive years, 1149 and 1150, of the same Ramón Berenguer IV, Count of Catalonia. I remember these two monasteries when they were as beautiful as any buildings in the whole of the Iberian peninsula, when they rivalled with Tomar or Batalha, miles away in Portugal, and it would have seemed they could only emerge, now recognized, in enhancement upon themselves. This has not happened, at least in the case of Poblet, because like the abbeys in Portugal it has been hideously tidied and restored. They are among the losses of a lifetime, but destroyed in peace and not in war. Santas Creus, to take the smaller of them first, is modest and not exceptional in scale, with a picturesque village within its walls, 'cloisters in flower, and in the month of March, violet-scented and loud with bees'. So it was, at least, when last seen though there is no knowing how much it may have been 'restored' and damaged since then. But I have seen Santas Creus, too, when it was neglected and little attention had been paid to it for a hundred years since the peasants sacked it in the first Carlist War, when with its walls and battlements it was more like some old fortress broken down in flowers. The church, built by French Cistercians straight from France, is rather empty-looking but for the canopied, alabaster tombs of the early Kings of Aragón.[2]

Poblet, with the Cistercian monks back in it, was founded from Fontfroide, in Navarre, and before the fatal spring cleaning that has done it so

---

[1] Though, an *aficionado* of Spanish names, I have been to Madrigal de las Altes Torres in the perfect circle of its mediaeval walls.

[2] This pair of canopied tombs of Don Pedro II and his son Don Jaime II, it has been pointed out by Mr Royall Tyler, closely resemble the canopied tomb of their enemy, King Robert of Anjou (d. 1343), in the convent church of Santa Chiara at Naples.

much damage, was among the wonders, not of Spain only, but of all Europe. It lies within a battlemented wall a mile round, within which are gardens, orchards, stables, slave quarters, hospitals and guesthouses, indeed all the appurtenances of a little independent kingdom. The huge church, now much spoilt, has some royal tombs, but the conventual buildings are of greater interest. The great cloister has its Glorieta, a fountain pavilion in form of a hexagon; there is a chapter-house with windows opening to another cloister, and over it what, *pace* Mr Bernard Bevan, must be 'the most imposing dormitory ever erected by the Cistercian Order', with nine bays of arches. Most beautiful of all buildings is the *Palacio del Rey Martin* with its traceried windows of the late fourteenth century and its outer stair. But that conditions at Poblet were not only of Cistercian austerity and simplicity, and that there may have been cause for the Catalan uprising of 1865 which attacked it as 'a nest of Carlism' is argued in the names of two subsidiary buildings, the sinister-sounding Torres de Locos and the Chocolatería, as also, a ruined castle, near by, which was the summer palace of the abbots, making of Poblet a monastery on the scale of Glastonbury. Perhaps, too, in the mysterious presence and death here (1732), as a monk, of the Jacobite, Philip, Duke of Wharton, former president of the 'Hell-Fire Club'. To my knowledge it has never been explained what he was doing here. He died at Poblet, we are told, 'in extreme poverty, without a friend or servant'; that is all. And coming down to the coast again from the olive groves and carob trees we are soon in the golden light of Tarragona, on the 'aprica littora' of the Mediterranean Sea.

In the very different landscape of High Castile there remains the Cartuja de Miraflores, outside Burgos. This is a royal foundation contemporary to the chapels of Eton College and King's College, Cambridge. Indeed, but for its being built of golden and not grey stone, it bears a resemblance to these two buildings, except again that its ceilings have not the fan-vaulting which is peculiar to Perpendicular England. But the chapel of the Cartuja, smaller in size than either of them, contains tombs and a retablo in the richest Gothic rivalling that of Henry VII, of a richness that, having seen the Certosa di Pavia, we may think would be intolerable were it the work of Italian builders in an Italian building. The chapel is in fact by Hans and Simon of Cologne, architects of the spires and the chapel of the Condestable in Burgos Cathedral, and arbiters therefore of the character of Burgos Gothic. The glory of the Cartuja is its monument to Don Juan II and Isabella of Portugal, whose grandmother was the Plantagenet Philippa of Lancaster, daughter of John of Gaunt. It is an eight-sided tomb of white marble in front of the high altar, star-shaped, and formed by the intersection or overlapping of two super-

Opposite: St Hugh of Grenoble Visiting the Refectory
of the Carthusians by Francisco de Zurbarán

imposed squares. The effigies of the King and Queen, parents of Isabella the Catholic, lie side by side, under canopies, he with a sceptre, she with a book in her hand, in richly worked and embroidered dresses, and in a plethora of heraldry. On the wall beside them is the tomb of their son, the Infante Don Alfonso, the hope of Spain, at whose death their daughter Isabella became heiress to Castile. The Infante is kneeling at a *prie dieu* under an arched canopy, with carvings of children playing with vine tendrils at the sides. But our eyes go to the golden *retablo* rising behind the altar, to the kneeling figures of the King and Queen at the foot of it, the carved scenes with innumerable figures, and at the top the gold pelican vulning her breast, which is to say, feeding her young with her own blood. In the land of *retablos*, it is the finest *retablo* in all Spain; and like the tombs it is the work of the sculptor Gil de Silóee whose origin is of more than passing interest. For it appears that he was brought to Burgos from Germany by the bishop, Alonso de Cartagena, who had been born a Jew, and that Gil de Silóee himself, was Jewish, for his father was a merchant of Nuremburg called Samuel and his mother's name was Miriam. Gil de Silóee was, we may think, the only considerable artist of Jewish origin to appear in Europe till the last century, and probably the greatest artist in the plastic arts that the Jewish race has so far produced. If it would be a mistake to attach too much importance to the Moorish or even Jewish ground plan of the double tomb in the Cartuja, the design in fact being that of the star of David, it is certainly true that it has something a little curious and ambiguous. An earlier bishop of Burgos had been Pablo de Santa María, a Jew who had been married to a Jewess as a young man, and who was not baptized a Christian till he was forty years old. They had a son, Gonzalvo, who was made bishop of Siguenza; and within a generation of their time the Inquisition was demanding proofs of *limpideza* of blood, arresting on mere suspicion of keeping the Passover, or not eating swine's flesh, and eventually driving all the Jews from Spain. If in knowledge of this strange and dangerous origin for the sculptor, we climb the wooden steps and look over the iron railings at his effigies once more, it is to notice in some of the detail a handling that now seems unlike any other work of the Middle Ages and that is due, it could be, to the Oriental blood in him. There is nothing else to admire in the chapel of the Cartuja except the high pinnacled priest or abbot's stall, or would it be merely fanciful to attach an Eastern aroma to the rosaries of pressed rose leaves that are sold at the Cartuja, and that smell of roses?

From Burgos it is about two hours' drive to the Benedictine monastery of Santo Domingo de Silos with its double-storeyed cloister of the middle of the twelfth century, rival to Monreale and to Moissac, and called by Mr Bernard Bevan 'probably the most beautiful cloister in Europe', though he dismisses the tradition that its capitals 'unsurpassed for wealth of invention and perfect execution' were carved by Muslim slaves as 'very doubtful'. Here again, the handing back of the monastery to the monks though admirable of intention has not improved its picturesque content as much as might have been imagined. But we are now approaching a part of Northern Spain where weeks or months could be spent in visiting lonely and forgotten Romanesque churches that belonged to monasteries. The reason for them is that they were on the pilgrimage route to Santiago de Compostela, the *camino francés* some five hundred miles in length from the French frontier through Burgos and León, a pilgrimage so well organized that in Mr Bernard Bevan's words it was 'like a huge tourist scheme', and was covered in thirteen stages not intended to be traversed on successive days. The monasteries were in fact rest houses like motels or *gites d'étape*, mostly in the hands of Cluniac or Benedictine monks. Important stopping places along this road were Sahagún, Carrión de las Condes, and Fromista. At the second of these I have to admit that I found the Renaissance cloister in the monastery of San Zoil ugly and disappointing, but, then, it is of the wrong date, some four hundred years after the spirit had gone from this, the most famous of European pilgrimages. In Spain where it could never be humanly possible to see everything, the Romanesque arches and capitals in San Martin de Fromista look to be most wonderful, though French in inspiration from Aquitaine whence the pilgrim routes started, and in fact at Fromista one could as well be in the abbey church at Souillac. Nothing could well be sadder or more depressing than the memory of Sahagún upon a rainy autumn day, darkening to winter, a town sighted with its old towers from the high road and approached, as who would not do so, if only for its name. Its Benedictine abbey, to which the early Kings of León retired from their struggles with their neighbours and with the Moors, is but a ruin; the soldiers of Napoleon having melted down its silver altars and completed the destruction. Once it was mother house to a hundred and thirty Spanish monasteries; but the ruin of Sahagún, or such another town as Benavente, is something too unutterably sad upon a weeping, rainy day, and we went away from Sahagún without the heart to enquire further through the puddles and the splashing mud into 'the convent of nuns of San Francisco' where in Richard Ford's day a hundred years ago, there were still 'some horseshoe arches and oriental reminiscences'.

Many miles further on through the rain on the road to Lugo lies the district of the Bierzo, where are the ruins of many convents, this secluded valley having been the Thebaid of Northern Spain in the time of the early 'Gothic' chieftains or 'sheikh-shepherds'. Beginning at Villafranca del Bierzo, the metropolis of this land of thyme-clad hills and trout-filled streams, there is the huge Franciscan convent founded by the famous Pedro de Toledo, Viceroy of Naples, the very name Villafranca being the Villa Franc of the French pilgrims on their way to Compostela. The country between here and the shrine of St James at Compostela is one of the most unspoilt parts of Europe, and as thick with monasteries as the northern provinces of Portugal, most of them of early date and lying in ruins, but culminating in the three huge old abbeys of Lorenzana, Celanova, and Sobrado de los Monjes, the first of which should be of interest as having a Baroque front by Fernando Casas y Novoa, architect of the west front or Fachada del Obradoiro of the cathedral at Compostela with its quadrangle, processional flights of stairs and the snapdragons lolling their lion-tongues from the crevices of its golden towers. Both other monasteries, Celanova which is on the road to Portugal, and Sobrado are largely the work of a local seventeenth-century architect, Pedro de Monteagudo, Sobrado de les Monjes having a thirteenth-century kitchen and no fewer than three cloisters.

If we now transfer to Catalonia and Mediterranean Spain, it is to find Ripoll rebuilt but for its splendid figured doorway of the twelfth century, and the other great Benedictine monastery of Montserrat so rebuilt that it is not worth the visit. Nor, the Collegiata or La Seo of Manresa apart, which was so much extolled by Street: 'in our large towns in England there is nothing we now want more than something which shall emulate the magnificent scale of these Catalan churches. They were built in the Middle Ages for a large manufacturing or seafaring population; and we have everywhere just such masses of souls to be dealt with as they were provided for' – is there much in the way of monastic building among the practical Catalans whose outlook was so like that of the mercantile Venetians. With Poblet and Santas Creus we are in Aragón, but not even at Zaragoza is more to be expected of a city that has already the upkeep of two cathedrals. The provincial towns of Aragón; Calatayud, dust-coloured like its troglodyte dwellings, and with a Dominican convent with a patio of two storeys, is in the land of the Mudéjar, church towers often standing detached from the main body of the building like a minaret, a feature that comes to its climax with the green-tiled towers of Teruel, sadly damaged in the Civil War, but it was as Oriental-looking a city as any in North Africa;[1] while no one who has

---

[1] Mr Bernard Bevan, *op. cit.*, p. 108, mentions Teruel as the only place in Spain where this tiled decoration remained to any large extent. 'The cathedral tower has purple and olive-green colonnettes. San Salvador had a roof of white and apple-green tiles, while other churches had tiles of canary-yellow and cobalt-blue.' Until their expulsion, which was only finally put into effect in 1610, the majority of the population of Aragón was Muslim.

witnessed the astonishing wildness and isolation of a town like Morella, often hidden in clouds, could expect rich monastic foundations in so barren a landscape. Indeed the only thing of the sort in Aragón, Poblet and Santas Creus apart, is the huge old Cistercian abbey of Veruela, on the Ebro, north of Zaragoza and near Tarazona, a Cistercian foundation such as one might find in the north of England though in this very different landscape, and a marvellous place to scramble about and spend the day in before the Jesuits took it over who have been here for a hundred years.

It is near Valencia within sight and smell of the orange groves that one would expect the monasteries to begin, and at the Cartuja de Portacoeli one is only mildly disappointed. It is a mirage like the Fata Morgana or Delibab of the Hungarian puszta that pursues us or rather entices us all down the coast of the Levante where, at least, the landscape is not 'an immense, treeless, grassy plain, relieved only here and there by the huts of the shepherds, surrounded by small groves of acacias, and there are magnificent sunrises', but this Carthusian monastery 'once renowned for its frescoes and rich marbles' and 'exquisitely situated among pinewooded mountains' is a deserted ruin, and a not inspiring one, at that, nor does this anticipation of the old warm South fulfil itself till we are in the Cartuja de Granada. Here, at last, is an architecture attuned to the warm vibrations of the South. It seems to have been the invention of a single mind, Francisco Hurtado y Izquierdo (1669–1725), a native of Córdoba, and the more deserving of that qualification of genius because in his early works at Córdoba and in Granada he shows few signs of his aberrant fancies. Those had to wait till he started work at the Cartuja, in a pair of halls attached to the church, the *sagrario* and the *sacristía*, the first of these, at least, with its outer walls of jasper and porphyry, and with the tabernacle in the middle with its salomonic columns of red and black marble, was finished in his lifetime, but the mystery lies in the fact that the much more personal and characteristic *sacristía*, without parallel except for another work by him that we have to mention, was not begun until five years after Hurtado died. How, then, was it accomplished? Did he leave the most detailed drawings? For the effect of the *sacristía*, its pilasters of red marble with white and pink veins, apart, and its doors and presses of ebony and tortoiseshell, inlaid with ivory, mother-of-pearl and silver, and with silver handles – the work of a Carthusian monk, Fray J. M. Vazquez – comes from its facetted pilasters in stucco and their many edges and volutes, from the wavering and rising and falling line of the cornice, from the innumerable white edges fluttering and never touching, and this effect though governed by strict rules has much the character of an improvisation. They are indeed plangent, twanging sounds in architecture of which the melody is complicated upon eye and ear, with more than a hint of Moorish ancestry in its wavering purpose. How could the hand of another man, Luis de Arévalo, a mere stonemason, with the help of a stuccoist, carry this out to his intentions?

But the *sagrario* which, as said, he at least completed in his lifetime, must have expanded the fame of Hurtado to the hebdomadal conversations of the taciturn-to-rule Carthusian fathers, and the order came to him for the *camarín* and *sagrario* at the Cartuja of El Paular, in the pinewoods near Segovia, and in a very different climate from that of Granada. The *camarín* at El Paular, as elsewhere in Spain a kind of dressing room for the robing of the statues of the saints, attained down a long dark passage at the back of the high altar, is in the form of a Greek cross with a tabernacle in the middle that rises to the domed ceiling. Beyond this, a red and gold lacquer door leads into the *sagrario*, also on the plan of a Greek cross, and which once had paintings in the dome by Palomino, the 'Spanish Vasari', whose work as chronicler has obscured his not inconsiderable merits as a painter.[1] This pair of strange halls in the Carthusian monastery of El Paular with their unmistakable echoes of the horseshoe arches in the mosque at Córdoba, and their use of coral and grey marbles and lapis lazuli, are something unique and although they seem to prophesy the Mexican style there is in fact nothing much resembling them in Mexico, except for one astonishing and solitary example, the façade of the Santuario de Ocotlán, near Tlaxcala, with pink shagreen-like bricks netted or lozenged in white mortar for the bases of its pair of towers, elaborate white belfries above this in two tiers or storeys, and a frontispiece of white fretted pilasters *à la Cartuja de Granada* with a hooded, shell-like projection to cover them and keep sun or rain off the statues. But now a further mystery supervenes for it is suggested by one authority that Hurtado had no hand in the *camarín* at El Paular, and that it is by his follower, F. X. Pedraxas, who was born eleven years after Hurtado died. It was Pedraxas who built the octagonal *sagrario*, a little masterpiece of its kind, at Priego,[2] between Córdoba and Granada. So perhaps it was really Pedraxas who built both the *sacristia* at Granada – after all it was attributed until very recently to Arévalo before anyone had heard of Hurtado – the *camarín* and *sagrario* at El Paular and the *camarín* at Priego.

[1] Antonio Palomino (1653–1726) was to be seen at his best on the flat ceiling of Los Santos Juanes at Valencia, which was fearfully damaged in the Civil War. The church has been restored, but not the frescoes by Palomino.

[2] The *sagrario* at Priego is in the Church of the Assumption (Cathedral), and therefore does not come into our present subject. I was only able to visit Priego and see its churches, 'discovered' since I wrote my book on Spain in 1949, in August 1962. Alas! that there can be but few more discoveries of the kind, for they are beautiful indeed. For Hurtado and X. F. Pedraxas, *cf.* R. C. Taylor, 'Rococo in Spain' in the *Architectural Review*, July 1952, and 'Francisco Hurtado and his school', *Art Bulletin*, 1950; and Antonio Gallego y Burin, *El Barroco Grenadino*, 1956.

Mr R. C. Taylor ascribes to him, too, the red wood choir-stalls of the cathedral at Guadix which do recall the fluttering cornices and fretted pilasters of the *sacristía* at Granada, in the light of which it may be F. X. Pedraxas and not Hurtado who emerges as perhaps the most interesting and certainly the most original Spanish architect of the early eighteenth century.

Andalucia, however, is a disappointment if it is monasteries we are looking for, despite the finding for oneself as is only possible in Spain and nowhere else, of at any rate one other church beside the cathedrals of Seville and Córdoba which has a court or patio of orange trees, it is in this instance at Lebrija just before Jerez – there should of right be mosques with cloisters of orange trees but I have never found one – and beyond Lebrija, near a ruined Moorish castle, are the ruins of the euphonious-sounding Cartuja de Gigonza. The Cartuja of Seville, now a dreary majolica factory, is the more disappointing if we hear it called the Cartuja de Triana, that being the Gypsy suburb whence come the *bailarinas* and the *toreros*, which is now built over with blocks of flats. But it had the paintings of Carthusian monks by Zurbarán which are in the museum at Seville; and is it calling in the Old World again to redress the balance of the New if we invoke the experience of going to a remote part of the town where are convents, San Clemente, Santa Clara, Santa Paula, with *artesonado* ceilings and *azulejos* on the walls and the murmuring of the nuns in their high, latticed choir? Where in the courts on a spring evening I have seen children dancing the *sevillana* with that thrilling interval between the two halves of it which has made me wonder if Domenico Scarletti during his years in Spain took from this the inspiration for his 'paired' sonatas – but on this particular evening tiring of the Sierpes, which has now lost all its character, we are looking for the convent where 'Yemas de San Leandro' are sold at the convent grille, and find it at last, and coming in at an overhanging porch, cross a little court and knock at a hatchway where a brass-studded revolving hatch in answer to the hidden voice slowly turns and sends round a little wooden box like a packing-case with the Moorish-looking and tasting sweets inside, and while we wait for the hatch to turn again and bring the change, there is an instant in which to look up in the unlikely moonlight, new born not many moments before, at another church tower seen in steep perspective climbing above the porch only a few feet away, and this is the immortal Seville as we may never know it again and only hear the hints of it in music, when the theatre is darkened for Lindoro to prelude on the strings as he begins his serenade. This done, and the dark falling, there is at any rate one monastery of the warm South to be seen for tomorrow. This is the Cartuja de Jerez, near to the vineyards and bodegas, among the cactus hedges. It has a façade which I have apostrophized elsewhere as being in 'Apulian' style, pertaining to the school of Lecce, of which it is indeed reminiscent; a façade in two storeys of eight columns each, with urns and statues, an architectural frontispiece of fanciful and high order, and three huge and deserted cloisters. This Cartuja once owned many of the vineyards; like Jervaulx and other monasteries of the Yorkshire dales it was famous for its horses, but they were Andalucian barbs and not white horses of Jervaulx or Coverham, or Cleveland bays; and the Cartuja de Jerez had many paintings by Zurbarán (1598– 1664) who was impelled by his temperament to surpass himself in his paintings of Carthusian monks.

Repairing north again through Estremadura, the solitary nature of the landscape, its rocks and rock roses (cisti) flowering white with chocolate or carmine blotches or markings, or sometimes rosy-red of flowers, and on occasion more thin or papery of petal, and like a hellebore of mind to become arboreal and be a rock rose, no human being in sight and but the lone eagle soaring overhead, all helps but to heighten expectation and make more unlikely the finding of a great monastery in this wilderness of oaks and cork trees given over to herds of swine and wandering flocks of migratory or nomad sheep. Yet, here it is, the Hieronymite monastery of Guadalupe, now in the occupation of Franciscans, an enormous group of buildings more like a castle, with its church standing above a flight of steps in the triangular village square. All at Guadalupe is on a big scale. Even the monastery garage is a huge empty church.

In the morning, for it is a necessary experience to stay the night, we are shown round the monastery. The church holds out many promises, but its splendid *rejas* (iron screens) and weakly Escorial-like wall-tombs of kings and princes apart, is a little disappointing. Not so, however, the rest of the monastery, least of all its brick two-storeyed cloister of horseshoe arches in Mudéjar style, indubitably the work of Moors, and the fountain pavilion or Glorieta in its middle, which more than one writer has compared to the covered fountains in the courts of mosques at Cairo. In the *sacristía* are no fewer than eight paintings by Zurbarán; and where indeed could this Estremaduran master, born near Badajoz, be seen better or to more advantage? At Guadalupe his theme is St Jerome and the Hieronymite monks, not the Carthusian fathers; and these pictures are among his masterpieces, even though we may miss that painting in Seville of Carthusians at refectory, in which Zurbarán makes such play of loaves of peasant bread and mugs and plates of blue and white pottery, investing them with the degree of delighted attention they might evoke in someone just emerged from a costly water and fruit juice cure – still lives so frugal and different in spirit from those of the Dutch painters and a tribute in themselves to the therapeutic virtues in ascetic living.

At Guadalupe, none the less, there are precious marbles where simply would do, and it is a stair with steps of red jasper that leads up to the *camarín*, an octagonal chamber with vaulted apses and nine large paintings by Luca Giordano, enticed or strayed far indeed from his native Naples. There are innumerable and wonderful treasures to be seen, some of them in a little room prettily called the *joyel*. How could it be that Marshal Victor took away nine cartloads of silver from Guadalupe?[1] What happened to it? Was it melted down? At least the vestments are left, a collection only rivalled by that in the cathedral at Toledo; vestments of silk and damask with the arms of the Catholic Kings upon them; with others which were the gift of the Empress Isabella, the beautiful, Plantagenet-looking wife of Charles V, who was an Infanta of Portugal; and the embroidered altar frontal given by Henry II of Castile, the same who sent Clavijo as his ambassador to Tamerlane at Samarcand.

It is with a heavy heart that one goes away from Guadalupe in the knowledge that with much that may be better so, there can never be such things again; and it is no lightening of our mood to arrive at the Escorial for an ending. But in fact this eighth wonder of the world – and it is significant that if there be a ninth it is Radio City or the Rockefeller Center – a church and semi-detached palace more than monastery, cannot have been as uncomfortable to live in as Versailles, and with double that span of history it is of less ill omen and not so depressing. But this is no place to detail its wonders so imbued are they with the Habsburg and Fleming, Philip II. The monks were Augustinians, Black Canons of the same order who built Canons Ashby, a mile or two over the Northamptonshire meadows from where these lines are written. The Escorial is a palace with monks living in it, and the church with Pompeo Leoni's gilt-bronze monuments to Charles V and Philip II and their families is a Royal Pantheon if ever there was one. But of what contingency would it be to the Escorial in its rôle as a monastery were we to describe paintings by El Greco and Hieronymus Bosch; write of Goya's tapestries in the Royal apartments; or of the grand stair of the monastery with its frieze of the Capture of the Connétable de Montmorency at St Quentin and the Apotheosis on the ceiling with portraits of Charles V, Philip II, and the imbecile Charles II, all by Luca Giordano – a painter of improvisatory talents only comparable to those of a Rossini or a Donizetti, and with the most inbred of dynastic patrons there have ever been; did he not fresco the gallery of the Palazzo Riccardi in Florence with the Medici as

---

[1] And, as well, 'the silver lamps, the *custodía* made by Juan de Segovia, the silver throne of the image, the silver angels, the 85 silver lamps, the gilt lamp taken at Lepanto, the diamonds, pearls, gold, and jewels, the offerings of kings'. Richard Ford, *op. cit.*

Royal Foundations in Spain and Portugal

Effigy of Charles V in the Escorial. With the Emperor are the Empress Isabel,
Queen Leonora of Portugal and France, Maria of Hungary and Donna Maria,
widow of Maximilian II

Double tomb of founders of monastery of Las Huelgas at Burgos, Don Alfonso VIII of Castile and his wife Eleanor of England

Isabella of Portugal from double tomb by Gil de Silóee in Cartuja de Miraflores, Burgos

Figure of Dona Ines de Castro attended by angel maids-of-honour on her tomb at Alcobaça

Abbess of Sigena (Aragón) attended by her court of nuns in the cloister of the convent. A photograph of 1912

Wooden coffin of Beatriz Cornel, one of the noble nuns of Sigena, painted in the fifteenth century

Sacristy of Hieronymite monastery of Guadalupe founded by Alfonso IX of Castile, with paintings by Zurbarán

Moorish patio in convent of Santa Clara at Tordesillas, former palace of Alfonso X
of Castile, built 1340–5

Top left: Eighteenth-century engraving of *Capelas Imperfeitas* at Batalha

Bottom left: Manuelino doorway by João de Castilho (1519) at entrance
to Sacristy at Alcobaça

Right: Three Cistercian Monks of Alcobaça from Nuno Gonçalves' polyptych of
St Vincent, painted for the monastery of San Vicente in Lisbon

Church of convent-palace of the Knights of Christ at Tomar decorated in Manueline style by Diogo de Arruda

gods of light among the deities of Olympus, they being the later half-Habsburg Medici of whom the strange busts greet one at the top of the staircase in the Uffizi? Whence it would be but a step further to visit the grand kitchen of the Escorial, 'a department worthy of two hundred monks', so writes Ford, or walk a little way to see the Casita del Principe de Arriba, 'the paltry maisonnette built by the booby *infant* Don Gabriel', but in fact this miniature palace is full of the most delightful small objects and curiosities of a kind to be seen nowhere else, and one wonders what this Bourbon prince had done to deserve Ford's censure. All of which has but small concern with the Black Canons of the Escorial.

Portugal is a kingdom which for its small area and population put as much energy into the building of monasteries and convents as into its exploration of the oceans and the founding of its scattered empire of small trading posts. Or, its detractors would say, into the building of homes for wasted and good for nothing lives. But we are alive but once and, lazy or not, were they not lucky to have escaped the coal-mine, the cotton-mill, even the 'rush-hour' to reach the office-stool in the new packing-case building? That Northern Portugal was in fact a monkish paradise only equalled by the mediaeval monasteries of the English fenlands and of the Severn Valley, and by Southern Bavaria and the Danube valley in the eighteenth century, will emerge from these pages. But this is for the end of the chapter; and before that there are the four great monasteries near Lisbon, the capital itself, and the other provinces.

An extraordinary picture of the late or tainted flowering of Portugal is to be gathered from various sources, but chiefly from two Englishmen who in their very different ways could qualify for being under suspicion themselves were it not that moral censure is more easily swallowed if it comes from the hand of either or both of a pair of writers who are far from setting up their own images as plaster saints. Augustus Hervey, later third Earl of Bristol, was a skilled naval officer who landed at Lisbon between bouts of what amounted almost to privateering for prize-money, and on disembarking proceeded to 'paint Lisbon red', in the course of which he paid many visits to the convents, where it must be explained that young ladies of good family were pensionnaires, something like the corrodies or life boarders in mediaeval English nunneries, and probably the majority of them would eventually leave the convent in order to get married. The nunnery of Odivelas was his particular goal, a Cistercian foundation of Dom Diniz in the early thirteenth century, where Philippa of Lancaster, daughter of John of Gaunt, died with three of her half-Plantagenet sons at her bedside, including Prince Henry the

Navigator; but in Hervey's time the convent had altered its character and the nuns were Bernardines. It is said to have contained seven hundred professed nuns, and as many more novices, servants, and others. As the editor of Hervey's Journal points out:[1] in the large unreformed communities, there was a large floating population of lodgers and pensioners, ladies whose husbands were overseas (in Brazil, Goa, Macao, or in Mozambique) 'and who wished to be chaperoned, wards in chancery waiting till they came of age, and ladies who had been sentenced to a period of seclusion in a convent for moral escapades. The choir sisters, too, were probably selected more with an eye to their vocal than to their virtuous qualities.' The King of Portugal, João V, the builder of Mafra, had a mistress Paula Teresa da Silva, known as Madre Paula, who was a nun of Odivelas and by whom he was the father of an illegitimate son, Dom Gaspar, who became Archbishop of Braga; while by her, or by another nun who was a Frenchwoman, he had two more bastard sons, Dom José who became Grand Inquisitor, and Dom Antonio, the three bastards being known collectively as the 'Meninos de Palhava' (Palhava meaning 'worthless straw'). The two last named of them were visited by Beckford in 1787. But the illicit amours of the King were not as scandalous as it might seem because as monarch he had the right of entry to the convent. Absence of such privilege was no impediment to Augustus Hervey.

The convent of Odivelas and probably threequarters of the buildings in Lisbon were destroyed in the earthquake of 1755. But life had resumed something of its old tenour when Beckford first came here in 1783. He lived in Portugal again in later years; but the surpassing curiosity is that his *Letters from Spain and Portugal* were only published in 1834, the year when by strange coincidence the monasteries and convents of which he wrote such vivid accounts were suppressed. By literary subterfuge his letters are dated 1794, though it is clear he only wrote them nearly forty years later, not long before he had them printed, an alternative technique in fact to that of writers who describe places before they have been to them. But it is to be noted that it is outside the area of Lisbon proper and beyond the earthquake zone that Beckford finds his best subjects, for in his time the capital had not recovered from the disaster, if it has ever done so.

It is strange indeed that the abbey of Belém, not more than a mile or two from Odivelas, should have survived. But what new can one say of the church of the Jerónimos, as it is called, with its giant pillars which give the impression of entering an Indian temple, and with its still more peculiar

---

[1] Edited by David Erskine Kimber, London, 1953. It was only by luck that Hervey missed the Lisbon earthquake of November 1755. His is the best account in English of pre-earthquake Lisbon, but his subsequent accounts of it are quieter in tone and the effect of it was to clip his wings.

double cloister that is in Manoelino style, yet at the same time less Oriental and more credibly the work of Boutaca or Boytac, an architect from Languedoc, who here at Belém at any rate, is a Frenchman emerging from the Gothic into Early Renaissance. It is possible to prefer the cloisters as they were many years ago, when swarming however inappropriately with orphans who could have been drawn by Cruikshank for additional illustrations to *Oliver Twist*, to Belém in its present condition after it has been scrubbed and hospitalized into a national shrine, in the course of which much that was unique and beautiful has gone never to return again. But that has happened, and is happening all over Portugal, and those persons are lucky who can remember what it was before.

Of nowhere in Portugal is this more true than of Alcobaça. Long ago, in 1926, this old Cistercian abbey, despite having been degraded into a cavalry barracks was, at least, left alone and allowed to decline slowly in the tatters of its old pomp and finery. Having read Beckford's *Excursion to the Monasteries of Alcobaça and Batalha* as a schoolboy not many years before that, how exciting the moment of turning one's back on the village street with its shops full of the local chintzes and printed cottons, climbing the steps onto that obelisk'd platform in front of the church, and coming in through the seven-course Gothic doorway in that heavy, twin-towered façade! How unforgettable that moment of first setting foot in one of the old abbeys! Nothing, it is true, could quite spoil the impression of those tall, white Cistercian columns. The tombs of Dom Pedro and Dona Ines de Castro, with their effigies lying feet to feet so that he should be the first to see his ladylove on the day of Resurrection are still in their chapel, their bodies as I have said elsewhere, being attended by angel maids-of-honour who smooth down their robes and hold their crowns in place. Elsewhere, all the enchanting junk and bric-a-brac of ages has been swept away. The Sala dos Reis, a marvellous old vaulted room, with its *azulejo* panels and its fantastic statues of the Kings of Portugal, robed as though for a masque at the Court of King Florestan, has been tidied up and put to rights as though by the fussy matron of a new hospital. The pair of Manoelino doorways, the pride of Alcobaça have been allowed to remain at the entrances to the Sacristy and a chapel opposite, of a flashing whiteness and formed, seemingly, from lopped stems and limbs of trees and snapped boughs of coral. Beckford's 'temple of gluttony', with a river running through it, is bare and empty; the kitchen where, dining at the high table and served with sinuous undulating graces, or so he hints, he was given lampreys, swallow's nest soup and shark's fin prepared by a Chinese lay-brother to the latest fashions of Macao. Not all of which is impossible, because Alcobaça, ever since Pope Pius V made it into the head monastery of the Cistercian Order in 1580, had become a haunt of luxury and grown immensely rich. It was famous for its orchards and kitchen gardens, of which probably the huge peaches of Alcobaça are the living relic.

The abbey of Batalha, which should on all accounts be seen after and not before Alcobaça, is certainly one of the wonders not only of the Iberian peninsular, but of all Europe, but it does badly need the monks back in it in order to prevent its being too heavily accented as the national monument of Portugal and tomb of the unknown soldier. That there is something reminiscent of an English abbey or cathedral about the exterior of Batalha, founded by Dom João I after defeating the armies of Castile in 1388, is indisputable, and it is as rich a Gothic exterior as any in the world to walk round owing to the constant varying and recession of its angles and projections. The interior, scrubbed and cleaned with devilish energy, is largely spoiled so that even the Founder's Chapel with its eight clustered columns and octagonal lantern has somewhat the air of a megalomaniac mayor's parlour in a town hall. The double tomb of Dom João I and Philippa of Lancaster is less fine than that of Dom Pedro and Dona Ines de Castro at Alcobaça. The cloister and the Unfinished Chapels form the marvel of Batalha and it is not only the latticed screens of the cloister, but more especially the fountain pavilion in the corner of the cloister, with the cusped arches of that well house and the Manoelino traceries like portable screens, that are unique. There is no such cloister in all Italy or Spain, and only this in Portugal. The Unfinished Chapels, also the work of Boytac, who built the cloister at Belém, an octagon which was intended to have the tomb of Dom Duarte in its middle, are entered through a great doorway of fringed and cusped stone carved to an intricacy of detail worthy of the temples of Halebid in Southern India, or of the red sandstone chapels of Banteai Srei.

Tomar, fourth of the great abbeys of Portugal only for convenience of reference, it is more pleasant to recall as it was unspoilt and unblemished by restoration nearly forty years ago, when in a personal sense even the journey thither was an exploration into the unknown. This convent-palace of the Knights Templar, then, after 1314 of a new Order, the Knights of Christ, who held spiritual jurisdiction over the Portuguese conquests in Africa and India, covers a long hillside. As we come nearer to it, the pierced parapet running along the roofline of the church, and repeating over and over again its pattern of the square cross of the Order and the armillary sphere of the navigators, has somewhat the look of a crenellation, a fringe or necklace of coral, a simile not unsuited to this Order whose pennon flew on the Portuguese caravels as they sailed the Indian seas. It is the exterior of the church under that coral-like ornament that has one above another the two Manoelino windows with marine motifs and they remain, whatever has been before or since, among the most startlingly original works of art in the world. For my personal taste I find the lower of the windows, that composed of knots and cables, heavy and indeed ugly; where the upper one, which is a round or rose window but framed by a tie-sail tied in with ropes and bellying in the wind, has at least the merits of originality. The corner buttresses, flanking the windows, have sea-anemone bases and go up in a welter of cork floats and cables towards the coral-like fringing of the parapet. These odd inventions, surpassing even the architectural exploits and eccentricities of Boytac at Belém and Batalha, are the work of Diogo de Arruda, an architect from Evora;[1] and after them the interior of the church, the early work of the Knights Templar, which is on a sixteen-sided plan with a central octagon, built on a Syriac model and relating itself indeed to the Dome of the Rock at Jerusalem, is solemn and ancient but has by now, it is almost certain, been largely spoiled. The huge monastery with its seven cloisters is, or was, an evocation of a past that went back as far as the castles of the Military Orders such as le Krak des Chevaliers, now in Syria; but perhaps the Knights of Christ, until emasculated and turned into ordinary monks in 1523 when their Grand-Mastership became hereditary in the Crown, could be better described as neither Naval nor Military but, in the full sense of the term, a Marine Order. The cloister of the Filippes, built under the Spanish usurpation, is in heavy-handed, even top-heavy Palladian, a curious contrast to the madrepore-coral motifs of the Manoelino seen above it on one side; and the gigantic T-shaped dormitory of the monks, the kitchen and the calefactorium would have made subjects for Magnasco, a fantasy both chilled and improved at once on seeing the cool and exquisite little chapel of N. S. de Conceição, halfway down the hill to Tomar, in the pure Italian, even Brunelleschian manner, and also pertaining to the monastery. That this little jewel of pure Renaissance architecture should be from the same hand, that of Diogo de Torralva, as the Palladian cloister, is not the least mystery of Tomar.

With the four abbeys is to be classed the palace-monastery of Mafra though it is on a level of expensive monotony all its own. This insensate extravagance of Dom João V, with whose other expenditure on such things as golden coaches, or the fantastic liturgical vessels and vestments of cloth-of-gold for the treasure of São Roque at Lisbon it is easier to fell sympathy, is the work of the German Ludwig or Ludovice from Regensburg. The King's apartments lay to one side of the church, the Queen's to the other, and at the back was the monastery. At least the pink, grey, and white marbles are fine, particularly in

---

[1] The Tower of Belém is by his brother, Francisco de Arruda.

the vestibule of the church which reminded Beckford not a little of the entrance to St Peter's, and in the church itself. The Library, in white and gold, is more interesting for what it may still hold mis-catalogued or not catalogued at all, than for itself. But it is the unutterable dullness of the Royal apartments that deadens, and in the end destroys the memory of Mafra.

With what relief one turns from Mafra to Coimbra, and to that Library in the University, the most rewarding of Dom João V's extravagancies, for it is the most splendid of Library Halls anywhere in the world! Coimbra, itself, and the district round it is rich in monasteries and nunneries. In the city there is the Augustinian Mosteiro da Santa Cruz, hideously mauled, with its blue and white *azulejos* knocked about or wrenched out as by a rogue dentist in the days before dentistry became an art, but still preserving its Manoelino traces, and it is to be hoped not having seen it these last few years, its red and gold Rococo organ. The choir-stalls in the *coro alto* are wonderful affairs with high-pooped ships shown on them depicting the Portuguese voyages to the Indies and there are a sacristy and chapter-house and a Manoelino cloister of more responsible and sober mood. Coimbra has old churches, the Carmo, São Bernardo, the Terceiras (Franciscans), and São Tomas (Dominicans), all with cloisters and *azulejos* even if no longer used as churches; and there is one large old convent, that of Santa Clara-a-Nova, on the other side of the river, though several others, and the Colegio do Carmo in particular, had, and may still have beautiful and half-forgotten things in them. But Santa Clara-a-Nova, passing on the way yet another convent, the Bernardine nunnery of Celas, with octagonal church and nuns' choir – is exceptional. Here, the interest centres in the Saint, Queen Elizabeth of Portugal, foundress of the convent in the fourteenth century; but the church is the work of a later architect, João Turriano (1649–77). It has a high stone roof, the Gothic tomb of St Elizabeth and such later details as a red and gold portable organ in the choir, and the twin to that in the upper choir or *coro alto*. There is, also, the double cloister of Dom João V with its obelisks upon the roofline and Doric columns for the piers, a more successful composition than any of the interior courts of Mafra.

We are now nearing, and have indeed all but reached, that paradise of monks for which we held out the promise, but before that it is necessary to go down for a last time into the South in order to visit Evora, capital of the Alentejo, and another town which for its small population has a great number of convents. Let us only mention in a single sentence before it becomes monotonous, the Convento da Graça, with its peculiar Michelangelesque façade of stone giants or Atlantes sitting in pairs upon the pediment, under stone globes which represent flaming grenades; the former Jesuit college with its huge cloister and stairs lined with *azulejos*, and little eighteenth-century theatre for religious plays; the Loios with Renaissance tombs and *azulejos*; the Franciscan convent; the convent of Santa Clara, with tower of open brickwork like the hint of Cairo; and outside the town convents in plenty to explore; the Cartuxa only one of its Order in Portugal, with huge cloisters lined with tiles; São Bento de Castris, of the Bernardines, with tiled two-storeyed cloister and refectory; the convent of Espinheiro of the *azulejo'd* church and magnolia'd cloister; and doubtless many others. And with no more ado for it is not many miles away we are at Beja in the Convent of the Conceição, where lived Mariana Alcofarado who wrote the *Love Letters of a Portuguese Nun*. It is a convent of Poor Clares, and the golden chapel is one of the wonders of Portugal; no less so the chapter-house of the nuns, a high-vaulted hall with lustred tiles. But this is as far as we need penetrate into the South, and leaves us free for Northern Portugal where we find the promised land or Arcadia of the monks and nuns.

Here it would be better to begin with the two or three better known and more accessible specimens of the kind, and first among them the church of São Francisco at Oporto which represents the 'igreja todo de ouro' of Portugal to perfection. It is a Gothic interior with whitewashed walls, but on reflection its interior is like some impression of a tropical forest transferred in seventeenth century masque-fashion to the sacred stage. I have written of it elsewhere as a 'golden cavern', but in fact as though for verisimilitude it is only every other one of the clustered columns that has become overgrown with vines and lianas and a visionary flora of the Amazonian forest inspired and instigated, it could be, by the gold dust of Brazil. There are golden gates, glittering with gold that are like magical entrances to the side chapels; there is a marvellous proscenium arch, for it is no less than that, to the high altar; and it is only surprising that the coruscating pelmets over the side chapels have no epiphytes rooted high up in their golden boles and on their gilded stems. Yet more poignant, and perhaps of more romantic impact, is the chapel of Santa Clara of which I have written elsewhere and can scarcely now attempt a fourth description. Let it be enough to say that there are five side altars to each side with grilles over them for the nuns to look down into the church, but these are not like the opera-boxes of Bavarian or Neapolitan nunneries. They are latticed grilles to hide the inmates of a sacred harem. The raised choir of the nuns, or *coro alto*, I would not write of otherwise than as a golden mystery, so poetic and beautiful is its effect. But some feat of the sort is expected, if improbably fulfilled, in this city where two churches of nuns, the Carmelites and the Ordem Terceira do Carmo, standing side by side, have the whole façade of one of them covered with a picture in blue and white *azulejos* of Carmelite nuns taking the veil. The fourth and last of the more easily seen of the golden churches peculiar to Portugal being that of the Convent of Jesus at Aveiro which, also, I have attempted to describe before. I will, therefore, confine myself to but mentioning the chapel, well and truly 'rutilante de dorures', the delightful and naïf paintings of the life of Santa Joana, daughter of Dom Afonso V, a nun here, and like the nun-princesses of Las Huelgas a lady of Plantagenet descent, and but drawing notice to details of such ravishing elegance as the pair of portable organs in the coro alto the keyboards of which could well be haunted by angelic or seraphic hands.[1]

There remain one or two town monasteries or nunneries to be mentioned, such as the chapel of the Carmo at Guimarães, no less than a paradise for the pelmet hunter, with a wonderful triple helmet over the three windows or openings of the nuns' choir, a chapel that is in fact more like a drawing-room; or the convent church of São Gonçalo at Amarante with the beautiful obelisked bridge with bastioned cut waters leading to it, a fine façade, a pair of cloisters, and an organ-case upheld by a pair of tritons with a merman with two black tails between them. But Amarante could almost be in Italy. Except for that organ-case there is little that is specifically Portuguese about Amarante, if its *festa* or *romaría* is another matter and in respect of certain pagan practices unlike any other.

The true architecture of Northern Portugal, to be studied at Braga, at Bom Jesus, at Lamego, at Barcelos, simply put, is of granite outline and accent and of whitewash body. It is in this medium that they achieved an architectural style that is their own, if of export to Brazil. The phenomenon of what was surely a farming and peasant population being suddenly gifted, as it were, with an extraordinary elegance of expression is a feature only paralleled in Bavaria where it has never yet been explained how or why they responded in this way to the Rococo; and here it must be said that if there are no fresco'd ceilings in Northern Portugal to compare with those in Bavarian or Austrian churches, the Portuguese exteriors are much more varied and interesting, the oval plans of the churches are often enchanting (more so still, it would seem, in the Minas Gerães in Brazil),[2] and what Portugal lacks in sculpture compared to Ignaz Günther and others, and to the Bavarian stuccoists, they make up for in their *azulejos*, their gold woodwork, and the astonishing fantasy displayed in their pelmets and their organ-cases. And, lastly, it is an Atlantic and not a Mediterranean architecture as that term explains itself all the way from

---

[1] No doubt the *ovos moles* of Aveiro, a sweetmeat made of eggs and sold in little wooden barrels, are a relic of the nuns of the Convent of Jesus. These sweets, much resembling the *yemas* of Seville, are on sale even at the railway station.

[2] That this so I can now state from personal experience of Ouro Preto and other towns of the Minas Gerães, the most beautiful of them being the most remote of all, at Tiradentes.

Other Monasteries in Spain and Portugal

Walk to Emmaus. Twelfth-century relief in cloister at Santo Domingo de Silos near Burgos

Romanesque cloister of Benedictine monastery at Santo Domingo de Silos, with relief of the Entombment

Façade in 'Apulian style' of Cartuja de Santa Maria de la Defensión at Jerez de la Frontera, built 1571 by Andrés de Ribera

Sacristía of Cartuja de Granada,
executed 1727–64 by Luis de
Arévalo and Luis Cabello, and
perhaps designed by F. X. Pedraxas

Detail of Tabernacle in Sagrario of
Cartuja de Granada, designed by
Francisco Hurtado y Izquierdo

Ermita de San Nicasio (1771), called *L'Aurora*, one of the elaborate rococo churches at Priego near Cordoba

Zurbarán's painting of *The Apparition of the Virgen de la Merced to St Peter Nolasco*, founder of the order of *Mercedarios Calzados*

Opposite page

Top: Convent of the Carmelites in Lisbon, one of the many monasteries in the city destroyed by the earthquake of 1755

Centre: Convent of São Gonçalo at Amarante near Oporto, approached by a bastioned and obelisked bridge over the river Tamega

Bottom: Nossa Senhora da Conceição, convent of Poor Clares at Beja in southern Portugal

Golden church of São Francisco at Oporto, looking through 'proscenium arch' towards high altar

a façade, let us say, like that of Elche in the Spanish Levante, which is a pure expression of the South, to the Khazue Faraoun, the famous rock-cut temple in the gorge at Petra, to show the style is immortal or endemic to the Mediterranean and not the invention of one race, one religion, or even one civilization of many tongues and races. This architecture was before, it has always been latent, and it came again.

Northern Portugal is a little pastoral pine-wooded vine-growing community resembling, so far as conditions for building and decorating are concerned, those obtaining in eighteenth-century Bavaria, or, as argued in the opening chapter of this book, in the Middle Ages in parts of Norfolk and Lincolnshire. In all three localities mentioned the monks and nuns took their full share, putting the old abbeys and convents of Northern Portugal in a category to themselves, quite apart from the four great abbeys of the South, Belém, Tomar, Batalha, and Alcobaça. They are deserving of at least as much admiration in their different way as Melk or St Florian, as Ottobeuren or Zwiefalten. Looking over my notes, were I marking them with asterisks as in the account I wrote of the temples and gardens of Kyoto after a stay of a month in that ancient capital of Japan, I find I would so distinguish some eight or ten monasteries or nunneries in Northern Portugal.

We can begin with Arouca, a Cistercian convent which has latterly aroused a certain interest, compound of the beautiful sculptures of nuns in the church and of its comparative and welcome inaccessibility, being situate about twenty miles from the high road between Oporto and Aveiro. It is another of the Royal nunneries like those of Las Huelgas of Sigena, of Aveiro, all described in this chapter, to which Queen Mafalda, daughter of Dom Sancho I, and divorced wife of Henry I of Castile, retired about the middle of the thirteenth century on her return from Spain. The embalmed body of this sainted lady, dressed for a Court ball, reposes in a coffin of glass and silver; there is one of the most graceful of the golden organ-cases of Portugal; but the *clou* of Arouca are the over life-size granite statues of Cistercian nuns with painted faces in the choir. That is to say, there are saints of the Cistercian Order on one side, and famous nuns of Arouca on the other, all by an otherwise unknown sculptor, Jacinto Vieira of Braga, of date 1720–25. These nuns are of great beauty in their white coifs and white habits with the long sleeves. And the huge buildings of this deserted convent are inspiring and romantic to high degree.[1]

Yet another old convent is at Lorvão which can be reached from Bussaco. It lies deep in a valley, and has memories of the same order as at Arouca with

[1] It is probably safe to conclude that the *morcelas* (*boudins au sucre*) of Arouca are a surviving relic of the nunnery.

its bodies of two nuns, daughters of Dom Sancho I, who are buried here in silver coffins. It was at Lorvão that a few still professing nuns were discovered some sixty years after the suppression of the religious orders in 1834. They were half-starving; but one conjectures they may have maintained themselves by engaging in the local industry of making toothpicks out of white willow-wood. The church is notable for its splendid choir-stalls, two dozen of them to each side, with comfortable armchairs in the front row for the novices and servants. Again, the conventual buildings at Lorvão are huge and picturesque in keeping.

Travanca, like Lorvão, deep in a wooded valley, is an old three-aisled church of Benedictine monks that dates from the twelfth century. It lies only just off the road from Amarante to Guimarães, and was largely rebuilt later. In the sacristy the chests of drawers for the vestments are painted in green and gold with *chinoiseries* of *scénes champêtres et familiales* of about 1750. The writer has not been to Travanca but it must certainly deserve a visit. This monastery of Travanca, with those of Santo Tirso and of Tibães, have been ascribed to the architect João Turriano (1610–79) son of the Italian, Leonardo Torriano of Cremona. But, first, another Benedictine convent, that of Pombeiro, also near Guimarães, must be mentioned; it, also, lies deep down in a wooded valley. The pelmets and golden woodwork are remarkable and charming.

Santo Tirso, a Benedictine monastery rebuilt in the seventeenth century by João Turriano, himself a Benedictine friar, is in the middle of a small town, and has not been improved by conversion into an agricultural college. Again, here, with much else that is more serious than beautiful, and a double-storeyed cloister, the gold woodwork is of unbelievable fantasy and grace, qualities which if they can be conceded to the stuccowork of a Johann Baptist Zimmermann cannot be denied in fairness to the forgotten and unknown craftsmen in the Portuguese churches.[1]

Fifth, but by no means least of the old abbeys in this north of Portugal, is Tibães which is on the Ponte de Lima road only a few miles from Braga, passing the early church of São Frutuoso on the way, where the conventual church of the nuns has the usual, beautiful gold woodwork, gold pelmets and a raised choir (*coro alto*) surmounted by cherubs holding chains of flowers. But the huge monastery of Tibães, once the chief house of the Benedictines in Portugal is the attraction, with its four cloisters, church with elegant pelmets and golden proscenium arch, and a garden with flights of steps and statues. This, too, is one of the deserted monasteries to wander

---

[1] Again, at Santo Tirso, the local speciality of *tijelinhas* (*petits gâteaux d'amandes*), may date from monkish times.

about in, penetrating into the chapter-house, or trying to attain the *coro alto*.

If anything, the Cistercian convent-church of Bouro is more picturesque still, empty and deserted as it is, and lying on another road out of Braga towards Caldas do Gerez. It has life-size statues of the Kings of Portugal in plumed helms and 'King Florestan' dress on its façade, like the statues in the Sala dos Reis at Alcobaça. The convent buildings are in private ownership and half in ruins, with roofless kitchens, refectory, and chapter-house. The church, which is still in use, I do not remember in detail, but the impression left by these abbeys and nunneries with traces of early work and such a wealth of Rococo detail is something that is to be found nowhere else in the world.

And, finally, there are a pair of convents with confusing names, São Miguel de Refoios and Refoios de Lima, which lie in different directions and are in fact quite a way apart. São Miguel de Refoios, a Benedictine monastery, lies down country lanes some twenty miles east of Fafe which is, itself, some miles from Guimarães. It is right out in the wilds and should repay the trouble of getting there. One account praises it for 'elegance of design, masterly execution of detail, and nobility of proportion', and calls it 'one of the most admirable specimens of the Rococo style'. It has many gold carvings in the 'style contortionné de l'époque', a phrase which tells us all we want to know. Refoios de Lima, which I have seen, is by contrary in one of the richest parts of Portugal, with tall vines festooned with grapes, when I was there, growing to either side of the road, and small *quintas* or manor houses one after another in the Arcadian scene. The little country town Ponte de Lima is pretty, too, in a riverine way. Its church is an exceptional pelmet centre, now we have come to accept these as the equivalent of Italian or Bavarian *stucchi*. The side chapels are framed, two at a time, by one single pelmet like double or twin stages held in by one single proscenium arch. The convent has become farm buildings; the kitchen with tile panels of fish and game, the refectory, the cloister, the chapter-house with clerical figures in *azulejos*, can all be seen. Refoios de Lima is just another of the old abbeys of Northern Portugal, and there must be yet others still unknown, with wood-work and pelmets that are gilded with the gold of Brazil, or have touches of green or scarlet, and with their fantastic organ-cases held up by figures of satyrs or of mermen.

5

Monasteries in France

An easy way of entrance into the splendours of the greatest monarchy in Europe in its luxurious decline towards its sunset is to be procured from the pages of the *Almanach Royal*, 'presenté a Sa Majesté pour la première fois en 1699', but the edition lying before me is for 1774, the last year in which Louis XV, 'Le Bien-Aimé, Roy de France et de Navarre, de la troisième race' was reigning. I open it at the page giving 'Abbayes et Abbez Commendataires, leur taxe en Cour de Rome, et leur revenu', nineteen pages of them in close print, followed by 'Abbayes de Filles', seven pages of these, more than forty entries to a page, making a total of, shall we say, more than seven hundred houses of monks and nearly three hundred convents of nuns, with some surprising items among them, as for instance Anchin, with titulary abbot 'la Cardinal d'Yorch', brother of the Young Chevalier and last of the Stuarts, 'revenu, 70,000 livres'; Corbie (an ancient abbey of Benedictines), near Amiens; and St Sever, 'revenu 100,000 livres', though I am not certain which St Sever that may have been, and neither is Anchin (near Arras?) easy to identify. But the shadows of plurality and of absenteeism obscure the 'Abbez Commendataires' when we read, among many others, of Cercamp, a Cistercian foundation near Amiens, 'revenu, 30,000 livres', that its titular Abbot was Archbishop of Trajanopolis, *in partibus*.[1]

No less interesting are the one-line entries in the section Abbayes de Filles; the Abbaye aux Bois, near Paris, income 23,000 livres; but the Benedictine nunneries of Jouarre, near Meaux, and Notre Dame de Roye, near Soissons, enjoyed incomes of 50,000 livres a year, while Notre Dame de Saintes had 60,000 livres and the more famous Fontevrault, near Poitiers, where both monks and nuns lived under the rule of an abbess who was always a lady

---

[1] 'It is almost impossible to convert the currency of the distant past into today's money in any really satisfactory fashion. The value of the livre in the eighteenth century was probably about 10d. In terms of today's purchasing money it must be between 15s. and 20s.' *Cf. Louis XVI Furniture*, by F. J. B. Watson, London, Tiranti, 1960, p. 43 footnote.

of high degree, 'a singular establishment thus combining members of both sexes', which survived for nine centuries until the Revolution, had 80,000 livres a year for income. On the other hand, Remiremont among the fir-woods of the Vosges and in Franche-Comté, a Benedictine nunnery founded by St Romeric in the seventh century. Later a chapter of noble canonesses, the 'Dames de Remiremont', 'only admitted after the most rigid proof of noble birth', but whose vows were only temporary and who were allowed even to leave their vocation and marry, a lay-convent of which the abbess was ranked as a princess of the Holy Roman Empire receiving her consecration at the hands of the Pope in Rome – its abbess according to the *Almanach* for 1774 being 'la Princesse Christine de Saxe' – is given as having an income of a mere 30,000 livres a year.[1]

The impression derived from looking through the pages of the *Almanach Royal*, already, then, in its seventy-fifth year of publication, with the ecclesiastics coming immediately after the Royal Family and before even the Maison du Roi or the Service de Monseigneur le Dauphin, is of a ramshackle mediaeval kingdom of hazardous and impossible survival persisting almost into modern times. It is like reading a Court Almanach of Imperial Russia from just before the First World War. Its unwieldy bulk and mediaeval machinery of government more than other intrinsic faults or shortcomings were the destruction of Tsarist Russia, and on the authority of the *Almanach* alone the same fate could have been prophesied for Bourbon France. It may have worked perfectly under Louis XIV, 'le Roi Soleil', with his classical (but how French) profile! and the curls of his periwig floating out over his armoured shoulders, but so did the Russian system under the iron autocracy of Nicholas I of the frightening, military presence and the 'eyes of pewter', as Herzen describes him, but in either instance within the span of another generation or two the machinery had broken down. In the pages of the *Almanach Royal* the eighteenth century is but a veneer upon a mediaeval surface, and if the least piece or corner of that becomes detached we perceive below it the riddled body crumbling from age that had come down from the first Capetian. When we read of a Roche-Aimon, Cardinal and Archevêque Duc de Reims, a Roche-chonart, Evêque Duc de Laon, or other of the ecclesiastical peers of France, it is not these prelates in their lace and purple that we see, as in portraits by Rigaud, but, rather, it is the belfries of Laon, jackdaw haunted, with the strange figures of the oxen looking down from the second storey, the rose-windows of Chartres, and we have nearly attained our theme or motif proper which is the mediaeval monasteries and nunneries of France.

But despite its important, or even predominant place in monastic history,

[1] Remiremont was in Lorraine, which was only reunited to France in 1766.

as a subject this is easier of access than it is of examination. For, I think, two reasons. Because, first of all, what was not destroyed or mutilated over a great area of France during the sixteenth century by the Huguenots perished in the Revolution. And, secondly, for the reason that the strict Trappist and Jansenist reforms of the next century did not encourage any luxury in building. What energies were then left in the body of religion were exercised more in austerity and seclusion than in display. That apart, there was from earlier times much to destroy and the destruction was carried very far.

The genius and force of mediaeval France had gone into building, and in any case it was the cathedrals of France, their stone fabric more than ever their intrinsic content of tapestries, paintings, jewelled monstrances, or gold embroidered vestments, as in Spanish cathedrals, Toledo, Burgos, León, Seville, that were incomparable and marvellous. Chartres, Reims, Amiens, by contrast, excelled in themselves and not in the works of art they contained. Mediaeval France was not as rich as Plantaganet England which was in possession, do not let us forget, of from a quarter to a third of the area of France; neither was it as rich as, at any rate, the united Spain of Los Reyes Catolicos, Ferdinand and Isabella. But in the stone fabric of her mediaeval monasteries and nunneries, as in her cathedrals, France must have excelled over every kingdom in Europe. The Gothic of the Île de France apart, the finest and best Romanesque architecture was French in origin and practise, and so were the therapeutic and spiritually cleansing buildings of the Cistercian monks. The French had the greatest building drive and the engineering skill, the genius for sculpture and for stained glass, and beside them even mediaeval Italy is inferior until the stirrings of the Renaissance and the revival of classical forms with their hereditary suitability for the Latins who we never find at their ease in the polychrome Gothic of the Italian *quattrocento*.

In so many of the old abbeys that are scattered all over France only the church remains; or the conventual buildings if still standing have been adapted to other uses nearly always of a dismal kind. It was a justice bereft of poetry that turned the double abbey of Fontevrault, which housed two hundred and thirty nuns and sixty monks till the end of the eighteenth century, where two Plantaganet Kings of England Henry II and Richard Coeur de Lion lie buried, and to which in softer times 'Mesdames', the daughters of Louis XV, came as pupils, into a prison occupied by five hundred women, twelve hundred men, and three hundred boys,[1] even if the nave of the church is no longer divided

---

[1] Or Cîteaux, a place of as much importance in French history as the palace of Versailles, into a 'Reformatory, Religious and Industrial Penitentiary for juvenile offenders, placed under the care of six priests, eighteen sisters of charity, and sixty lay-brothers.' Such was the fate of Cîteaux under Napoleon III.

into four floors and used as the dormitory of the prison. But where the stone shell is standing the accumulation of ages in nearly every instance has been swept away. Almost every tomb has gone. So have most of the other works of art, to which rule the treasuries of Conques and of Saintes are the exception. At some of the most famous and important monastic sites of all, hardly one stone stands upon another. In very few cases, and those of little import, was the abbey church made, as in England into the cathedral of the town. This had been part of the colonizing of our Norman Kings, who found the great Benedictine abbeys of early foundation ready for their purpose. Gloucester, Worcester, Westminster, Canterbury, and still others are of this provenance, but in France there was little if anything of the kind. For one thing the abbots, and in particular those of the Benedictine communities, were by long custom appointed *in commendam* by the King. In England, the cathedral-abbeys had an abbot and an archbishop as well to divide the duties between them. But in France, far from being an instrument of local policy, the abbots *in commendam* were absentee landlords who seldom if ever spent their revenues on the monasteries to which they had been appointed.

It has been calculated that in the first years of the sixteenth century, at the beginning of the reign of François I, there were in France more than six hundred Benedictine abbeys, six hundred and sixty Cluniac houses, two hundred monasteries of Cistercians, and sixty Chartreuses, houses of Celestines, Premonstratensians, Regular Canons in proportion, with some four hundred houses of friars, a figure which it is interesting to compare with the nine hundred religious houses to be found in England a little earlier than this. The number of religious communities, if not double that in England, was at least half as much again. But the Huguenot troubles following close upon this period destroyed many monasteries and ruined or impoverished others. By the time France had made another of her sensational recoveries from disaster, for the reign of Louis XIV in this instance, the religious spirit was expending itself in austerity and self-starvation as at La Trappe of de Rancé, and it could be said that there was no future in religious building. The Wars of Louis XIV ending in many battles lost did nothing to improve this deteriorating situation. But neither could it be expected to better itself under Louis XV by which time the soul had gone out of it, and the large number of persons of quietist and pietistic tendency leading the religious life could neither affect nor change the spirit of the age. It is enough to see the range of eighteenth-century buildings at either, or both, Cîteaux or Clairvaux to feel the truth of this. Cîteaux, the mother-house from which spiritual wonders in the way of architecture spread to all parts of France, and into England and Italy, Portugal and Spain, was to have been rebuilt after 1760 as a quadrangle with two very long sides, seven hundred and fifty feet in length, with two flights of windows and with pavilions at the ends. Luckily, only one block of this hotel-like extension which in its existing portion lacks the proportion and fine hand of Gabriel was ever completed. Both here, and at Clairvaux and at Cluny, it is the same story, and the best feature are the wrought-iron railings to the simple but grand stairs. It is no different at the famous mother-house of the Premonstratensians, now like Zwiefalten a lunatic asylum, except that the scale is heightened into magnificence and the side blocks of the Louis XV conventual buildings alone with their three floors of long windows, huge Ionic pilasters rising through their three storeys and great bow-shaped projections in the centre, could be the fresco'd and adorned twin palaces of a Prince Palatine, at the very least, or of a Prince Bishop.

There is in all respects both more, and less, of our subject in France than in other European lands; in pursuit of the former aspect of which it is only necessary to turn the leaves of such a compendium of patient if not always inspired observation as Augustus Hare's four-volume tour of France, on nearly every page of which opened at random there will be mention of an abbey or nunnery. But the other side of the picture is that in only perhaps a third of these instances is there anything left to see. We are to expect, therefore, more, and yet not as much as in England where some of our monasteries turned cathedral have come down, choir-stalls, cloister, chapter-house and all, with the addition of Elizabethan and Jacobean tester-tomb blazoned with heraldry, wigg'd monument, and cherub'd wall-tablet, and only the Benedictine monks are missing, so whole and entire it can appear to be till we look closer into it. There is in France nothing quite of this kind. But neither in France is there an Escorial, a Descalzas Reales, or a Las Huelgas, a royal monastery or nunnery with all its belongings that has survived, unscathed almost, into modern times. There are not the huge Franciscan and Dominican churches, Santa Maria Novella and Santa Croce of Florence, the Frari and Santi Giovanni e Paolo of Venice, Santa Chiara and San Domenico Maggiore of Naples, built in rivalry to each other in Italian towns. There are not the Jesuit churches of Sant' Ignazio or the Gesù to dazzle the mind with altars of silver and lapis lazuli and trick the eyes with false perspective. Nor, although the French perfected, if they did not indeed invent the Rococo, and although their craftsmen surpassed all other techniques of the kind in the grace and invention of their furniture and in such marvels of fancy and execution as their gold snuff-boxes, had they the proper mood of religious conviction working itself out in exuberant gaiety, that produced a Zwie-falten, an Ottobeuren, or other of the monastery churches of J. M. Fischer,

France: Romanesque Abbeys of the Benedictine Order

Christ in Majesty on tympanum in the narthex at Vézelay

View into church of La Madeleine at Vézelay, where pilgrims congregated at the start of their journey to Santiago de Compostela

Saint-Sernin de Toulouse, once
occupied by Benedictine monks,
one of the stages on the pilgrimage
route from Provence to Santiago

Church of Saint-Étienne in Abbaye
aux Hommes at Caen, founded by
William the Conqueror and his
wife Matilda

Porch at Moissac, another of the churches on the route to Santiago

Left: Saddhu-like figure of prophet Jeremiah on *trumeau* at Moissac

Right: Jeremiah at Souillac, perhaps by the same artist who carved figures in porch at Moissac

Left: Porch of Saint-Gilles, on the pilgrims' road from Arles to Santiago, carved in Provençal Romanesque style

Right: Cloister at Moissac with richly carved capitals and relief depicting St Andrew at corner

Right below: Cloister (completed 1228) of abbey of Mont-Saint-Michel, built on a rock overlooking the English Channel

Below: Basilica of Sainte-Foy at Conques built by Master Hugh under Abbot Odolric (1039–65)

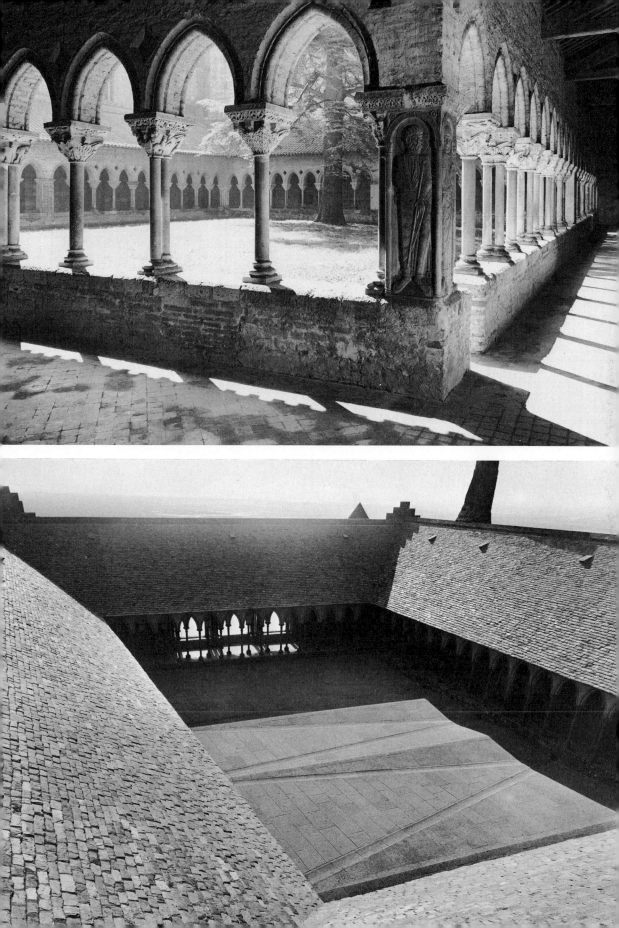

Gothic choir (1450–1521) of church of Mont-Saint-Michel, built on top of other abbey buildings

Dominikus Zimmermann, or the Asam brothers. Had the French but been experiencing a different phase of mental and spiritual activity, had it but been an age of conviction and not of cynicism, this altered temperature could have produced the supreme wonders of the Rococo. But there were faults or holes in the vessel and it could not hold water. Yet after their bloodletting the French were in a trice from end to end of Europe as soldiers and law-givers. But only for a score of years, and then they were back within their own frontiers again, though in another mood that gave them the golden age of their painters and their writers.

Cluny, in its day the fulcrum of monasticism and the biggest church in Christendom, is an utter and entire disillusionment to see. There is not more left of its great church than there is of ancient Babylon. Of its nave of eleven bays, its double aisles and its tiara or corona of radiating chapels, there are the stone traces or vestiges, and nothing more. All was torn down during the Revolution and in the first years of the Empire.[1] The conventual buildings must have had somewhat of the aspect of a walled city. By 1245, when St Louis came here to see Pope Innocent IV, it was large enough to accommodate the Pope, the King of France, twelve cardinals, the patriarchs of Antioch and Constantinople, the Latin Emperor of Byzantium (Baldwin II, of the House of Flanders), seventeen archibishops and bishops, the Queen-Mother, the Comte d'Artois, the Prince of Aragón, the Duke of Burgundy, the Comte de Bourbon, and knights and ecclesiastics in profusion, beside its own garrison of three or four hundred Benedictine monks, without causing the monks to move out of their quarters in order to make room for others. But it is of little use to discuss the ancient Cluny which to all intents and purposes has gone completely.

It is very different at Vézelay. Here, in spite of, or even because of its restoration by Viollet-le-Duc, is one of the major architectural sensations of the Western world, a statement which I do not think anyone who has seen it would venture either to contradict or to deny. It is in part the siting of Vézelay on its hill with the little parish church of Saint-Père-sous-Vézelay at the foot of it, built by the monks where the earlier monastery had stood, which preludes and then introduces the sensation. The arcaded church tower of Saint-Père, of a marvellous complexity yet elegance in its arcading, with its statues of archangels blowing their stone trumpets at the corners, and with its peculiarly large porch or narthex with the triple arches which must have

---

[1] The reconstructions of this third church of Cluny by Professor Kenneth J. Conant (of the Mediaeval Academy of America) give some impression of its towers with their three tiers of windows, and of the fantastic number of radiating chapels like a brood or clutter of chickens around their mother.

been intended for the shelter of pilgrims during showers and before and after the heat of the ascent, has a beauty of excitement and expectation all its own. It was built after the abbey was finished, in the same way that most if not all overtures are written when the opera is completed, and its architects and stonemasons had well in mind the heightening of the drama on the hill above achieved by means of a huge narthex or Galilee, less sacred than the rest of the church, where men kept their hats on and children played, and where the main door opens into the church under a Romanesque archway which is almost hysterical in the excitement of its now faceless, carved figures with their fluttering garments. It is the view from here into the church when the great doors are open which is the glory of Vézelay, the lifting of the sacred curtain, a perspective view into its procession of arches which is as strange, and as Oriental indeed, as any view of the horse-shoe arches of the mosque at Córdoba. The impression perhaps diminishes a little as one reaches the choir which is three-quarters of a century, or two human generations later in date than the porch or narthex. It is a little more ordinary, and could be elsewhere in one of several places other than Vézelay, because it has moved into Gothic out of the Romanesque. Probably Vézelay was allways finer than Cluny; or so we will assure ourselves turning back for a last look again into this chalky vessel of a church, particoloured red upon its chaky whiteness.

Saint-Sernin de Toulouse – did it not stand in a great city and were not its brick contaminated, for it is built of brick not stone – its octagonal tower rising in five storeys, double aisles that form quintuple avenues in brick, and five radiating chapels with apsidioles or paired chapels two to each side, is on the scale and should be on the aesthetic level of Vézelay, but such is not the case. Not even from outside the east end of Saint-Sernin, looking up at the octagonal tower with its diminishing tiers like a telescope reminiscent of the cupola of the Certosa di Pavia, though Saint-Sernin being the taller and more tapering in its five storeys lacks that hinting of the tomb of Humayun, or other Mughal building, as, also, the Certosa's suggestion of an over ornate and battlemented gasometer; not even with its covey or brood, its proliferation of nine chapels in all clustering to its mother-body, does Saint-Sernin de Toulouse compare with Vézelay.

But neither can the Abbaye-aux-Hommes, nor the Abbaye-aux-Dames of Caen, be entered in this argument, despite the plain speaking of the Norman style at Saint-Étienne, the church of the first mentioned abbey; twin towers of immense height, with blind arcading in two storeys; *bifora*, round-arched windows in pairs above that, under narrow, thin clerestoried towerets, turrets, at the corners and in the middle of each tower-face, making a dozen turrets in all clustered below each of the plain spires – neither can this pair of Benedictine abbeys founded by the Conqueror and his wife Matilda just before the success of an adventure that defeated both Hitler and Napoleon be mentioned in the same breath as Vézelay.

The wonders of Benedictine architecture and sculpture are to be enjoyed in remote places in France and not, as in England, in big towns. At Souillac, in the Dordogne, in the writhing animal-composed columns of the portal and in the wild-looking, long-haired prophet Isaiah of the doorway, his hair and beard like the beard and hair of an Indian *guru*, and in general the fanatical, *saddhu*-haunted air of Souillac or in the cloister-capitals of Moissac. And not only in that cloister beautiful as it is, but in the sculptures in the church at Moissac, some of them in spite of their Christian imagery seeming to derive from Roman consular dyptychs and inspired therefore by ivory carvings. But elsewhere at Moissac, in the tympana of the arch and at its sides, there are figures as *saddhu*-like as the Isaiah of Souillac, if indeed the attenuated prophets of the great door at Moissac are not from the same hand, and the question arises as to whence did this indubitably Oriental influence reach to them.

There is a theory that it came from Mozarabic Spain. The Mozarabes were Spaniards who remained Christian but had become Arabized, and even spoke Arabic. The melon domes of their early churches, their horseshoe arches and *artesonado* ceilings showed the Córdoban origin of the Mozarabic style, so much so that where they made carvings or illuminated manuscripts it is as though with Muhammadan fanaticism they are practising arts forbidden to the Muslim. This would seem to be the answer, and it is this that gives to the sculptures of Moissac and of Souillac their unique and unlikely air.

The Cluniac monks who ordered in detail, if they did not themselves carry out the sculptures at Moissac and Souillac, as indeed at all Benedictine foundations of the eleventh and twelfth centuries, had but limited sources of inspiration to draw upon. Prior to the naturalistic copying of leaf and vegetable forms, at once the glory and the bane of Gothic, they could copy such classical capitals from Roman Gaul that were to hand, and that apart must look for motifs from Oriental silks, brought perhaps from Apulia, but of origin from Sicily, or Byzantium, and used for vestments or as wrappings for the bones of saints. It is from such sources that the capitals in Cluniac churches carved with pairs of eagles, or pairs of horsemen face to face, or even with a pair of elephants, are derived and of course their Oriental origin is felt at once. But, also, the other source was from illuminated manuscripts, 'an art in which Mozarabic culture found its extreme expression',[1] a perfervid

[1] *History of Spanish Architecture*, by Bernard Bevan, London, 1938, pp. 47, 48.

example of which, according to the same authority, is a Commentary on the Apocalypse by Beatus of Liébana, a Spanish Mozarabic monk, a work which was read widely for four centuries and of which twenty-three copies still survive. It is suggested that it was the fiery Apocalyptic or Pentecostal figures from this manuscript, their fanaticism inspired by self-starvation and self-inflicted penance and expressed in distortion and attenuation, that were the origin of the trumpet-blowing angels of the tower at Saint-Père-sous-Vézelay; of the attenuated, thin prophets of Moissac, pale of skin, but in the canon of height of the giant Nilote tribes, the Dinkas and the Watutsi; and of the *saddhu*-Isaiah figure from Souillac. Prophets and apostles that could have come from the same sculptor's yard appear in the pillars of the portal at Beaulieu (Corrèze) where was a famous Benedictine abbey (which I have not seen). All these strange figures might indeed be the work of Christians who had become Arabized, and who, as I have put it, 'with Muhammadan fanaticism were practising arts forbidden to the Muslim'.

How different is the ultra-Roman Romanesque of Saint-Gilles, the Benedictine abbey a few miles from Arles! But, then, it is in Provence where so many classical remains are above the ground, Arles being in this respect another Capua or Tarragona. The inspiration here, as at the cathedral of Saint-Trophime in the town of Arles, comes from Roman sarcophagus sculpture adapted to the purpose and formed into triple portals. Saint-Gilles and Saint-Trophime indeed are so similar in style that they are almost interchangeable, except that Saint-Gilles is the larger of the two. Even the clothes worn by the carved figures on the fronts of both churches hang down in long folds and are like fringed togas. The new emergence is in the crouching animals below the apostles' feet. This is the beginning of another and fresh art, while the processions of small figures are of sarcophagus monotony and as dull as that.

Into the multitude and wonder of the Romanesque abbeys of France before the Cistercian reform it would be difficult to enter fully within our limits of space, it having been well remarked of old that 'in the western provinces where the influence of the antique was little felt, the distinctness and harmony shown in the monuments of Provence – it could be called the influence of the Roman sarcophagus and triumphal arch – 'has given way to more fantastic and wilder character. This is especially the case in the portal of the church at Souillac . . . and in the main portal of the abbey church at Conques' from which ending of the sentence one may differ in opinion for though perhaps the most impressive and wonderful of all the Romanesque abbey churches there is nothing of the fanatical Orient about Conques. But, rather, the great double arcading of its interior galleries suggests a mosaicless San Vitale or

Santa Sophia, the capitals of its columns apart, while the horseshoe arches dividing the ambulatory from the choir are no more than a distant echo from the East. But the church at Conques must always be something of a wonder and apart because of its treasures, and in particular the reliquary statue of Sainte-Foy, a seated statue encrusted in gold and jewels, of ancient Peruvian more than Christian aspect, and that could pass for the legendary golden statue of Mama Oello, mother of the Inca Huayna Capac in the Temple of the Sun at Cuzco. Then, again, the siting of Conques in a remote green valley of the Rouergue makes of it something special and on its own.

Another of the masterpieces of Benedictine architecture is the abbey of Saint-Benoît-sur-Loire, which is near Orleans. It has a porch or Galilee of splendid, strong columns with rounded arches, these pillars in the phrase of Viollet-le-Duc forming a quincunx, which is to say a grove of columns four in a square and one in the centre, with effect somewhat similar to that of looking from a passing train into the hop-poles in the Kentish fields. And this pattern of columns is repeated in the high-vaulted chambers over the porch, only there it is to be enjoyed again in open air but behind immensely elongated openings more than windows. The interior of Saint-Benoît-sur-Loire is of the same order of magnificence, and achieves that by plain surface, and where that is broken, by majestic movement, as in the circular motion of the ambulatory between the columns of which one looks back to the marching columns of the nave.

What can be said, in order to avoid monotony and make them individual, of other abbeys: Saint-Savin, near Poitiers, founded by Charlemagne, cruciform in shape, with three aisles, an immensely high crochetted spire, and much early and not particularly arresting wall-painting? Of Paray-le-Monial, near Mâcon, and of La Charité which is not far from Nevers; the first of these of plain but glorious exterior with its towers, but an interior which it is difficult to disentangle in memory from the relics and the veneration of the echolalic, 'la Bienheureuse' Marguerite Alacoque; and the second more memorable in its simplicity, of truncated length with half its nave lost and gone for ever like another Pershore, but with a tower unsurpassed in its round-arched arcaded splendour and wonderful exterior view of its Byzantine-looking apse? There are so many others, many of them in forgotten villages; not omitting such singularities as the 'lanternes des morts', something as individual to a particular part of France as the monastic tithe-barns of England, and several of them of monastic foundation, the pattern of them being possibly something as strange and unique in itself as the openwork lantern or arched rotunda, two floors of open rounded arches and a closed octagon above, only relic of another abbey founded by Charlemagne, at Charroux, near Ruffèe; or, again, there is something as unique and extraordinary as the 'fountain' of Valmagne, near Montpellier. This beautiful architectural capriccio of the early Middle Ages, if it is still *in situ* and not demolished or removed to an American museum, is an octagonal fountain house in a corner of the cloister. The fountain has eight jets from which the water splashes, and above its bowl the fountain rises in an obelisk which, again, is eight-sided. An open arcade surrounds the fountain, and from each angle of its eight sides springs only the rib of a stone arch, the eight of them meeting and then falling together so as to form a cusp or stone drop above the fountains. It is in fact an openwork canopy of stone over the fountain in the middle. All at Valmagne is on a small scale, though most beautiful in idea and in execution, and one does not know whether to equate it with the Perpendicular chapel over the sacred spring at Holywell in Flintshire, another capriccio of the Middle Ages, or say more boldly that only the well house or lavabo in the cloister at Batalha can compare with it. Thirty years ago the open stone trellis-work of the fountain at the abbey of Valmagne certainly brought to mind the sound of waters and the stone grilles or lattices of Batalha. But, also, its cloister was filled with orange trees, and where else in Europe is there a cloister of orange trees but in the cathedrals of Córdoba and Seville, and at the abbey of Valmagne?

The mention of this abbey, which was a Cistercian foundation, brings us to a further stage or development in France. It must include an abbey as tremendous in its history and contents as St Denis, where the Kings of France were buried and sixty-three abbots had ruled for nearly twelve centuries until the French Revolution. It is a gloomy journey thither through the reddest suburb of Paris and past the Métro station of Lenin, and anticipation of its past glories is made no happier by previous reading of Chateaubriand's *Les Girondins*. He describes its desecration under the Revolution, starting with the destruction of the bronze doors of the abbey which were the gift of Charlemagne. The tombs were broken open and robbed, and the bodies dragged out and thrown into a huge trench which had been filled with quicklime and was called in irony 'le cimitière des Valois'. Pepin, the founder of the Carolingian dynasty and father of Charlemagne, Chateaubriand tells, was no more than a pinch of greyish cinders that blew away upon the wind. The mutilated heads of Turenne, of Duguesclin, of Louis XII, of François I, rolled upon the paving. Only the body of Henri IV, thanks to the Italian embalmers, kept its historical physiognomy and could be recognized by its scented beard, combed out into a fan-shape as in his portraits. Louis XIII was but a mummy; Louis XIV a black and shapeless mass of unguents.[1] Louis XV came out last from the Royal tombs, and Chateaubriand says the infection of his reign came out

[1] 'Homme disparu, apres son mort, dans ses parfums, comme pendant sa vie dans son orgueil.'

even from his sepulchre, and that a mass of powder or sulphur had to be burnt in order to disperse the mephitic smell from the corpse of this prince (he died of smallpox), the scandals of whose life had brought defilement upon the theory of royalty. And Chateaubriand, the advocate of monarchy, concludes that nothing that was royal was judged innocent, and that the Revolutionaries wished to repudiate the long past of France, and tear out all the pages of her history in order to date everything anew from the Revolution.

After so tremendous a tirade it is difficult to know what to expect from St Denis, especially in the knowledge that all its tombs and monuments were removed in 1793 into a Musée des Monuments Francais in Paris, where they stayed till 1816, and were gradually returned stone by stone to St Denis where they were eventually restored and re-arranged by Viollet-le-Duc. The original shell of Abbot Suger's church remains, as black now as any railway engine, but due now, it is said, for attention in the campaign for the cleaning of the monuments of Paris. In the interior of the abbey are the tombs of Louis XII and his queen, a twelve-arched structure with their kneeling figures on its roof; likewise the tomb of François I and his queen by Philibert de l'Orme; and the tomb of Henri II and Catherine de Medici, more united in death than in their lives, by Germain Pilon; monuments 'in which French sculpture attained its classical perfection', but it is not easy to disassociate them in one's mind from the horrible fate of the corpses they contained, or to forget the hideous slum boulevard upon the way here which has to be passed again. Such is the abbey of St Denis, and all its monuments in metal were melted down. The stone sarcophagi remain, empty of their bodies, and St Denis is an empty shell from which the purpose, or the life in death, is gone.

Let us repair, then, to the abbey of La Chaise Dieu in Auvergne, which has as much of stormy history as many a minor principality; like some fortified castle a little lacking in works of art except for tapestries, and where the last of its abbots *in commendam*, the Cardinal de Rohan, Archbishop of Strasbourg and Grand Almoner of France, banished here after the affair of the Diamond Necklace, may have been in a little of the same situation as the retired Casanova when librarian in the dark library at Dux.[1] Abbeys only less famous than this have entirely disappeared, with the corollary or the anomaly, according to the way you look at it, that there are these telling and significant relics in the form of churches belonging to abbeys of only local fame and that play no part in history. This is of application to countless Romanesque churches,

[1] The late Arthur Symons told the writer of his experiences in the library at Dux, where his meals were sent up to him, and reading the love letters written to Casanova he thought more than once that a shadowy figure was there, too, reading the yellowing pages over his shoulder.

but particularly in Burgundy, and from the region of Poitiers and Angoulême into Auvergne and down south as far as Toulouse and Albi.

This new wave of building was Burgundian and began from Cîteaux at the instigation of St Bernard of Clairvaux. It was a branch or offshoot of the Benedictine Order, St Bernard, himself, passing his novitiate at Cîteaux, and then becoming first abbot of the new and reformed monastery at Clairvaux. This was in 1115, and within a quarter of a century of that date there were sixty thousand Cistercian monks who had adopted the white robe in distinction to the black habit of the Benedictines. By the middle of the next century there were eighteen hundred Cistercian monasteries from Sweden to Portugal, and fourteen hundred convents of Cistercian nuns. Manual labour was enjoined upon the Cistercians, and their monasteries were built of purpose in remote places. The reformed Benedictines were opposed to all the splendours of the Cluniac churches in matter of architecture and the dependent arts. Or so they started, though their stern principles became altered and softened in two centuries.

The architecture of the Cistercian monks, alike their churches and their conventual buildings, is of cleansing, therapeutic sort, the only historic parallel in rapidity of growth being the first mosques built by the Moslem conquerors. Those are different in spirit, but possessed of the same austerity of purpose. The Mosque of the Ommayads at Damascus, and the early mosques in Cairo and in Kairouan, speak another language but the grammar and the essential purpose and meaning are the same. Or it is using the same means to different ends. For the prime aim of the Cistercians was to isolate themselves from other human beings. They were husbandmen, farmers and market gardeners and, at least in the earlier generations, they eschewed learning. The arts, architecture apart, they looked upon as luxuries. On the one hand the Cistercian monks planted the vineyard at Clos-Vougeot, built the cellars and made the still existing wine-presses known as the *Vendangeoirs de Cîteaux*, as against which in exposition of their principles they made it one of the clauses of the Cistercian *Carta Caritatis* that no Cistercian monk should compose verse.[1] But if they denied themselves poetry in its direct sense they exposed themselves to its irradiation in many other ways. Their self-denial, as nearly always, brought its own rewards, and as ever, in substitute or as alternative to what was missing in their lives.

Cistercian architecture carried to the furthest ends of Europe, to Casamari and Fossanova in Latium, to Poblet and Santas Creus among the Catalans, to Rievaulx and Fountains in Yorkshire, and Alcobaça in Portugal, naming but those that come first to mind, in virtue of its ubiquity was both Burgundian

---

[1] *Art in Mediaeval France*, by Joan Evans, Oxford University Press, 1948, p. 64.

Later Monasteries in France and Belgium

Church of La Chaise-Dieu (Auvergne), rebuilt by Pope Clement VI,
a former monk of the abbey

Left: Fountain in cloister for monks' ablutions at Valmagne near Montpellier

Right: Cloister in Chartreuse of Villefranche-de-Rouergue founded in 1450

Of comparison only with Valmagne the *Pavilhão* or well-house in the *Claustro Real* at Batalha in Portugal

La Grande Chartreuse, founded by
St Bruno about 1080 and inhabited
by Carthusian monks until 1903.
The high-roofed buildings date
mostly from the seventeenth
century

Carthusian or Cistercian nun by
Jean Barbault, a painter who
worked and died in Rome in the
late eighteenth century. At
Petworth House

Cistercian abbey of Noirlac, subsequently porcelain factory, orphanage and shelter for refugees from the Spanish civil war

Prémontré, mother-house of the Premonstratensians, rebuilt in the eighteenth century, with subsequent fate as glass-works, orphanage and finally asylum

ANN·1654· ÆT·62
OBIT·6·AVG·1661·

Mère Angélique Arnauld, Jansenist nun of the Port-Royal, by Philippe de Champaigne,
whose daughter was a novice in the same nunnery

Church of Cistercian abbey of Valloires in northern France, with sculpture by the
Austrian Josef Pfaffenhofen and wrought-iron grilles by Jean Veyren

Pulpit in Cathedral of Notre-Dame at Antwerp, supported on statues representing the four continents. Carved in 1713 by Michel van der Voort for Abbot Saint-Bernard

Béguinage at Bruges founded in the thirteenth century, with gateway of 1776

Abbaye de Forêt, Brussels. Drawing by the seventeenth-century artist R. Cantagallino

and international in style. We have seen that the final plan for Fountains Abbey was brought over from Clairvaux by the third abbot, who had been a friend of St Bernard, and this degree of personal intervention from the mother house of the Cistercians, far from being unusual seems generally to have been the rule. Probably one or two of the monks in every case were skilled masons, and if they were not Burgundian by birth had served a term or two of indoctrination and training in, as it were, bush-fighting and guerilla warfare in the Cistercian college or university at Cîteaux. Here the object of the course, quite as deliberately as it sounds, was to give instruction in the building of monasteries in remote places, or in fact in the founding of religious colonies in all their detail, down to kitchen, dormitory, lavatory, farm buildings, even to tithe-barn and fish pond. It must be remembered that a French accent, whether Norman, Angevin, or Burgundian, was nothing strange in twelfth-century England. But the plans went out from Cîteaux to the same degree to other lands. Certainly there has been no comparable growth to this which led to 'three thousand six hundred tributary convents of the Cistercian Order', and which combined in its first buildings something of the austere temperament of the early Moslem mosque builders with the clear utility in detail of the Mennonites and Shakers. The Cistercian buildings are therapeutic in the sense that a fast, a Lent, a Ramadan, a water-cure, are healing and cleansing to the spirit.

A principal part of the Cistercian cure or treatment was in the choice of site. And we may think, in the choice of name. Fountains, or 'Fontes' as it was called, with the six springs still rising within its confines has already been noted; as, too, Whitland or Albalanda and Strata Florida, both in Wales, with Welsh-speaking novices from the noble families of Wales; and Blanchland of the night stair, near the Scots border. Such names had their origin in the French Cistercian monasteries, and we would hope and expect to find the best of the names in France. Noirlac, l'Abbaye de l'Eau, l'Abbaye aux Bois, Fontfroide, Clairelieu, Clairefontaine, Vauluisant, Valcroissant, Clairmarais, Belleaigue, Hort-Dieu, Belleaux, Bellecombe, Valhonnête, l'Abbaye de la Belle-Étoile, l'Abbaye de la Joie, are some of them. Little indeed is left of most of them, it being perhaps typical of this last which was near Hennebont (Morbihan), that 'nothing remains except a parlour belonging to its later buildings, decorated in the time of Louis XV.[1]

[1] Thus, Augustus Hare in *North-Western France*, p. 368. But Miss Joan Evans, in her recent work on *Later Monastic Architecture in France*, Cambridge University Press, 1964, illustrates (plates 300 and 307) a curious little guest house at the Cistercian nunnery of La-Joie-Notre-Dame with a high pitched roof and, also, the Abbess's lodging, a substantial red and white Louis XIV building with a flight of nine windows on three floors.

It would be easy to expatiate or dilate upon these names. Was the abbey of Noirlac, where church, cloisters, and conventual buildings are still standing, in or near the forest of Meillant, really so called after a dark pool near it? And l'Abbaye de l'Eau (Eure et Loir), a convent of white Cistercian nuns, was some part of it built out on piers or piles into a lake or river, as at the Château de Chenonceaux? There is no sign of this in an engraved view of 1696.[1] Perhaps l'Abbaye aux Bois is not difficult to site and accommodate in the mind. Fontfroide, near Narbonne, with a cloister 'of roses and oleanders' and a twelfth-century chapter-house of Cistercian purity and economy of line, Clairelieu and Clairefontaine, they, too, are eloquent of pure airs and waters. Vauluisant and Valcroissant are of a different world, that of Thomas Traherne and his standing cornfields of 'orient and immortal wheat, which never should be reaped, nor was ever sown'.

Clairmarais (Pas-de-Calais) in the mere sound of it might be set opposite and nearly in sight of Romney Marsh and Dungeness. Belleaigue (Puy-de-Dôme) was derived from Bella Aqua, as was Aiguebelle (Drôme) from Aqua Bella, though Belleaigue could be among jagged hills of which a pair of peaks, as at a certain convent in Auvergne, are known as 'têtons de l'abbesse' by the peasants; and Hort-Dieu which surely was a nunnery within a walled garden. Bellum Pratum or Beaupré was another abbey indicative in name. Or Clairvaux itself, addressed by a monk from Grandselve, in the woods, with the words 'Salut, vallée sacrée, vallée pieuse, claire vallée, plus claire que les plus claires métaux'; or for an epithet expressing light, Rivus Nitidus, Rieunette; or, for content and happiness, Carus Locus, Cherlieu, or Silva Benedicta, Sauvebénite; Carus Campus, Cercamp. Such names serve to give a better idea than anything else but the abbeys themselves of what the Cistercian ideals were, and of the moving spirit within the white habits of the Cistercian monks and nuns.

Unity of plan conferred its own individuality upon their churches. The rich carved capitals of the Benedictines were not permitted; nor were sculptured portals, nor stained-glass windows; and in the phrase of Miss Joan Evans 'from a distance a Cistercian abbey looked more like a great farm' or agricultural colony than a monastery. By the same rule, a dorter, an infirmary, or a refectory, had the nobility and austerity of the Cistercian churches. The refectory at Royaumont (Oise) with its tall, graceful columns, plain capitals and the stalk-like vaulting that springs so lightly from them, or the infirmary at Ourscamp (Aisne), plainer still as to its columns and their capitals, but with a healing of the mind and spirit in those three aisles of air

[1] *L'Architecture Cistercienne en France*, by Marcel Aubert, Paris, 1947, vol. II, p. 180. Vauluisant (Yonne) is illustrated from a print of 1692 on his vol. 1, pl. 132.

and the vaulting above them, such are buildings of utility that yield in no respect to the churches of the Benedictines.

The Augustinian, or Black Canons, who were allowed to retain their own property, were of another spirit altogether from the Cistercians, little more being expected of them than that they should attend Mass and be responsive to their religious duties. Owing to their private means the collegiate churches of the Augustinians were rich in gold and enamel work and in sumptuous reliquaries. At the same time their laxity in mode of living, compared at any rate with the austerities of Cîteaux, made it that their churches have no particular or distinguishing style. Notre-Dame-la-Grande de Poitiers is the richest in sculpture of all the collegiate churches, as to its exterior at least, but here again it lacks fire, and there is even something a little silly about its pepper-pot turrets with their scaled tops like the lids of beehive honey-jars and in the flat relief of its sculptures.

Neither did the mendicant and preaching orders, the Franciscans and the Dominicans, find architectural expression in France as in Italian towns. To some extent perhaps because, Paris apart, there were no French cities in the Middle Ages with the population of Venice or of Florence. But also the Franciscan temperament altered as it crossed the Alps, and the Dominicans spent so large a part of their energy in teaching and in disputation. It is not to be expected therefore that we should find in France buildings and attendant works of art sponsored by the mendicant orders upon the scale of those in Italy or Spain where the Franciscan and the Dominican Orders had their origin. But neither did the Carthusians in France build any Chartreuse to compare with those of Pavia, Florence, Pisa, Naples, Padua, Burgos, or Granada. Or, in other words, they kept to the pure Carthusian ideals in nearly every instance and were not suborned into the use of gilding and rich marbles. Two examples of this contemplative Order in its purity are at Villefranche-de-Rouergue and at Villeneuve-lès-Avignon, in the first of which one still feels the presence of the white monks in their square-toed black shoes, so familiar from Certosa and Cartuja in other lands. But it is a fifteenth-century building, now turned into a hospital, in a late Gothic which becomes nearly odious after the wonders of the Romanesque, its best feature a pretty cloister; while, at the other Chartreuse mentioned, that of the Val-de-Bénédiction, it is the Carthusian absence more than presence for the works of art are gone, it is in ruin and delapidation, and only the walls and towers around, in golden stone, forestall the distant view of Avignon.

The Chartreuse de Champmol is of another dispensation for it was in fact not French at all but Burgundian, being in the suburbs of Dijon which was only annexed by Louis XI after the death of Charles le Téméraire in 1477.[1] What are in their very essence Burgundian and not French are the tombs of Philippe-le-Hardi, founder of the Chartreuse, and of Jean-sans-Peur and Marguerite de Baviére, the first of these being the work of Claus Sluter, who by no stretching of the imagination could be considered a Frenchman, or other than a Fleming or, indeed, a Dutchman, tombs which are no longer in the Chartreuse for which they were intended but are in the Salle des Gardes of the Hôtel de Ville or Museum at Dijon. Both tombs are famous for their trains of mourners or 'pleurants', and the second of the tombs much in the same style as its predecessor is, curiously, by a Spaniard, Juan de la Huerta, from Aragón. But Claus Sluter is to be seen again at Champmol in the famous Puits de Moïse with its statues of the Prophets, a work of ugly but unarresting realism, interesting for its early date since Sluter died in 1406, but anticipating in some sort the Nuremberg masters, Adam Kraft, Peter Vischer, Veit Stoss, of a hundred years later, the last of whom carried this realism of the late Gothic as far as Cracow where his name is restored and reverenced as Wit Stwosz.

If there be a French Escorial it is La Grande Chartreuse, which begins in monotony and ends by impressing itself as one of the long lasting memories of France, and not only from the writer's predilection for the Carthusian monks but because it may not be too fanciful to see in its architecture the epitome or embodiment of some traits in the national character. Here is the expression of their frugal habits in the midst of the richest and most fertile land in Europe, and of their innate conservatism and their economy. The gloom and chill of the buildings with their high gables of slate are much enhanced by the climb to La Grande Chartreuse through the forest and into the Désert up a gorge cut and hollowed from the rock, and through a gateway that a seventeenth-century traveller saw hung with the heads of bears killed in the woods. The monastery was rebuilt more than once, and in its present state only dates from 1676; but although typical of that time in its mere bones, and speaking the same tongue, La Grande Chartreuse is as French in its patient economy and its reticence as ever the ostentation and the pompous splendours of Versailles. One comes away having seen little but long passages and bare walls and a bearded monk or two in his white robe,

---

[1] The first family of Dukes of Burgundy descended from the second son of Robert I of France (d. 996). On their extinction, Burgundy was reunited to France and then became the appanage of Philippe-le-Hardi, fourth son of Jean I of France. There were but four dukes of the second royal race, Philippe-le-Hardi, Jean-sans-Peur, Philippe-le-Bon, and Charles-le-Téméraire killed by the Swiss before the walls of Nancy in 1476. The Dukes of Burgundy possessed themselves of Flanders, the other half of their dominion, by the marriage of Philippe-le-Hardi, with a daughter of the Counts of Flanders on the extinction of their male line.

in the knowledge indeed that there is little or nothing more to see, but this little is much to remember, not least at a Certosa or a Cartuja in a hotter land.

That the French Carthusians are not to be dismissed lightly as patrons of art is proved in their churches at Lyon, at Bordeaux, and at Toulouse – and at the latter, in particular, with its caryatids and *boiseries* – three cities in which during the late seventeenth and the eighteenth centuries the same conditions applied to some extent as in Italian towns of that date. They are town monasteries, that is to say, as in Venice or Naples.

A recently published work on *Later Monastic Architecture in France*,[1] in appendix or supplement to the same author's monumental works on the earlier history of French aesthetics, yields the results of her journeys of many thousands of miles in pursuit of her subject in all parts of France. Among the surprises in her book are the royal abbey of Chaalis (Oise), a Cistercian abbey built under Louis XV to the plans of Aubert, architect of the stables at Chantilly, but it has to be admitted far less splendid than those suites of 'de luxe' apartments for the horses of the Condé; La Valasse (Seine-Maritime), a Cistercian abbey like a much pedimented country-house; and La Couronne, an Augustinian abbey near Angoulême, with entrance piers carrying trophies of coats-of-arms and great scrolled volutes at their sides. Valloires, of the Cistercian monks, near Abbeville, is something unique in France for it is the Rococo of Bavaria, or rather, of monasteries like Stams in the Tyrol, transported to the Channel. It has wrought-iron grilles, stucco angels above the high altar, and an extraordinary curving and floreated ironwork stem like the stalk of a burgeoning palm tree that climbs from the altar to support the host, all due to an exile from Austria, a certain Pfaffenhofen, living here for no certain reason, and responsible for these works of art so far removed in spirit from their native land.

The French convents or nunneries, as might be expected, being less of an anachronism are truer to their time. The little chapels of the Visitandines have much character and individuality, and in particular that at Nevers which is an earlier building in the baroque of Louis XIII. It is tall and narrow of façade, of pocket size; and other chapels of the Visitandines, later in date, have the same duodecimo character while yet assertive of their Lilliputian size. The chapel of the Ursuline convent at Versailles by Richard Mique, the architect of Marie-Antoinette's *Temple d'Amour* in the gardens of the Petit Trianon, is a minor curiosity in a town where everything is neglected in favour of the palace. It was built by Queen Marie Leczinska, whose father King Stanislas had employed this architect at Nancy when beautifying the city with new buildings. Its façade, placid and sentimental in the manner of that vapid

---

[1] *Later Monastic Architecture in France*, by Joan Evans, Cambridge University Press, 1964.

temple, has a portico of four Ionic columns with bas-reliefs appropriate to the mood, and after the death of his Queen the chapel was opened by 'le bien aimé' in person, just two years before he died. Two years passed by with much expensive nonsense in the way of buildings at the Hameau, the Belvedere and Marie-Antoinette's little theatre, and Mique whose character may have been as empty and harmless as his architecture, was beheaded like his Royal mistress by the guillotine.

The monks are persecuted and driven out and return, if they come back at all, in abject poverty. For the nuns there is more public sympathy, and the number of them to be seen in the streets of French provincial towns is surprising. Beautiful relics of their past, if not wholly within our category, are the chapels of the Pénitents-Noirs and the Pénitents-Gris at Avignon, with their *boiseries* and pictures by Mignard, Parrocel, and the painters of the local school. Other survivals are the pharmacies of convents; at Tournus (l'Hôtel-Dieu); at Carpentras, where according to report there are paintings of *singeries*; at l'Isle-sur-Sorgue, also near Avignon, where the Rococo church with much gilding has pictures by the same masters, and the pharmacy has jars of blue Moustiers pottery upon its shelves; and at Baugé, near Angers. There are, too, the sweetmeats of the nuns; the *sucre d'orge* (*berlingots*) made by the *réligieuses* (Soeurs de la Charité) of Moret, near Fontainebleau; and other sweets no longer made by the nuns, but following their recipes and still sold in the towns; the *griottes*, candied cherries in chocolate steeped in cherry brandy of the Benedictine nuns of Montargis; a sweet of eggs and milk, moulded with caramel and cooked in a *bain-marie*, the secret of the nuns of Château-Châlon, in Franche-Comté; and the *gaufrettes*, *craquelins*, cracknels shaped like the letter 'S', and *pets-de-nonne*, a kind of lemon-flavoured cake, of Beaume-les-Dames, where was formerly a convent of noble ladies of the Benedictine Order. Such are but a few relics of the old convents, and a direction in which a little part however minute of the French genius found expression. Doubtless, there are many more than these few.

From such sweet flavoured trivialities which are in reminder it is only a step over the border into Belgium where the Béguinages offer an experience of tranquillity and gentleness to which there is no parallel in the modern world. The Béguines in their black robes and white linen headdresses of the Middle Ages may not be nuns in the precise meaning of the word for they take no vows, but they are more nun-like than the nuns and are never seen bicycling, driving cars, carrying shopping baskets, or ferrying droves of school children across the traffic lights. They dwell in an inaction, limpid and perfect of its kind, each Béguinage under the aegis of a *Grande Demoiselle*, in walled enclosures, sometimes of whitewashed walls, in little gabled houses of brick and stone with green shutters. At Courtrai the Béguinage is a huddle of little steep-roofed houses crowding together as though for company and warmth; while at Bruges and Ghent the houses are grouped round open grassed spaces, half cathedral close somewhere in England and half village green, and only lack a pond in the middle with a few ducks and a pair of swans as aloof and slow of movement as the white-coiffed Béguines.

In Bruges, a city of nuns, one must see the church of the Dames Anglaises, who are identical with the Englische Fräulein of Osterhofen in Bavaria (see p. 79), an Order founded by Mary Ward at St Omer in 1609, their church at Bruges being an Italianate interior of rich marbles collected in Rome. It even hints at the chapel at São Roque in Lisbon which was one of the extravagancies of Dom João V, where the marbles are of the same Italian provenance, and it is a most curious thing to find in Bruges of the quiet waterways and crow-gabled houses. But Flanders in the eighteenth century was full of English nuns of the old Catholic and Jacobite families, there being just before the French Revolution, nine Carys in four nunneries, seven Tempests, seven Ropers, six Gascoignes at Cambrai, six Knatchbulls at Ghent, six Blounts, and five each of the Bedingfields, Throckmortons, Lucys, Hornyolds, Fermors and Sheldons.[1]

For an end to all of which monks and nuns there should be mention of the Abbey of St Hubert, deep in its forest, where was an ancient Benedictine monastery famous for its black hounds, of which three or four couples were sent yearly by the Abbot to the Kings of France. As late as 1788, d'Yanville, Master of the Royal Hounds, writes: 'the St Hubert hounds were formerly much prized; but they have no doubt degenerated, for out of six or eight that the Abbot of St Hubert gives each year to the King, it is rarely that one is kept in His Majesty's packs; some have been trained as *limiers* and have turned out quite well.' These black hounds of St Hubert are mentioned earlier by Charles IX (1550–74) in his book *La Chasse Royale*; and it is thought that a pack of them was given to the monks of Margam Abbey in Glamorganshire in the Middle Ages, from which the Welsh fox-hounds are descended. But the famous old abbey like its black hounds has degenerated and is now a reformatory. Perhaps at Echternach, just over the border in Luxembourg, where the curious dancing procession of St Willibrod still takes place, and where was another Benedictine abbey, much the same way of life must have been

[1] Mr Tudor Edwards, in his *Belgium and Luxembourg*, Batsford, 1951, p. 19, who gives these figures, names the Benedictines of Brussels, Ghent, Ypres and Cambrai, the Poor Clares of Dunkerque, the Augustinian canonesses of Louvain and Bruges, the Carmelites of Antwerp, Lierre and Hoogstraeten, and the Sepulchrines of Liège as the most important of these Anglo-Flemish communities. All of them fled to England at the French Revolution, where all except the Augustinian canonesses or Dames Anglaises of Bruges still remain.

maintained as at the Abbey of St Hubert, to judge from a remaining relic of its past in the form of a little Rococo garden pavilion of the abbot's in a landscaped park.

Back in Flanders there is the group of Norbertine or Premonstratensian abbeys largely rebuilt in the late seventeenth century; the Abbaye du Parc, outside Louvain, with much heavy stuccowork in deep relief, sculpture in fact more than stuccowork, in its library and abbatial apartments, and with huge paintings by Verhaegen (1724–1811), a late lingerer into another age, but no more so than Laurent Benoit de Bez (1731–1812), architect of many of the Belgium monasteries, others of this group of Norbertine abbeys being those of Averbode and Grimberghen. Of what Order were the monks of the Abbey of Tournai who were keen florists and had 'auricula theatres . . . made of planks, and covered with a high enough roof to give air to those upon the top tier? It is best to paint the back of a black colour, in order to make the colour of the flowers stand out well, and to paint the flower pots green, while square pots, not round, are recommended. Many fanciers have been at much trouble to make these "theatres" substantial and to lavish decoration upon them. They have painted, at the back, pictures which serve as ornaments to their gardens when the "theatres" are not staged with flowers. Fanciers are recommended to go and see the auriculas in such "theatres" between 20th April and 10th May.' Thus, a *Traité de la Culture parfaite de l'Oreille d'Ours ou Auricule*, published anonymously, in 1732. And the author extols the monks of Tournai, who have not fewer than fifteen of these 'theatres', and who 'receive one with a politeness and affability more easy to imagine than describe'.[1]

And there were the Jesuits of Namur, in whose church of St Loup the doomed Baudelaire had a seizure which brought on his final illness, but not before he had on a previous visit written of its interior, this 'merveille sinistre et galante, l'intérieur d'un catafalque, terrible et délicieux, brodé de noir, de rose et d'argent'. But St Loup is little enough of its kind and we would wish that this genius of poetry and of the critical word could have seen Zwiefalten or Ottobeuren, or how many others of the abodes and temples of the monks and nuns which have been theme and subject of these present pages.

---

[1] It was probably the Benedictine Abbey of St Martin, largely rebuilt in 1763 by Laurent Benoit de Bez, and much damaged in the last war.

Monasteries of the Eastern Church

Cowled doorkeeper of Petropavlovsk in Roumania

Nuns of Hurez (Roumania) at
dinner in courtyard of convent

Ecclesiastical crowns and other
treasure preserved in the Grand
Lavra on Mount Athos

Simopetra monastery on Mount
Athos founded in the thirteenth
century by the hermit Simon

Monastery of Gračanica near
Priština in southern Serbia

Fresco of *St Nicholas Stilling the Storm* on outside of church of Voroneț, in the Bukovina

The Hermit St Luke of Stiris (d. 976/9), patron of monastery of Hosias Loukas, depicted in a mosaic in the church

Pantocrator mosaic in dome of church at Daphni

Monk of Meteora standing by the
winch by which supplies are
brought to the monastery

Two of the Meteora monasteries,
Rousanou and Aghios Nicolaos,
built on rock-pillars rising from the
Thessalian plain

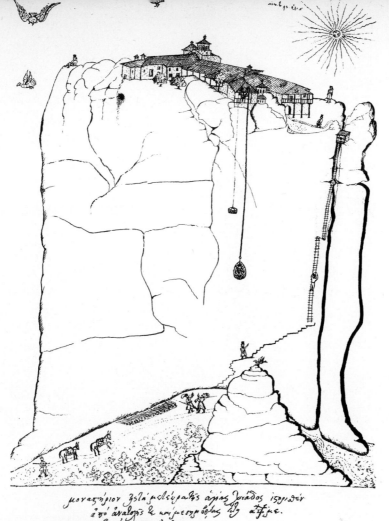

μοναςηριον Ψελα μεδεώρακος αγιας Τριαδος ιςορηθεν
άπο αναλογης κ και μεσημβρίας της αψίμε.
Μοναςτη επια Προνιας

Meteora drawn in the eighteenth
century by the Russian
V. Grigorovich Barsky

Leaf from a double triptych by
El Greco showing a holy mountain
with aspects of Sinai and Meteora

Troitsa Lavra, the monastery of the
Trinity and St Sergius outside
Moscow, dominated by Rastrelli's
bell-tower

Cathedral of the Assumption
(1559–85) and Chapel on the
Fountain in the Troitsa Lavra

6

Monasteries of the
Eastern Church

I WOULD like to begin this sketch of the monks and monasteries of the Oriental Churches, for that is all it can pretend to be, with recapitulation of an experience of Roumania in 1937, for as much as any visit to Mount Athos, or to the rocks of Meteora, it brought one within the span of a few moments into the Eastern Middle Ages. We were at Valcov in the Danube Delta, a town of canals and little bridges inhabited by Russian-speaking Lippovans, a race of Cossack affinity, who engage in sturgeon fishing, where the caviar sheds are the only sight to see. Valcov is in the Dobrudja, a province of Roumania which was ruled by Turkey until 1878, and the still Turkish-looking and sounding village of Babadag with its mosques and minarets was not more than forty miles away. Just the journey thither through the Danube Delta had been an adventure, there being nothing like it this side of the Yellow Sea. The Delta is a watery wilderness of giant willow trees stretching out mile after mile in tropical heat, with storks and cranes and pelicans and other aquatic birds in their tens of thousands. But at Valcov the atmosphere changes again. It is no longer the Far East, and in the evenings, floating under the bridges, you hear nostalgic Russian songs sung to the accompaniment of balalaika and guitar.

We spent a day or two at Valcov, visiting the predominently red-bearded Lippovans in their wooden house, where there was ever a samovar on a table in the middle of the living room with a sugar-cone dangling over it from the ceiling. This the fishermen would get up and lick before sitting down again to drink their tea. There had been talk of a strange monastery near Valcov, a monastery where the monks were so old and poor that it was painful to see them. It was a place, obviously, to which a curious aura attached, and everyone in Valcov seemed to know about the Petropavlovsk

Monastery though no one had been there. The harbour officials held firmly to their opinion that it was better not to go. They even invoked the spirit of patriotism. It was not a place to be shown to foreigners by a loyal Roumanian. These were things that were better kept hidden. It had the effect of course of making one the more determined to get there. So off we went early one morning in a motor boat.

The way to it led down one of the last side streams of the river Danube before it reached the Black Sea, and after some three-quarters of an hour there were apple orchards and the cupola of a church was visible among the trees. We landed, and came to a wooden church which was painted white, with a wooden shed to either side. No one was in sight. And that was the monastery of Petropavlovsk. But then a door opened in one of the sheds, and out came three tall, gaunt figures, bare-headed and with white beards, wearing coats and trousers of some cheap, checked cotton. They were like old-fashioned tramps and vagabonds leaving the workhouse at the first sign of spring. But it was really that they heard our voices and had come out to see the strangers. It is now twenty-seven years ago since that morning, and reading through the account of it I wrote at the time I find it interesting how I have forgotten much of the detail, but how the impression of that extra-ordinary place remains as strong, or even stronger than ever in my memory.

I remember the inside of one of the wooden huts, with icons hung upon the walls, and places, quite a number of places laid at a long plank table. That, and the meal which was ready waiting, and consisted of no more than a thick slice of bread, black bread, placed upon as many wooden platters. One would have expected cabbage or beetroot soup, but not a sign of it, nor, as yet, of the inevitable mug of tea. And then it would appear from my account that we went into the church; that the three monks or caloyers we saw had been left behind to see to that frugal meal, and that the others were all in church. I do not remember the service, but I will never forget the monks who formed the congregation, and who were of a strangeness nearly defying description. Near the door stood a tall, cowled figure who was some kind of sacristan or doorkeeper. He was so infirm that he had to support himself with both hands upon a crutched stick of cudgel-like thickness. His habit was a long gown of rusty black, with a red line or piping at its edges. A black cowl covered his head; but the weird feature in his dress was the leather helmet fastened on his left shoulder. This, at one and the same time, called to mind the knights' helm to be seen sometimes hung high on the wall over a tomb in country churches in England, and fashioned reputedly from boiled leather, and the crash-helmet of a 'ton up' motor cyclist. Next to him, another cowled monk with an identical helm upon his shoulder stood so deeply engaged in prayer that one dare not look at him. Right at the back stood an old bearded simpleton, the holy idiot of Petro-pavlovsk, in long patched coat down to his knees and tramp's trousers, talking to himself aloud and drowning the chanting with his chatter. And all the time bearded faces were peering at us through the open doors of the screen or iconostasis. Now came a moment when all crossed themselves with a wild fervour, and in peculiar fashion, calling aloud the name of Jesus in its two syllables while they did so, and the service was ended.

The ten or twelve monks now came stumbling out into the sunlight, each with his leather helm upon his head, the shiny brim of it showing, and the black cowl over that. The monk who was porter or doorkeeper came towards me, walking wearily, leaning upon his stick, and I could not look at him. It seemed to me that the spirit of my mother, who had died two months before, had entered into him. The transmigration expressed itself in the long trailing walk of the poor old monk. Also, for some reason, perhaps the same reason, he would look intently at me. I found it altogether too poignant to look at him. The abbot too was a person of saint-like appearance. I learned from him that two hundred *lei*, the equivalent of about five shillings, was sufficient for all their needs for a day; so that two pounds would maintain the monastery for a whole week. With the abbot, and always by his side, was his grandson, a boy of some twelve or fourteen years old. After he had performed his military service he would return to them, and his grandfather hoped that he would feel the call to become a monk. Or would he, I wondered, after only a taste of a soldier's rations? But this small boy was the person in whom the pathetic hopes of this extraordinary place resided, and it was his shrill treble that we had heard joining in the service. We went into their cells and saw their straw pallets and the few attempts at sewing or carpentering which was all their feeble hands could perform. By which time they had picked bunches of flowers and given them to us, and those of the monks who were strong enough came down the long path to the shore and saw us embark again and go away.

Who and what these monks were it is difficult to say. They lived on their island in the Danube Delta in virtual isolation. When asked their history, they replied that there were other monasteries of their Order, far away, with whom they were not in communication, in the Dobrudja, and that the only other monastery to which they were related was at Ismailia, the Danube town we passed upon the way to Valcov. Even of this they professed almost entire ignorance. That they were dissenters from the Orthodox Greek church was evident in the service at Petropavlovsk, which was incomprehensible to Roumanians. It was almost certainly a monastery of Raskolniki, or Old

Believers, a Russian sect of seventeenth-century origin who were exiled because of their religious tenets to remote provinces of the Russian Empire. Not one of them can be alive in 1964. Were it not that in any case they were too old to be living now, they will to a certainty have perished during Hitler's war. But that boy of twelve or fourteen, the abbot's grandson? What can have become of him? He would only be forty years old now, and may have memories of his fourteenth-century childhood for that it must have been, allowance made for a few such things as printed books or a box of matches.

Pre-war Roumania had other opportunities contingent to our subject. In what other land of the Orthodox Church could as large a convent of nuns be seen as that at Hurez? Not in Soviet Russia, certainly; nor yet in Greece where nuns are few and far between. And although there were, and still are now, monasteries like Rila in Bulgaria, there are no convents of nuns the size of Hurez. It is true that Hurez started as a monastery, and that the monks were dispossessed and nuns installed there about a hundred years ago; but when we saw it Hurez was a nunnery, and one could imagine it as nothing else so entirely had feminine feeling and atmosphere imposed itself upon its masculine antecedents.

Hurez is in a beautiful valley in Oltenia, the province of Roumania where the finest of the local rugs are woven with their patterns of strewn flowers. Its entrance is through a towered gateway into an interior court with the church and its cupolas standing in the middle. Nothing could be more different from what we have seen hitherto in these pages. All round the court is a double flight of whitewashed colonnades, with a staircase inside an open porch or pavilion leading to the church and other, smaller, matching pavilions along one side. This court, when we were at Hurez, had flowering window-boxes along the entire length of its balustrades. And now into the church which was only founded in 1692, in the age of Versailles and Hampton Court, but we are in another world from those. The frescoes on the wall are in strict Athonite tradition according to the book of rules, more monotonous than interesting their unfamiliarity apart, the only deviation being the portraits of the donor of Hurez, the Hospodar Constantine Brancovan and his wife and children. Their brocade dresses edged and trimmed with furs may have given the painter, who was certainly a monk, his excuse to come outside his text book and paint something that his eyes had seen. Even so, it is a fresco that comes down in direct tradition from the mosaic of Justinian and Theodora at San Vitale in Ravenna. It was painted three centuries after the fall of Byzantium; but what is an iconographical formula a thousand years old in comparison to the thirty centuries and thirty dynasties of the Pharaohs? A still closer link with Byzantium at Hurez was a round scarlet cushion or footstool with the double-headed white eagles of the Emperors worked upon it, for the founder claimed Imperial descent through the Cantacuzenoi. Outside in the autumn sun the living, not the dead life of Hurez was carrying on. Peasant women were carrying in loads from the vineyard or the orchard, or bundles of faggots from the woods. And in one corner of the court, in the shadow of the church, trestle tables were set up and they were at their dinner. Great cauldrons of soup were carried up, huge hunks of bread, and bunches of white grapes. It was a scene of a thousand years ago; the monks or nuns and their serfs lived in this manner in any great Byzantine convent of the tenth century before the coming of the Turks. As for the nuns of Hurez, I have forgotten to say that their dark habits were completed by the *camilafca*, a little round black hat, inimitable in smartness, and surely of an early date and a relic of Byzantine fashion.

Hurez, one presumes, must be gone. Where else in the Balkans, or in all the region of Oriental Europe, can there be a nunnery to compare with this? Not, of a certainty, the convent of the Pantanassa with its seven nuns at Byzantine Mistra in the Peloponnese, even if only in its church and nowhere else in the world are there the mortal remains of a Roman or Byzantine Emperor. For a stone coffin there is said to hold the bones of one of the Palaeologi. But the nuns are as poor as almswomen and add to a meagre living with their needlework. The tiny convent of the Pantanassa does not in the least resemble, as did Hurez, a Byzantine country house of a thousand years ago, perhaps in some Asian province of the Empire, as I have suggested, before the arrival of the Seljuks, the first wave of Turks.

But such again is perhaps the true picture of the monasteries of Mount Athos. And equally, if the architecture of the monks is our present subject, it can hardly be enlarged to include the communities of Coptic anchorites in the Sketian and Nitrian wastes, despite the traces of Mesopotamian and Sasanian influence in their desert churches. Nor can the great walled monastery of St Catherine on Mount Sinai, any more than that of St John the Divine on Patmos, enter into our category if it is architecture and the attendant arts for which we are searching, as distinct from manuscripts, or the scarlet bulls of Eastern Emperors and Patriarchs. This is not a history of anchorites, nor asceticism. The monasteries just named, and in particular those of the Nitrian Lakes, however interesting in point of history pertain more to archaeology than to aesthetics, in order to appreciate which we should have seen them as they were when visited and written of by Curzon in his *Monasteries of the Levant* (1833). At the convent of St Macarius, while Curzon plied the blind abbot with rose-pink rosoglio and persuaded him to part with precious manu-scripts, we would have seen the Ethiopian monks, his 'Abyssinian eremites', dark of countenance, in his words 'black as crows', tall, thin ascetics in tunics and cloaks or togas of light yellow wash-leather, made, they told him, of gazelle skins; true disciples, Curzon thought, of the great Macarius, the founder of these secluded monasteries (d. 394 after sixty years of austerities in various deserts) 'and excellently calculated to figure in that grim chorus of his in-vention, or, at least, which is called after his name, *La Danse Macabre*'. No doubt such are experiences that in their land of origin could be paralleled today.

The very strictness of the rule of monks of the Orthodox Churches, not more severe than those governing the lives of monks of the Western world, but more unyielding in their insistence upon minor points of liturgy and in endless argument upon formalities of doctrine, made it that their energies over the centuries were occupied more with argument than with the beauti-fying of their monasteries. Their way of life did not call for great dormitories or cloisters; their churches were in practise smaller and did not soar up into flights of imagination. It took them some hundreds of years while the dis-putes of iconoclasm were raging in all acrimony to decide whether, or not, their conscience would permit of carved images in their churches. And, of course, during endless and often bloody argument many offending works of art were thrown on the flames or otherwise destroyed. It was their inherit-ance of argument, or the tendency toward that, from the ancient Hellenes, a trait still further complicated by admixture of Armenian and other Eastern blood, that occupied too large a part of the nervous temperament of the Byzantines, that filled their tortuous histories, but, contrariwise, kept their field of aesthetic expression within rigid bounds.

During these ten centuries between Justinian and the last Christian Emperor of Byzantium, a chasm of time as wide nearly as that between William the Conqueror and our own day, it is probable that their monasteries and con-vents indulged in a multiplicity of small chapels rather than any one large building comparable to our abbey churches. Their preference was for small churches built side by side. Even when there are churches with large areas of Byzantine mosaic, Torcello, Cefalù, or the Benedictine Abbey of Monreale, outside Palermo, it is to be remembered that as to the first mentioned the scene is Italy and not Byzantium which would in itself explain and excuse the larger scale, and that as regards the latter two, both were the foundation of Norman kings of Sicily, of the House of Hauteville, at only a remove or two from the kings and monks who built our Norman churches. Travellers in Greece will appreciate the distinction between Eastern and Western Christianity if they think of the multiplicity of little domed and colour-washed chapels on the isles of Mykonos or Santorin and contrast them in their minds with the single big church, probably too big for its congregation, that is typical of most of the rest of Europe, from villages in Norfolk or Lincoln-shire to towns or villages in Southern Italy or Spain.

The original, and Oriental conception of a monk as a solitary recluse and anchorite persisted longer in the East, and was not diverted in the direction of teaching, nursing the sick, or into the forming of Military Orders to fight the infidel and reclaim the holy places. That they had large monasteries never-theless is true, as witness the Akimiton in Constantinople where the 'sleepless ones', three hundred of them in three stints or watches, chanted monoton-ously all day and night. It has been calculated that later in Byzantine history the monasteries owned as much as a third of the land but, also, if a general pattern of increasing civilization can be traced over Europe as a whole from, say, the twelfth century onward after many centuries of savagery and stag-nation since the collapse of Rome, it has to be taken into account that the great days of monastic building in the West came just before and after the growing impoverishment of Byzantium and the fall of the capital to the Crusaders in 1204, and that Byzantium for that reason alone missed this archi-tectural upsurgence, and was left out of it. During the two centuries of their restored Empire (1261–1453), which there is reason all the same to call their third or minor 'golden age', the Byzantines were too poor to embark upon ambitious building schemes, monastic or other, and they were too harassed by the Turks.

It is this combination of circumstances that makes it hopeless to look for the past magnificence of the monastic orders in the greatest city of the Early Middle Ages which was, as well, the heir of Ancient Greece and Rome. Even were this not the case, the small scale of the Byzantine churches, Santa Sophia excepted, and the fact that Byzantine architects seem to have attached so little importance to the exterior, would have made a walk in that city at its great epoch, if only in this respect and none other, an architectural sensation or ex-perience less rewarding than a walk through other mediaeval cities, Siena, Venice, Nuremberg, or Cairo. Where the exterior or the art of façade is con-cerned, something ignored or unknown to the Byzantines, perhaps the most impressive and typical relic in Istanbul is the plain brick mass of the Fethiye Cami, or church of the Pammacaristos, a convent of nuns founded by the parents of Alexius I Comnenus in the twelfth century and further restored by a princess of the Imperial family. Before their tombs were desecrated by the Turks it was the burial place of the Comneni and Palaeologi, and therefore it was probably the most important of the later churches of Constantinople. So compact is its shape that it could be a reliquary in the form of a church, or the model of a church held in the donor's hand in an early painting. The squarish, brick bulk of it, in three storeys with round-arched windows and openings, and its five domes, big and little, are the pattern or set piece of Byzantine church building. It very nearly resembles the church of the Serbian monastery of Chilandari on Mount Athos, except that it is not so red and white in effect from its contrasting brickwork; and it would resemble, also, the Holy Apostles in Salonica were it not that the domes at the latter have tiled roofs and are not sheathed in lead. In fact it is typically Byzantine; and from being so very average or typical it is not very interesting.

How unlike this is to the Italian temperament that may make the façade into the most important feature and leave nothing to be seen inside, in which respect there could be no greater difference than between such bucolic and therefore natural instances of the Italians 'at their most Italian' in the façades and balconies of a Southern town like Lecce, and the small promise but great achievement of the little churches at Mistra in the Peloponnese! It may be that the Greeks, though as voluble, are lacking in sense or instinct for the theatre. The striving after effect, and a willingness to subordinate that to every other consideration, are not in the national character though it is this very thing that made of Italy the land where opera was invented and the home of painters. But neither in any way whatever are we to expect that their mental picture of monks or nuns will correspond to that of the Western world.

It is perhaps not too fanciful to suggest in this context two theories or lines of thought that are apposite and even contingent to one another. They are in connection with the classical Oriental cities of the Roman Empire; towns like Ephesus, or like Antioch. The latter city had streets of columns with double colonnades, one of them four miles long and crossing the city from East to West; and a gigantic palace built by Diocletian on an island in the Orontes, which island was later given over entirely to theatres and pleasure haunts and was joined to the rest of the town by no fewer than five bridges. What an extraordinary picture of luxury and therefore wickedness this must have presented to the Arab invaders coming out of the desert! They were cities of classical buildings undertaken during the twelve centuries since the building of the Parthenon, after architecture had gone through phases which are paralleled in Vanbrugh, in Bernini, and even Borromini. It was the statues of naked men and women still erect in the debris of the ancient world that shocked the Arabs and led them to prohibit the portrayal of human beings or even animals as one of the tenets of the Moslem faith. In the same way it is too childishly simple, and yet it may be no more than the truth, to argue that the 'pillar saints' or Stylites of the Eastern Church had their origin in the myriad pedestals and columns of the Roman towns. It is a wholly Eastern conception of holiness that may have owed its very invention to the ruins of ancient Rome; so Eastern indeed that the 'pillar saints' can be looked upon as the *saddhus* of the Christian world. If other ascetics were no less assiduous in the mortifications that they inflicted upon themselves the Stylites at least were more spectacular and had not to be sought out in the Sketian and Nitrian deserts. Indeed the whole point of being a Stylite was to bear witness in public. He must be seen standing conspicuous in the fallen cities of the pagan world; and though the habitat and observation post of the original and authentic St Simeon Stylite was on a hillside where later a church was built round all four sides of it, and not amid the ruins of a Roman city, at least it was in the midst of a large population and almost in the suburbs of Antioch. Had the Stylite proceeded to Rome, which was no impossibility for he could have reached it before either Attila or Genseric sacked the city, while an Emperor of the West was still reigning, might he not have mounted the Column of Marcus Aurelius where, at a hundred feet above ground with collar and iron chain round his neck to prevent his falling, he would have towered forty feet higher than upon his own pillar at Kalat Seman? But the 'pillar saints' had no appeal to this side of the Eastern Mediterranean, and indeed there are no traces of them further West than Athens.

The nearest approach to Eastern monasticism in the West is with the monks of any Carthusian monastery or with the hermits of Camaldoli, the latter so rare an Order that in order to see them at all it is necessary to visit their forest cells in the pine woods of the Casentino. Even so, a Chartreuse, whether it be a Certosa or a Cartuja, or in its native 'désert' in the woods of Dauphiné, has little or nothing to bring the Orient of the anchorites before our eyes. The aristocratic solitude of the Carthusian monks who are alone because it is their wish to be by themselves and not sleep in a dormitory or eat in common is different in spirit and not only in aspect from the tall hats, black gowns, and beards of Athos. Their hermits are tramp-hermits, of a type not seen in Europe since the Early Middle Ages. Perhaps the sound that stays longest in the memory from a visit to Mount Athos must be the striking of the hour, and the Byzantine hour at that, upon the *simandra*, an iron bar fixed to the wall, or a plank of wood carried round by a monk who strikes it with a hammer. By such simple means can a whole dead civilization come back to life, no less than when the pair of wooden clappers, giving forth sounds as of a woodpecker or some unknown but tropical woodland bird, as if every clacking conveyed its own warning that this was for the last time, iterates and reiterates and then really hurries, and slowly one whole side of the proscenium revolves as on a turntable bringing forward the seated musicians with their *samisens*, and it is the unforgettable opening of a Kabuki play. Or, more prosaically, when the three strokes of the mallet from the prompter's box return you to the French theatre.

Mount Athos, as Robert Byron said, is the 'station' or static capital or centre 'of a faith where all the years have stopped', having miraculously survived the last war and the German Nazi invasion of Greece and consequent massacre or 'liquidation' of other minorities such as the Spanish Jews in nearby Salonica. The monastic republic or Holy Mountain which was under Turkish rule until as late as 1913 has no equivalent in the living world, and only a distant rival in the hundred and more temples on that other holy mountain in the cryptomeria woods of Koyasan. But Koyasan never had its juridical autonomy as an independent state; nor were the prince-abbots of the Holy Roman Empire in their park-size dominions on the same platform of independence as this curious anachronism of the Holy Mountain which perpetuates, and even now in its thousandth year still reproduces its population, without direct intervention of male or female, by ritual process near to parthenogenesis.

There are twenty major monasteries upon the island, of which number nine are idiorrhythmic, permitting, that is to say, the ownership of private property, the rest being cenobitic with community of property; and there is a slowly dwindling population of five thousand monks, among them many solitaries and hermits living in little eyrie-like terraces only reached by ladder up and down the cliffs. As well, there are the monks of the monastic farms or granges, but of a condition of life very different from that of the tithe-barns of Glastonbury, or the happy convents of the Severn valley and the Vale of Evesham; different but, it is certain, not less beautiful for all accounts agree as to the loveliness of the landscape.

Foremost in interest of the score of monasteries on Athos is Vatopedi, which had a hundred monks within its walls, chiefly from Anatolia, where the many-cupola'd church is washed red-rust colour according to Robert Byron, or it is more accurately the colour of the red turf-roofed cabins of Dalecarlia, and which has in its treasury the jasper bowl of Manuel Cantacuzene, Despot of Mistra (1349–80), guarded or upheld by wingless dragons, or, at least, their wings are closed or sheathed. After Vatopedi must come Chilandari, the Serbian monastery founded by Stephen Nemania, who was son-in-law of the Byzantine Emperor Alexius III Angelos, in 1197. The church of Chilandari we have already compared with that of the Pammacaristos in Istanbul. But the monastery of Dioysiou could be more interesting still to the collector and lover of lost causes for it was founded by Alexius III Comnenus, Emperor of Trebizond, of that family famous for two centuries for their good looks, who affected a particular form of family hat indicative of their Imperial pretensions in that small kingdom of theirs on the South coast of the Black Sea, near to Armenia, and whom for no other reason it is a pleasure to mention for the mere sound of the adjective 'Trapezuntine'. This monastery was in receipt of annual income from the Court of Trebizond, from estates that it seems to have enjoyed until as late as 1580, and even now, so many centuries after the fall of the Trapezuntine Empire in 1462, prayers are intoned three times a day to the convent's bene-factor from that straitened, Turk-threatened corner of the Christian world. Robert Byron, who was never able to see it, writes of the Imperial Chryso-bull of Dionysiou 'as a foot and a half broad and fifteen feet long, with capitals three inches high emblazoned in gold and ultramarine, and with the word "Majesty" whenever it occurs in the document, always written like the Emperor's signature, in the Imperial scarlet ink'. It has two full length portraits of the Emperor and Empress, sixteen inches high, below which are 'two golden bullae, each the size of a crown piece, bearing the effigies of the two sovereigns, attached to the manuscript with clasps of gold'.[1] It must be among the most wonderful of all monastic treasures.

Afoot or riding on muleback it would be possible to spend any period of time from a month to three months in visiting all or most of the monasteries of Athos, not forgetting its extraordinary and nearly unforgettable abodes of hermits. There would be time to compare its frescoed refectories painted in all the rigours of the Athonian canon – the best may be those of Dionysiou and of Chilandari – and to admire as well the various *phiales* or colonnaded fountains in the courtyards of the convents – there are beautiful specimens at the Grand Lavra and at Vatopedi – the *phiales* being a Byzantine feature adopted and much elaborated by the Turks, as witness the fountain of Achmet III, the 'Tulip Sultan', at the gate of the Old Seraglio in Istanbul. Other monasteries beside those mentioned would be the Lavra, with its red, red church, one domed prototype of all Athonian churches; Zographou, of the Bulgarian monks, with its high tower-like walls resembling a Kasbah of High Atlas; Esphigmenou, a fortified Byzantine villa on the sea-shore, its chapels safely hidden inside its walls as though in fear of pirates; and, of course, the extraordinary Simopetra which in fact resembles its companion Dionysiou taken up and rebuilt on top of a precipice but in the result, as has been remarked often before, it is like no other building in the Western world and its only parallel or architectural equivalent would seem to be the Potala of Lhasa, this being an exaggeration for Simopetra is on a very much

[1] Robert Byron, *The Station: Athos: Treasures and Men*, London, Duckworth, 1928, p. 125. Written after two journeys to Mount Athos, and published when its gifted author was twenty-three years old.

smaller scale than the Potala. It cannot be true, as Robert Byron argues, that 'none but the most inspired genius could have produced Simopetra'; this is only to belittle by comparison the palace of the Grand Lama. Nevertheless, perhaps two sentences in his description of this monastic eyrie could not be bettered, as when he writes of 'a pedestal of twisted, golden rock leaping to the light with three blocks' of building, 'each built back one behind the other as the rock demands', and explains that 'the pedestal of rock rises at the back of the monastery to within three storeys of the roof, instead of, if the foundation walls of the front were windowed, approximately twenty storeys'. Its several storeys of rickety wooden balconies built out over the precipice below, and the absolutely level roof-line but heighten the drama. But Simopetra is of course the accident of untutored minds, and of the same order of negligent picturesque as those rock-peak villages of Calabria and the Abruzzi that seem to have been made to inspire the scene-painters of *Fra Diavolo*, or other Romantic opera of the early nineteenth century. Simopetra, Vatopedi, Chilandari, must be the highlights of Athos with all the romance of foundation by Byzantine and even Trapezuntine Emperors; the chryso-bulls and the scarlet ink of Comnenus and of Palaeologus; gaunt frescoes in the attenuated canon of Panselinos; or of the Cretan school, the spiritual ancestors of El Greco; portative mosaics of minute workmanship; the vicarious romance of revenues drawn till not long ago from Macedonia, Bulgaria, Wallachia, the Greek Islands, and even Georgia; daily life unaltered, and even the passage of time regulated as in the living days of the Byzantine Emperors; in general, the unique conditions and the equally unique pro-hibitions of Athonian life; the most beautiful landscape in all the Aegean; and it is little wonder if Mount Athos has been the holiday home, almost the hostel of more than one generation of British undergraduates between the two wars, since and before the day, of Robert Byron.

If the monastery churches of the former Serbian Empire before Kossovo's field – Decani, near the Albanian frontier, 'built of alternate bands of black and white marble and rosy quartz', the pillars of its interior frescoed appro-priately with stylite hermits; Gračanica, in Macedonia, high-domed, and tall and bleak of exterior; or the various churches helped by lacustrine environ-ment upon Lake Ochrida – are all a little provincial and lacking in mundane importance, though some have notable frescoes, it is the more surprising that Greece proper, probably the poorest part of the Greek-speaking Byzantine Empire, should have other monastic buildings of the first im-portance beside and in addition to those upon the Holy Mountain. Nothing in the whole of Byzantine art could be more awe inspiring and impressive than the mosaic of the Pantocrator in the dome of the monastery church at

Opposite: Docheiariou Monastery
on Mount Athos

Daphni on the Sacred Way from Athens to Eleusis. It is frightening and tremendous, a work on the highest level of imaginative creation, with awe and majesty even in the finger and thumb of that terrifying hand that holds the code of law. This masterpiece in an art that, however different in mood only reaches to the same heights at the Cariye Djami and at San Vitale in Ravenna, dates from the end of the eleventh century, and at a time when Athens was of no moment or importance owes its existence to the easy sea-passage between Thessalonica, the second city of the Eastern Empire where there are or were beautiful mosaics in the churches, or from the capital itself. In any other context it is difficult to explain its presence.

On the other hand in a much more remote part of Greece, in Boeotia, but not far inland from the Gulf of Corinth, stands the monastery of Hosios Loukas or St Luke in Stiris.[1] It is the marble facing of the interior walls and the inlaid marble floor almost more than the mosaics that are memorable at Hosios Loukas; but, also, it is superb in plan, in the manner in which its square plan becomes an octagon above the second storey of piers, by means of the squinches in its angles, then becoming a circle high up and resolving itself into a dome. Hosios Loukas impresses as only San Marco and San Vitale, and perhaps the Capella Palatina, impress themselves. It is of the order of Torcello and Cefalù.

Greece, too, has a natural wonder in the monasteries of Meteora which in a world sense are of the order of Petra and of Machu Picchu. Whether the ascent to one or more of them is not a mistake and a disillusionment is another matter for they are of no great interest whether in point of architecture or in works of art. But curiosity must be satisfied, even at the risk of turning one of them into a hotel. There were originally twenty-four of the monasteries all on the high rocks of this corner of Thessaly, near Trikkala, but their number soon fell by half, and now only five of them, the Grand Meteor or Meteoron, Hosios Stephanos and Hosios Varlaam are barely inhabited by a mere twenty monks.[2] The monasteries are in any event of late foundation, dating only from the fourteenth century and having little if any contact with the fading splendours of Byzantium. But their interest is that in their strange aerial isolation they are to be looked upon as the Stylites or 'pillar-monks' at their apogee. The 'pillars' are 'a series of twenty or thirty tall, thin, smooth,

[1] *Cf.* R. W. Schulz and S. H. Barnsley, *The Monastery of St Luke in Stiris*, London, 1901.

[2] 'The total population of the five monasteries now inhabited has never exceeded twenty in the last twenty years', *Meteora, the Rock Monasteries of Thessaly*, by Donald M. Nicol, Chapman & Hall, 1963. The monastery of Rousanou is now inhabited by nuns, and 'none of the Meteora Monasteries is quite so closely fitted to its rock as Rousanou. On the side facing the valley the walls are three storeys high, and on all sides their windows look straight down to ground level far below.' *Op. cit.*, p. 145. Quoted from Curzon's *Monasteries of the Levant*, 1834.

needle-like rocks, many hundred feet in height: some like gigantic tusks, some shaped like sugar-loaves, and some like vast stalagmites. These rocks surround a beautiful grassy plain . . . some of the rocks shoot up quite clean and perpendicularly from the smooth green grass; some are in clusters: some stand like obelisks. Nothing can be more strange and wonderful.' The ascent was by net or ladder (and not in the near future, it is to be hoped, by lift), which made the monasteries of Meteora impregnable in time of danger. The monks had fruit trees and grew a few vegetables, each monastery had its supply of water, and no marauders would be bothered to wait at the foot of the rocks for weeks or months until the monks surrendered. It must be the rocks rising out of that grassy amphitheatre that makes the wonder of Meteora, but its mystery is how the monks in the first place climbed upon their 'pillars'. However accomplished, it was a feat that once done could be repeated again to the extent, as we have seen, of twenty-four rocks with monasteries large or small on top of each of them. To their simple minds how curious the comforting thought of their brother-monks on rocky 'pillars' so near as the eagle soars; whether with snow upon the mountains in the siege of winter; on evenings of spring where of old the white mares of Magnesia coursed along the winds upon the plain below as, later, in the day of Curzon, the Albanian brigands, long gun on shoulder, in shaggy capotes of sheepskin and flaunting the fustanella; or safe on their rocky columns in midst of the Thessalian thunderstorm! In physical extraordinariness of situation there can be nothing to compare with Meteora; not the clayey Dolomites, the peaks or cowls of Guadix with their Gypsy-troglodyte inhabitants; and hardly, if at all, the rock monasteries of Cappadocia, mere chapels and hermits' cells with a few remains of frescoes. But, like these latter, which are in the middle of Turkey-in-Asia, the monasteries of Meteora are the conception of Oriental minds. They are the 'pillar-monks' or Stylites *in excelsis* and their monasteries qualify as a wonder of the East, not of the West.

They are Eastern, and of a spiritual ancestry extending to the banks of Ganges and beyond; and they are Oriental, but they are not Slav. It was the claim of Moscow in the later Middle Ages to be the heir of Byzantium and the 'third Rome', the first of such self-assumed titles having perhaps as much warranty as that of the Habsburgs to call themselves Holy Roman Emperors, be elected 'King of the Romans' and be crowned at Frankfurt. But the Slav temperament though Eastern in some respects dwells in an Orientalism of its own. What else is it but Eastern when we read, of the catacombs in the famous Pecherskoi Lavra, at Kiev, that 'the most distressing part of the scene is the row of small windows, behind which eleven martyrs had built themselves into a stone wall, leaving only those apertures at which to receive food. . . .'

In another part of the catacomb are the mummified bodies of 'ten more monks who had immured themselves in order to gain the kingdom of heaven. One martyr is exhibited who, in the fulfilment of a vow of continence, died from being buried almost up to his neck for a few months.' Is this in Russia, we may wonder, or in some lamasery in Tibet? But what was dead in Holy Russia was alive in the lamasery; and photographs are to be seen of a hand encased in a huge glove emerging from an opening in the wall of a gompa (monastery) near Gyantse, where a lama-recluse had immured himself for as long as seven years; of the hand emerging and feeling round, and then with-drawing because the buttered tea he expected was not there for him.[1] We may conclude that mediaeval Russia was half-way between Byzantium and the steppes that lead on to the tundra, a truism that becomes the more ap-posite when we read that the shape of roof in Novgorod, a city of churches and monasteries that was in direct touch with Constantinople, had to be altered from the Byzantine model so as to throw off the snow. Thus may have begun the bulbous domes that are characteristic of Russian churches.

Typical of the custom of building small churches side by side must be the three churches of the monastery of Yuryev, outside Novgorod. And the huge theme of Russian monasticism could be pursued to the six churches of Solo-vetsk, of evil repute as a prison, on an island off Archangel in the White Sea; and to Valamo on its island in Lake Ladoga. At this stage it is permissible to wonder why it was so many of the Russian monks and priests who are his-torical figures have been of giant height, from the seven-foot tall Patriarch Nikon of the seventeenth century who started his austerities as a monk on Solovetsk among the ice floes, down to the monk Rasputin who may have belonged to the sect of Stranniki or Wanderers; no one seems to know. And not only in Russia but all over the Eastern Church for it is to be remarked in Greece, though not apparently on Mount Athos; and one is led to conjecture that perhaps the ecclesiastics of Byzantium were of this giant canon, or so at least their saints and hermits are flattered in the frescoes.

There exists, it is little known, a kind of living excursion into what we would call for convenience the Russian world of *Boris Godunov*. It is to be enjoyed in the *Travels of Macarius*, Patriarch of Antioch, written in Arabic by his son Paul, Archdeacon of Aleppo,[2] there being the further curious touch that this diary of one of the Patriarchs of the Eastern Church should

[1] *The Fire Ox and Other Years*, by Suydam Cutting, New York, 1947, pp. 195-7.

[2] This manuscript which came into the possession of the Earl of Guilford when he was Governor of the Ionian Islands was translated into English by F. C. Belfour, and first published in 1836. More recently it was re-edited by his niece, Lady Laura Ridding, Oxford University Press, 1936. The visit of Macarius to Cozia took place on his return from, and not his journey to, Moscow; but I have put it by reason of narrative where it stands.

have been written down, not even in Turkish, but in Arabic. Macarius and his entourage set off from Aleppo in 1652 for Moscow where they hoped to obtain alms from the Tsar Alexis, father of Peter the Great, travelling by way of Moldavia and Wallachia, and only reaching Moscow after a journey, be it noted, of two and a half years. On the way they stayed at the monastery of Cozia, in Oltenia, which the present writer has seen, where the diary mentions

the balconies or galleries looking over the river, which drive dull care afar, banish melancholy and brightly clear the brain . . . and the beautiful fish called Bastrobus, which live only in waters rushing down from the hills . . . and resemble the fish Soltan Ibrahim, prettily marked with red spots . . . It is much famed throughout this country; and when salted is carried in presents to the Beg and the Agas.

Rambling on in this vein, but with more serious adventures and delays, they continue on their journey . . .

On February 17 the abbot of the Convent of the Assumption [at Jassy] invited the Patriarch and sent for him a sledge drawn by four black horses. I never recollect, without a sigh for past delights, those continual rides with the Patriarch in the coach or in the sledge, with the crozier held before him, and the heads of the monasteries on his right and left, while both his hands were employed in blessing the people in the streets and roads – the Turks looking on

– this last item being obviously a particular point of contentment – and they at last reach Moscow. Soon they are guests of honour at a banquet given by the gigantic Nikon, with the young Tsar Alexis present; 'the meal continued from early in the afternoon till near midnight, until our very souls groaned within us'. They are invited to the famous Troitsa monastery where 'the steward placed before us silver cups of cherry-water, cider, and mead, of astonishing flavour and coolness; but rest at night was, however, denied us by the gnats, bugs, fleas, and mosquitos, more numerous than the grains of dust on the ground'. On another day, after witnessing the arrival of wagons full of chained Polish prisoners of war, Nikon, who, as will be seen, did not dislike a practical joke, invited them to a banquet at which were present forty Lobani, 'dog-faced savages' from the Arctic, who were perhaps Samoyeds.

We shuddered with horror at the sight. When Nikon perceived that I was instigating our master to question them, he came forward and taking me by the hand, called to the savages to eat me, that he might have his laugh and jest with me, while I was quaking with fear . . . In his jesting he actually delivered a deacon into their hands! As soon as they laid hold on him they tore his clothes to tatters in scrambling for him; and it was with difficulty that he was rescued out of their grasp by redeeming him with fish and money, which the Patriarch gave them instead. The poor deacon, from fright and horror, lay ill for a long time afterwards.

Nikon who, we have seen, served his noviciate at Solovetsk, probably knew well this tribe whose land was 'along the coast of a sea of darkness, north of Archangel'.

In fact a hundred years after his time it was still the Russia of Ivan the Terrible (d. 1584). We are to think of the boyars standing on wooden benches at the entrance of the Tsar into the banqueting hall, in their long caftans of fur trailing on the ground, nine feet perhaps of fur robe with a fur cap three feet high on top of that, making a double wall or corridor of furs twelve feet high for the Tsar to walk down. It was the Tsar who would sit at a banquet in the Kremlin with an entirely naked anchorite at his side. The multi-domed church of St Basil in the Red Square at Moscow, near to the embalmed body of Lenin, is in honour of one of the holy idiot saints of the Russian Church, St Basil the Beatified. Somewhere in the labyrinth of its interior his iron chains and collar used to hang above his grave. Later on, another idiot, Ivan, called the Water Carrier and Big Cap, from his habit of carrying water for others and from the iron helmet which he wore as penance, was buried by his side. Dr Giles Fletcher, in 1588, writes of this type of anchorite; 'There are certain eremites who used to go stark naked, save a clout about their middle, with their hair hanging long and wildly about their shoulders, and many of them with an iron collar or chain about their necks and middles, even in the very extremity of winter'. But he adds: 'Of this kind there are not many, because it is a very hard and cold profession to go naked in Russia, especially in winter.'[1]

Monastic Russia is to be studied in the monasteries of the Troitsa and the New Jerusalem, outside Moscow. There are, or were, no fewer than ten churches within the enclosure of the Troitsa, which has crenellated walls nearly a mile long and of immense thickness, the peculiar and characteristic Russian 'twist' being given to it when we read that one of its towers, 'of Gothic architecture, is surmounted by an obelisk, terminating in a duck carved in stone, to commemorate the fact of Peter the Great having practised duck-shooting on a neighbouring pond.[2] This is an extremely minor matter of no importance whatever, but it carries a weight of meaning, and the sentence seems as it were complete and finished with the information that in 1764 the Troitsa was the possessor of a hundred and six thousand male serfs and, of course, their families. Perhaps the character of the Troitsa may best be expressed in the two halves of a sentence, when fitted together, that

[1] Some lines quoted from *Roumanian Journey*, by the present writer, Batsford, 1938, p. 92.
[2] Murray's *Russia*, 1875 ed.

mentions the great bell-tower of 'Count' Rastrelli and continues that the treasury of the Troitsa holds more pearls than there are in all the rest of Europe together. If we add to this that the four rooms of the sacristy containing its treasures are more interesting than the churches themselves, and that the refectory 'always smelling of cabbage soup' where the four hundred monks dined, was near an outhouse where the pilgrims were fed on rye bread and soup, and were permitted to sleep upon sacking in a kind of loft, we get perhaps the true picture of the Troitsa Lavra. Concluding with the Court procession of the same Tsar Alexis to the Troitsa in 1675, an account which says:

Immediately after the carriage of the Tsar there appeared from another gate of the palace the carriage of the Tsaritsa. In front went the chamberlains with two hundred runners, after which twelve large snow-white horses, covered with silk housings, drew the carriage of the Tsaritsa. Then followed the small carriage of the youngest prince, all glittering with gold, drawn by four dwarf ponies. At the side of it rode four dwarfs on ponies, and another one behind.

This 'youngest prince' being the future seven-foot Peter the Great. And we are left to imagine for ourselves the arrival of the cortege within those sacred walls.

The mention here of 'Count' Rastrelli is because this Russian-born son of an Italian sculptor who made memorable and heroic busts of Peter the Great, was responsible more than any one other person for our mental picture of eighteenth-century Russia – Russia, that is to say, emerging from the chrysalis stage that lasted from the time of Ivan the Terrible until the moving of the capital from Moscow to St Petersburg. Rastrelli was the great Baroque architect of Russia during the reign of the Empress Elizabeth (1741–62), daughter of Peter the Great. He designed the Winter Palace, but we return to him later for he built monasteries as well as palaces. There are at the Troitsa Lavra and elsewhere, it is true, chapels and also abbatial apartments such as those of the *hegumenos* or prior where it is evident that Swiss-Italian stuccoists from the Ticino of the same late seventeenth century or delayed Louis XIV school who worked in Denmark, at Clausholm in particular, and at the old palaces at The Hague, were at work. But, in general, the Russian Baroque appears and is brought to its climax by and with Rastrelli.

The monastery most nearly associated with the Patriarch Nikon is that of the New Jerusalem or Voskrasenski. It is here that he began to arrogate to himself powers that only the Tsar could rightly exercise, and that made his own fall inevitable. In his reformist zeal Nikon sent monks to Mount Athos hoping to renew and revitalize the rites of worship from that sacred fountain, not seeing that it was every bit as antediluvian in spirit as the Old Believers or Starosti whom he was driving into exile in the Arctic forests and into the far provinces of Russia because their religious conscience made it impossible for them to agree with him. It seems to have been his ambition to unite the five Patriarchal thrones of the Eastern Church, and he may not have been averse to uniting them in his own person. He fell from favour; the Tsar Alexis degraded him to the status of an ordinary monk, and Nikon was kept in prison for nine years and released only to die on his way back to the New Jerusalem, and die very much in character on a barge upon the Volga.

Other of the Moscow monasteries seem of greater interest than the New Jerusalem; that of Simonov with its six churches, where Augustus Hare noticed 'the bees humming in hedges of spiraea', but that can no longer be so in the midst of modern Moscow; or the nunnery of Novo Devichi, with its many domes shrouded 'in a veil of chain work', a nunnery of particular association with Tsarinas who retired thither, but of sinister history, for the Tsarevna Sophia was imprisoned there by her brother Peter the Great who suspected her of complicity in the revolt of the Streltsi in 1698, and had a hundred and ninety-five of the rebels hanged on a square gallows in front of her window, leaving three of them hanging there all winter, one of them holding in his hand a folded paper to present a petition. Thus, Augustus Hare, who minces not his words when regaling horrors. Or there is the Novopaski monastery, or the Donskoi; though no account of either sounds very interesting.

It could be that, the Troitsa apart, the most rewarding of Russian monasteries are those on islands in lakes, such as that of Valdai, the town where the sledge-bells are made, an island-monastery built by Nikon; or the Kirillo-Bielozersk monastery on an island in the White Sea, near Vologda, where there are in fact two walled monasteries, one within the other, and the greater with its nine stone churches lies between the first and second wall. The choice would seem to be between the wooden monasteries of the Far North where a simplicity obtained such as that which the opening pages of this chapter attempt to describe at the monastery of Petropavlovsk in the Dobrudja, or the monasteries more in the Greek-Byzantine tradition in Central Russia and the Ukraine. Here, too, some extraordinary effects are obtained, as in the so-called 'Kokoshnik' gables, shaped in the form of a Russian woman's traditional head-dress, gables that tower up one above another into the Russian sky. The church of the Transfiguration at Kizhi is typical of this, though not strictly applicable to our context for it is an ordinary church and not a monastery. But its date (1714) makes it the more unique if we consider what was being built in that year in every other European land. The church at Kizhi could be called more of a pagoda or a wooden toy than an architects' building.

It is to be noticed that where any originality obtrudes itself it is in a church built by a private donor. Here it may become obsessive as though insisted upon. If Kizhi, however fanciful and bizarre, could be the work of some capricious village carpenter, there are other Russian churches that look as though the donor would be satisfied with nothing other than something entirely new. Such are the churches at Fili (1693) and at Dubrovitzy (1690) built, respectively, by the Naryshkins and the Galitzines and, therefore, as Russian as could be, but neither of them monastery churches. The first is a circular church of three storeys with octagonal cupola or central tower and bulbous domes like so many hats crowning its chapels; while Dubrovitzy is in plan a trefoil like a clover-leaf with Baroque gabling over its chapels and even with statues, a feature that a thousand years of orthodoxy would have frowned upon. It, too, has a central tower in two storeys; but, somehow, the church at Fili is the more convincing and the more Russian even with the balustraded stairway leading to it, and the terrace round it.

Where the monks were left to themselves and had not the foreign-tinged ideas of boyars and noblemen imposed upon them, architectural adventure was confined to the roof-line where it was safe to indulge in a proliferation of onion domes that could be seen from afar above the monastery wall. It is difficult indeed not to think that the shallot or chive-like domelets of the Church of the Saviour 'behind the Golden Lattice' in the Kremlin were not of direct inspiration from the onion-bed. The nine golden domes of the little Cathedral of the Annunciation, on the other hand, also in the Kremlin, are of another, cheap Persian or Indian inspiration; they are domes of the Quajar dynasty, or of the Kings of Oudh. It is to be remarked further that the domes with the floreated crosses rising from them at the Church of the Saviour 'behind the Golden Lattice' are as the sprouting of the onion-heads. Or, at other places, the onion-dome was whittled or cut round till it became octagonal and, thereafter, sharpened to a point. The curious veils or nets of chain-work on the Russian domes were another innovation, with all of which decorative chicanery or avoidance of architectural hard work must be associated that incessant ringing of the church bells in Moscow that so tired and exhausted the Patriarch Macarius and his son. 'Nothing affected me so much,' wrote the latter, 'as the united clang of all the bells on the eves of Sundays, and at midnight before the festivals. The earth shook with their vibrations and like thunder the drone of their voices went up to the skies.' The services lasted for hours on end, all the congregation standing, 'and we scarcely ever retired till we were ready to drop. Ten large and small bells hang over each church's gate, which are ordinarily rung successively; only on Sundays and festivals they ring them all at once with no cessation from midnight to day-break.' And the Patriarch Macarius, with understandable exaggeration puts the number of the Moscow churches as 'above four thousand'. The long, un-kempt hair of the Russian priests and monks and the begging nuns in their black veils all belong to that earlier dispensation of the Eastern Church which in Russia, at any rate, did not attract the best brains; the educated, in that sense, implying those not of peasant origin for whom there was virtually no hope. In the Russian Church there was none of the tradition of learning of the Benedictine or the Dominican Orders. There were priests and monks of character like Nikon; and an occasional pedant of some learning like the Metropolitan Plato of the Troitsa who talked to his visitors in Greek, and was tutor to the Tsar Alexander I, though if he learnt anything from the archbishop it was to be an autocrat.

But 'the small, quiet, pretty rooms' of the Metropolitan Plato at the Troitsa, described, too, as being 'rose-coloured like a boudoir', bring us into another Russian century, that of Rastrelli. It was he who built the Smolny Convent in St Peterburg for the full-blooded Empress Elizabeth, worthy daughter of Peter the Great, who voiced at last her intention of retiring to it but died before she could fulfil her improbable ambition. The exterior of the Smolny Church is a little huddled to look at, but the white and gold interior is Russian Baroque and the expression of another and new age. To judge from what is probably Rastrelli's masterpiece, the Cathedral of St Andrew at Kiev, on its terrace overlooking the river and the other churches of that city, it is a pity he did not build more monasteries in the Ukraine. At St Andrew's the turrets supporting four of the five classical domes of a Russian church stand seperate from the main cupola and are not pressed and huddled against it as at the Smolny Convent, while the pink and gold iconostasis of the interior is of untrammelled spirit, revealing perhaps his Italian ancestry and his birth and childhood passed in Paris, being almost Catholic in mood. It was probably that the more southern climate of Kiev was better suited to Rastrelli's temperament than the short summers and the snows of St Petersburg. But, also, in spite of the vicissitudes of the Ukraine shown in the three or more sackings of Kiev by the Tartars, it had a living tradition of its own that was influenced both from Byzantium and from the Catholic and much hated Poles. The diary of the Patriarch Macarius calls the catacombs of the Pechersky Monastery at Kiev 'the glory of the Cossack country', and it is indicative of Little and not Great Russia that there should be monasteries in Kiev that were founded by the legendary, but actual Mazeppa. In the black-soiled and fertile provinces of Volhynia and Podolia there were Cossack villages for the one part, and the country houses of Polish landowners and Baroque churches and monasteries in Ukrainian style for the other.

Russia was the biggest and richest of Orthodox lands, its stormy history notwithstanding, but its very size spells out its own monotony. There must be some reason in calling part of Moscow outside the Kremlin wa ls the Kitai Goròd or Chinese City; and the writer may not be entirely wronlg who says that the taking of Kazan, the Tartar city, by Ivan the Terrible in 1552 was to Russia what the conquest of Granada was to Spanish history, adding by way of paranthesis that 'from time to time Kazan and the whole district of the Volga were overrun with swarms of beetles (*tarakani*) from China, but that in 1817 a more terrible enemy appeared in enormous swarms of rats – yellow, with a black stripe down the back, which destroyed all the native rats and mice'. Moscow, and also Kazan, has its Kremlin; and that this is an Oriental conception with its roots very far to the East of the Ural Mountains no one will doubt who has seen the Forbidden City of the Manchu Emperor, or even the gilded dragon-eaves gleaming above the white walls of the Temple of the Emerald Buddha at Bangkok.

Russia has its Kremlins and its Troitsa, its monasteries of the White Sea and of the islands in cold water lakes among the birch woods, but no Mount Athos, no Mistra, no Meteora. Those have the Imperial seal or cachet set upon them as surely as the signature in scarlet ink upon a chrysobull, howsoever poverty stricken their past, their present, or their future. They are living relics of that dividing of the Empire in AD 364 between Valens and Valentinian, and of that Orient part of it or second Rome which was still fulfilling its functions while our abbeys and cathedrals were building and when the capital city on the shores of Europe and Asia which had descended from classical times was struck down by the Venetian galleys and the Crusaders in 1204. Thereafter it got onto its feet again and stumbled on for nearly two hundred years more until 1453 – but having suffered its mortal blow at the hands of the West and in the face of the Turkish hordes who were the greatest military power in the world, nothing would have saved it.

Of that last rallying of its dying forces, Mistra, Meteora, and Mount Athos are in reminder, and they even continued with breath in their bodies after the fall of the city to the Turks and remain in static or cataleptic state until the present day. What could have been otherwise is but conjecture. That Eastern monasticism was of a form that would never owing to the rigidity of its rules and conventions, have rivalled the monasteries and convents of the West, whatever the circumstances, is arguable. Their structural system, the churches of Justinian, Santa Sophia, and San Vitale apart, would not have permitted of it. No cluster of churches, four or five together, or even ten or more as in Russia behind high monastery walls, could have rivalled with Ely or Durham, with Fountains Abbey or Glastonbury, with the town monasteries of Italy, or the Cistercian abbeys of France and Spain. The black-cowled monks of the Eastern Church had neither the learning nor the energizing forces of the Benedictine or Dominican monks. After the tenth century there was nothing much more to be expected of them. They were not to continue with the painted ceilings and the altars of silver and lapis lazuli of the Jesuits, with the high Baroque of the Danubian convents, or the wonders in elegance of the Bavarian Rococo. But, rather, they were to go on as they had begun, so that the interest of the Troitsa, the Lavra, the Pantanassa, big or small, is less in their substance than in that dead world of which they are the ghost or shadow.

Index